SALINA PUBLIC LIBRARY
1701 9100 229 763
W9-BWN-703

Cooperstown Confidential

BY THE SAME AUTHOR

Non-fiction

Double Vision: How America's Press Distorts Our View of the Middle East

Heroes and Hustlers, Hard Hats and Holy Men: Inside the New Israel

Members of the Tribe: On the Road in Jewish America

Devil's Night: And Other True Tales of Detroit

A Match Made in Heaven: American Jews, Christian Zionists, and One Man's Exploration of the Weird and Wonderful Judeo-Evangelical Alliance

Fiction

Inherit the Mob

The Bookmakers

The Project

Hang Time

Whacking Jimmy (as William Wolf)

Zev Chafets

COOPERSTOWN

CONFIDENTIAL

Heroes, Rogues, and the Inside Story of

the Baseball Hall of Fame

B L O O M S B U R Y

New York • Berlin • London

Published by Bloomsbury USA, New York

All papers used by Bloomsbury USA are natural, recyclable products made from wood grown in well-managed forests. The manufacturing processes conform to the environmental regulations of the country of origin.

LIBRARY OF CONGRESS CATALOGING-IN-PUBLICATION DATA
HAS BEEN APPLIED FOR.

Chafets, Ze'ev.
Cooperstown confidential : heroes, rogues, and the inside story of the Baseball Hall of Fame / Zev Chafets.—1st U.S. ed.
p. cm.
Includes bibliographical references and index.
ISBN 1-59691-545-5 (alk. paper)
1. National Baseball Hall of Fame and Museum. 2. Baseball—United States—History. 3. Baseball players—United States—Biography. I. Title.
GV865.A1.C37 2009
796.357'092'273—dc22
[B]
2009006601

First U.S. Edition 2009

1 3 5 7 9 10 8 6 4 2

Book design by Simon M. Sullivan
Typeset by Westchester Book Group
Printed in the United States of America by Quebecor World Fairfield

Dedicated to
Charley Roden, son-in-law extraordinaire,
Abigail Roden, latest but not least,
and
Malcolm Cook MacPherson (1943–2009),
beloved friend

Contents

Preface 1

ONE. Induction Weekend 7
TWO. Paternity Suit 21
THREE. James and the Vets 38
FOUR. A Question of Character 49
FIVE. The Monks 72
SIX. The Haul of Fame 85
SEVEN. Bad, Bad Barry Bonds 110
EIGHT. The Marvin Miller Affair 137
NINE. Lost in Translation 151
TEN. Mitchell and Clemens 163
ELEVEN. A Few Closing Thoughts 194

Acknowledgments 199
Appendix 1: Rules for Election 201
Appendix 2: Hall of Fame Members 205
Appendix 3: The Honor Rolls of Baseball 215
Notes 217
Bibliography 223
Index 227

Cooperstown Confidential

Preface

Soon after I started work on this book, I got in touch with Bob Lipsyte, a former *New York Times* sportswriter. We didn't know one another personally, but he had once written some good things about a novel of mine. Naturally, this disposed me to think of him as both wise and virtuous.

In an e-mail, I told Lipsyte what I was writing and asked if he would share his thoughts on the Baseball Hall of Fame. He responded with a question of his own: Why the hell was *I* writing a book on the subject?

Good question. I am not now, and never have been, a sportswriter or a baseball historian. As a kid in Pontiac, Michigan, I played ball, collected baseball cards, and rooted with all my heart for the Detroit Tigers to regain their past glory—or at least make it out of fifth place in the division. The Hall of Fame was a distant place back then, but it loomed large. Our baseball catechism began with the fact that Ty Cobb was the first man inducted into the shrine. Harry Heilmann, Mickey Cochrane, and Charlie Gehringer represented us in Cooperstown. So, after 1956, did Hank Greenberg and, the following year, "Wahoo" Sam Crawford. My friends and I were too young to have seen any of them play, but it didn't matter: we had a connection to greatness.

In 1967, I moved to Israel. Baseball wasn't played there (the national sport is freestyle political argument, no statistics allowed), and American games weren't broadcast on television because, at the time, Israel had no television. All I had were the box scores on the sports page of the *International Herald Tribune* and a subscription to *Sports Illustrated,* which arrived sporadically or—when *SI* ran a cover that interested Israeli postal clerks, on subjects like soccer or women in bathing suits—not at all.

Sometimes we American expat journalists played sandlot baseball in the park, much to the amusement of the Israelis, who preferred soccer. But that changed in the late seventies, when a group of American socialist hippies arrived at Kibbutz Gezer, a collective farm about a half hour's drive from Jerusalem. One of their first acts was to lay out a softball diamond. They also went about planting crops, some of which had more in common with Humboldt County than the Land of Milk and Honey. The kibbutzniks were good socialists; they believed in sharing. And so, within a few years, Gezer became the Cooperstown of Israel. Teams formed. Kibbutz Gezer fielded a squad of men and women, an act of gender-mixing that seemed revolutionary at the time, and also humiliating to the teams that lost to them. The Venezuelan embassy, one of the best squads, often showed up with drinks from the diplomatic duty-free store. So did the marine guards from the American embassy. All of them beat us, the foreign correspondents. My memories of those games are hazy, but I did take away one lasting lesson: not all substances are performance-enhancing.

Baseball never caught on in Israel, a fact that didn't deter a group of American entrepreneurs from attempting to set up a professional league there in 2007. A former U.S. ambassador to Israel, Dan Kurtzer, was appointed commissioner. Six teams were designated and began recruiting. Open tryouts were held in the U.S. for Jewish players who might want to combine a baseball career with a Zionist decision. This effort quickly yielded to the more realistic plan of importing players from Latin America. Two former major-leaguers, Kenny Holtzman of the Cubs and Ron Blomberg of the Yankees, were among the first managers. But even former big-leaguers didn't put fans in the grandstands. To be fair, there were no grandstands. The

Baptist Village near the airport had a baseball field but it prohibited beer drinking, and its team quickly folded. There were only two other "stadiums"—an improvised ball field in a Tel Aviv park and the diamond at Kibbutz Gezer. In deference to the Sabbath, league games were not played on Saturday; and they weren't played at night, either, because there were no lights. The games weren't broadcast or telecast, and the Israeli press, after a half-hearted attempt to explain the rules of the sport, more or less ignored the whole thing. Unsurprisingly, the Israel Baseball League folded at the end of its first season. Evidently Commissioner Kurtzer had failed to inform the investors that the average Israeli would rather undergo a colonoscopy than watch nine innings of baseball in the hot sun. Chalk it up to yet another failure of American intelligence in the Middle East.

I missed the demise of the Israeli League. At that time, I was living in Westchester, New York, not fifteen minutes from Yankee Stadium—enemy territory. But despite my boyhood hatred of the Yankees, I found myself gradually drawn into the saga. It was, I discovered, great to be a Yankees fan. Unlike the Tigers, the Yankees were in the pennant race every year. The team had a roster full of future Hall of Famers, and bought new ones every season. The New York media turned these players into familiar A-list characters, complete with soap-opera back stories. Did Jeter hate Rodriguez, or were they best friends? What was Giambi on, and could he get off in time to save his career? Andy Pettitte kept following Roger Clemens around like Robin trailing Batman—what was that all about? What did Joe Torre really think of Steinbrenner? And what the hell was A-Rod doing at Madonna's apartment in the middle of the night? Unwillingly, irresistibly, I found myself being drawn to my new home team. (Rooting for the Mets was never an option. They are in the National League, an organization I grew up regarding as more foreign than the Warsaw Pact.)

My son, Coby, was eight when I first took him to Yankee Stadium. I was a columnist for the *New York Daily News* at the time, and I scored two tickets in the newspaper's box, just in back of the Yankees dugout. (I had always wondered who sits in such great seats. The answer, it turned out, was mostly drunk sales reps from out of town.) As the Yankees were coming off the field from infield practice, pitching coach Mel Stottlemyre walked past, saw us sitting there and rolled a baseball across the roof of the dugout to Coby. With that gesture, I overcame a lifetime of Yankee-phobia and plunged myself back into the endless cycle of baseball fandom.

That season I also took Coby to Cooperstown, the first visit for both of us. One of the Hall's key selling points is that it connects generations, and I kept that in mind as we walked through the exhibits and the plaque room and stood in front of Ty Cobb and Babe Ruth and my boyhood hero, Al Kaline. Coby listened to my generation-connecting nostalgia with interest, but he was even more charmed by the memorabilia stores along Main Street. He bought a bat with his name inscribed on it, a little piece of baseball immortality of his own. He took a few practice cuts with the newly minted relic, and his expression reminded me of the look I had seen on the faces of pilgrims ascending the Via Dolorosa in Jerusalem, sporting "authentic" crowns of thorns from the Seventh Station of the Cross Boutique.

Religious language comes easily in Cooperstown. "Since its founding by Stephen C. Clark and its opening a museum in 1939," writes Jeff Idelson, the president of the Hall, "the Baseball Hall of Fame has always been the definitive repository for baseball's important relics and the museum has always drawn national attention as a showcase for the game's sacred past."

Every year, about 350,000 visitors come to the Hall of Fame.*

* The term "Hall of Fame" is a convenience; the full name is the National Baseball Hall of Fame and Museum. This takes in the National Baseball Hall of Fame (that is, the gallery of plaques) and the National Baseball Library and Archives.

Many regard themselves as "pilgrims" visiting a shrine, where they can gaze on hallowed relics and bow before the bronzed images of immortals.

It is hard to overestimate the power this confers. For fifty years, America has devoured its own iconic institutions: Vietnam killed John Wayne. Watergate did in the imperial presidency. Bill and Monica transformed the Oval Office from a chamber of awe to a room with a rug. The once-grand mainline Protestant churches stand empty. Catholic priests are openly despised by their former altar boys. The Declaration of Independence, it turns out, was written by a sexist slave master. After the 2000 election, half the country even believed the Supreme Court was in the tank. But Cooperstown has survived this carnival of iconoclasm and flourished. Not even Major League Baseball's image busters—strikes and lockouts, drug and sex scandals, multimillionaire .260 hitters and carpetbagging owners—have dimmed its aura.

Cultural historian Jacques Barzun once remarked that "whoever wants to know the heart and mind of America had better learn baseball, the rules and realities of the game." The sacred nature of Cooperstown is one of baseball's realities.

Certainly the media, critical and cynical about so much else, tend to speak of the Hall of Fame in reverential terms. There are debates every year about which players do and do not deserve to be elected, but rarely does anyone question the way the Hall actually works and who is in charge; what players do behind the scenes to get themselves elected; how "Cooperstown values" are sometimes used to enforce baseball's unwritten codes on its nonconformists and renegades; or the ways in which the Hall writes and promotes an official narrative of baseball's past and of the history of America.

America has few honors greater than enshrinement in the Hall of Fame of its National Game. The title HoF that the approximately sixty living members are entitled to add to their signatures confers upon them the closest American equivalent of knighthood. Election is an achievement of almost mystical significance. "If you don't feel an aura that's almost spiritual when you walk through the Hall of Fame, then check tomorrow's obituary. You're in it," pitcher Don Sutton said in 1998. Of course, Sutton was being enshrined at the time.

And shrines, as everyone knows, are full of mysteries and secrets.

ONE . . . *Induction Weekend*

There is one traffic light on Cooperstown's Main Street, and that's usually more than enough. The normal population is 2,032. But the last weekend in July 2007 was far from normal. Induction Weekend at the Baseball Hall of Fame is an annual event that always draws droves of fans from around the country to what the Chamber of Commerce calls "America's hometown." But in 2007, the place was overtaken by a crowd estimated by the Chamber of Commerce to be eighty thousand people. The previous record was fifty-five thousand fans, who had come in 1999 to honor three incoming superstars: Nolan Ryan, George Brett, and Robin Yount. This year, Cal Ripken Jr. was the draw. Tony Gwynn of the San Diego Padres was also being inducted, and Gwynn had his fans, but San Diego is a long way from Cooperstown. (Actually, almost every place is a long way from Cooperstown. The closest airport is at Albany, an hour's drive away.) These were Ripken people.

Cal Ripken was born and raised to be a baseball hero, especially to the white working-class fans of Baltimore. He was the hardest-working man in baseball. Tutored by his baseball-coach father to play "the Ripken Way," he ran out ground balls, chatted with reporters, signed autographs with a smile, and, most impressive, showed up to punch the clock every day for years on end. The Iron Man's record of 2,632 straight games eclipsed Lou Gehrig's fifty-six-year-old mark. He had 3,184 career hits. The Baseball Writers' Association of America (BBWAA), whose members serve as the electoral college of Cooperstown, picked him on 98.6 percent of the ballots. Babe Ruth—another son of Baltimore—only got 95.1 percent.

When Ripken retired in 2001, his fans made a quick calculation. He would be eligible for the Hall in five years, which took them to July 2007. They opened their datebooks and reserved every hotel and motel room in a six-county radius of Cooperstown. I found this out when I tried to book a place to stay and wound up crashing with friends near Albany.

The village of Cooperstown has changed very little since the Hall first opened in 1939 (and in 1939, it still looked a lot like 1839). This isn't accidental. Cooperstown works hard to maintain itself as what its leading citizen, Jane Forbes Clark, calls "a wonderfully accurate record of nineteenth-century American architectural history." The Clark family, which owns or controls everything worth owning or controlling for miles around (including the Hall of Fame), has even bought up land around the entry points to the village to ensure that nothing modern or crass greets visitors to the American Brigadoon.

Only Main Street departs from the Victorian theme of the village. Main Street's theme is pure commerce. During Induction Weekend, hordes of pale middle-aged people, shapeless but ample in their baggy shorts and baseball jerseys, surged up one side of the street and down the other, rummaging through the many baseball memento shops, scarfing burgers at baseball-themed restaurants, lining up to buy Hall of Fame autographs at signing tables positioned along the main drag, or just cruising for a glimpse of an immortal. Frank Robinson, looking slow and aged in a golf cap, drew applause as he emerged from the Home Plate Restaurant. Even fans too young to recognize him from his Orioles days recognized him from television; he had recently managed the Washington Nationals. Other Hall of Famers passed by in relative anonymity, but if you watched closely you could pick them out by their determined stride and straight-ahead demeanor. Eye contact with a civilian could mean a request for a free autograph, but autographs that weekend were a cash proposition. There were also hawkers and eccentrics up and down Main Street peddling various kinds of baseball stuff. Jim "Mudcat" Grant stood in front of a restaurant signing copies of *Black Aces*, his book celebrating the thirteen black pitchers (Grant among them) who'd won 20 games, and delivering a loud, more or less continuous lecture on inequities of baseball toward African-Americans. Across Main Street, a fellow named Randall Swearingen, who claims to have the world's largest collection of Mickey Mantle memorabilia, including a Harley-Davidson with a seat made of leather from Mantle's old gloves, was hawking copies of his latest book on the Mick. During a lull, Swearingen mentioned that he also had once been the sole distributor of Mickey Mantle–themed pinball machines, which were apparently once all the rage in certain Great Plains states.

Down the block, a store was selling sacks of old baseball cards for a dollar a bag. I knew from my previous visit with Coby that these were not a bargain. For every worthwhile player, there were fifty benchwarmers in the batch, a marketing technique that weirdly prefigured the bundles of bad loans mixed with good that investment banks were selling to the public.

Near the card store I ran into Jim Rice, the Boston slugger, sitting at a table manfully signing his name—without an HoF—on baseballs. As a player, Rice had been notoriously withdrawn and uncooperative with the media, and it had cost him Hall of Fame votes from the writers. Now he had just a couple years of BBWAA eligibility left, and he was trying hard to project a friendlier public image. Exclusion rankled him. "All these guys had big numbers," he told me, waving a very large arm in the direction of some of the immortals at a nearby signing table. "But I put up big numbers, too. Yes, I did. Did they dominate? Yes. But I dominated, too."

"Maybe you'll get in next year," I ventured.

Rice fixed me with a hard stare. "If the people had a vote, I'd get in," he said. "But I can't influence the writers. I can't even get a list of the ones who vote."

"I don't vote," I assured him. "I'm not a baseball writer."

Rice regarded me with a renewed interest; I might be a paying customer. His signature was going for thirty dollars a pop, high for somebody not in the Hall. There was economic logic to this. If Rice made it into the Hall (as he would in 2009), the value of his autograph would shoot up. Basically he was selling Jim Rice futures.

"I am writing a book on the Hall of Fame, though. Do you want to talk about your prospects?"

"No," said Rice.

"Maybe it will help you get in," I said.

Rice gave me a look of sheer skepticism. "Might make it worse," he said.

For certain ex-players without a Hall of Fame future, Induction Weekend offers a chance to meet old friends and teammates, to reminisce with fans, and to be somebody—even a little somebody—for a day or two. The pharmacy on Main Street was offering "one free autograph from major league pitcher John Montefusco of the Giants, with the purchase of a Coke." Montefusco had a very respectable thirteen-year career with four teams in the seventies and eighties, finishing with 90 wins and a lifetime ERA of 3.54. Good, but not great. Still, here he was in Cooperstown, a guy whose signature was not worth nothing.

Most young boys dream, if only for a moment, that they will someday be major-league ballplayers. They play until they reach their level of incompetence. Millions start in Little League. Tens of thousands make it to high school teams or the Babe Ruth League. A small percentage go on to play in college or the minors. A tiny elite get to the top. Since the dawn of professional baseball, almost a century and a half ago, just over seventeen thousand young men have made it all the way to the majors.

John Montefusco's name on a scrap of paper might not have much market value, but there were lots of people happy to get one for the price of a soft drink and shoot the breeze with a guy who once pitched to Hank Aaron. Seeing Montefusco made me think of the unsung heroes of my own youth—Yankee killer Frank Lary; first baseman Earl "Torgy" Torgeson; Charlie "Sunday Punch" Maxwell, the AL's top Sabbath slugger. I've met quite a few famous people in the course of a long career as a reporter, but I would rather share a Coke with Torgy or Maxwell than with Kofi Annan any day, and I bet most people would. Although, who knows? There are probably kids out there today who collect UN trading cards.

I stepped out of the drugstore and found myself face to face with Al Kaline. For some reason it hadn't occurred to me he would be here. Willie Mays, sure. Yogi Berra, Bob Gibson, Frank Robinson in a golf cap—but not Kaline. It was like running into Achilles. But there he was, sitting quietly at an autograph table on Main Street, next to former teammate Senator Jim Bunning, signing his name on baseballs with a shy, fixed smile on his thin lips.

Al Kaline and I broke into baseball together. In 1955, he led the American League in hitting with a .340 average, the youngest batting champion in history. He played in the All-Star Game outfield with Mickey Mantle and Ted Williams. The papers called Kaline (as they had once called Ted Williams) "the Kid." That was also what I called myself (to myself) on my first Little League team. As baseball years are computed, we were practically the same age.

Detroit back then was a rough sports scene. The Red Wings Gordie Howe was revered as not only the greatest player in the NHL but also the dirtiest; he once practically decapitated Rangers defenseman Lou Fontinato in a fistfight. Lions quarterback Bobby Layne was a reliable DUI after almost every home game. The raucous spirit of Ty Cobb hung over Briggs Stadium. But Al Kaline never did or said anything embarrassing—at least nothing I ever heard about.

Not every kid on the sandlot was a Kaline man. One of our pitchers, Jimmy Spadafore, idolized Whitey Ford, an act of treason against the Tigers we attributed to the fact that Jimmy was both a lefty and a Catholic. Jimmy had an ancient uncle who would sit on the front porch and curse loudly in Sicilian, probably at the fates that had deposited him in Pontiac, Michigan, instead of a civilized place like Brooklyn.

In the outfield we had two brothers, transplanted hillbillies named Hubert and Herbert. We called them the twins, although they weren't. For some reason, they both wanted to be center fielder Bill Tuttle. There was also a born-again Christian first baseman named Monroe who claimed to be a distant cousin of Tigers third baseman Ray Boone.

We almost never saw our heroes in person. Pontiac was an hour away from Briggs Stadium, and back then an hour was an hour. My grandfather took me to my first game—which, I soon realized, was his first game, too. We sat in right field, just behind Kaline. I had my glove with me, in case something got over his head. Late in the game, a bunch of kids jumped over the low wall and began racing around the field, trying to touch Kaline, with ushers and stadium security in hot pursuit. My grandfather nudged me gently and said, "Nu, why don't you go down there and play with the other boys?"

The only baseball fan among my immigrant relatives was my uncle Pinchus. He had the round red face and slightly slanted eyes common among Hungarian Jews. He also shared the Hungarian inability to learn languages. After fifty years in America, he barely spoke English. Pinchus was a pious man who wore a black silk skullcap of the kind often found in the loaner bin in the foyer of synagogues. He never attended an actual game. I doubt that he knew the rules of baseball. He couldn't follow the Tigers easily, either: his Hungarian newspaper didn't carry box scores. But he never missed a game on the radio. On Friday nights and Saturdays he would ask a gentile (or a grandnephew) to turn on the radio for him. I often wondered what he got out of it, since he couldn't understand the play-by-play.

My uncle's fandom, as it turned out, dated back to Hank Greenberg, the Tigers Hall of Fame first baseman. In 1934, Detroit began the month of September in a hot pennant race. A crucial game against

Boston was scheduled for Rosh Hashanah, the Jewish new year. Greenberg had promised his parents that he wouldn't play on a holy day, but manager Mickey Cochrane convinced him to reassess his priorities. Greenberg hit a home run in the ninth to beat Boston 2–1. The city celebrated Greenberg, but a lot of Jews were disappointed.

A reporter from the *New York Evening Post* traveled up to the Bronx to discuss the matter with Greenberg's parents. "It's not so terrible," Mama Greenberg said. "I see young guys go to the Temple in the morning and then maybe do worse things than Henry did." Papa Greenberg took a harder line, saying that he was putting his foot down and his son would not be playing on Yom Kippur. Greenberg listened to Papa and sat the game out. As it turned out, it didn't matter to the team—the Tigers had already more or less clinched the pennant—but for Greenberg, it was one of the greatest public relations moves in baseball history. Edgar Guest, a nationally syndicated poet (such a thing actually existed back then), expressed the general mood in a tribute called "Speaking of Greenberg."

Come Yom Kippur—holy fast day world-wide over to the Jew—
And Hank Greenberg to his teaching and the old tradition true
Spent the day among his people and he didn't come to play.
Said Murphy to Mulrooney, "We shall lose the game today!
We shall miss him on the infield and shall miss him at the bat,
But he's true to his religion—and I honor him for that!"

If that's what Murphy said to Mulrooney, you can imagine how Uncle Pinchus felt. Hank had taken one for the tribe. His Rosh Hashanah lapse was forgiven, a temporary flaw, like Moses smashing the tablets in a fit of pique. From that day on, the Tigers were the Jews in my uncle's opinion, and the rest of the American League teams were goyim.

As a kid, I scoffed at this kind of ethnic patriotism, but with time I have come to see that you can't be a baseball fan in a vacuum. We love the players and teams that we can identify with. How different, really, was Pinchus from the Baltimoreans who packed Cooperstown to pay tribute to Cal Ripken? They, too, were a tribe: white middle-class folks who had grown up in the city and fled to the suburbs, refugees in their own minds, whose main tie to the metropolis of their nativity was their love of the Orioles.

Al Kaline was a member of this Baltimore tribe, a working-class German-Irish kid who married his sweetheart right out of Southern High School, moved to Detroit, and stayed there for fifty years as a player and broadcaster. Team loyalty and traditional conformity are highly prized virtues in the baseball culture, which prefers its heroes plain and modest. Individuality and charisma are often discouraged as "hot-dogging." Players don't usually get into Cooperstown with the baseball equivalent of end-zone spikes or 360-degree dunks. This was especially true in the American League of my youth, where the dashing, athletic style of the Negro leagues was actively discouraged by the simple expedient of hiring very few black players. The Tigers were less hospitable to African-Americans than most; their first player of color, Ozzie Virgil—who didn't arrive until 1958—was from the Dominican Republic. Since integration, the fans of Detroit, and other American League cities, had grown increasingly nervous about the growing gap between us and the National League. Kaline was a great white hope, proof that you didn't need to be a Mays or an Aaron or a Clemente to be great. There's no record that Kaline shared or encouraged this view—and none that he didn't. He was always the strong, silent type.

Standing in line waiting to meet Kaline, I could see his acne scars. As a kid, another thing I had loved about Kaline was his courage. He knew how to play through zits (although he had them erased on his baseball card). I used to imagine him keeping a tube of Clearasil in his locker. For a moment my cynical adult self wondered what other substances he might have had stashed in there, but I dismissed the thought as unworthy. I can no more picture Al Kaline using steroids than I can Davy Crockett hunting bear with an Uzi. Besides, I owed Kaline. Although he didn't know it, he gave me a gift that had lasted me a lifetime: a magic number.

When my turn came, I introduced myself as a writer working on a book. Kaline took this in with an expression of polite wariness. Like other great players, he has spent many years deflecting hero worshippers, groupies, cranks, reminiscers, irate critics, hustlers, guys down on their luck: an entire universe of needy strangers. He glanced over my shoulder where the line of paying customers—at sixty dollars a signature—was stalled. "Sounds interesting," he said. "Why don't you get in touch with me and we can discuss it? The Tigers PR department will know how to reach me."

"The Tigers," I said, as if I were hearing the name for the first time. "Right, the PR department."

"Great," said Kaline with a smile of well-mannered dismissal.

"PR department," I repeated. "Right?"

"Right."

And that was that. I wanted to say: Al, I know you don't remember me, but we broke in together. I'm the kid in right field with the weird grandfather who wanted me to run out on the field that night. And .340? That's my number.

As a ten-year-old I had taken my first and last ride on a monster roller coaster. Back on solid ground, I wondered how I would know if I was ever truly frightened out of my wits—so scared that I was actually mentally incapacitated. I needed a secret watchword, a wit-detector, something so fundamental that forgetting it would be a sign of total breakdown. I chose the one thing I knew better than my own name: Kaline's championship batting average.

I focused on .340 through teenage traumas, took it with me to the army, and invoked it in the midst of a near-drowning in the Sea of Galilee. In Tel Aviv, during the first Gulf War, every time I had to fit a gas mask onto my nine-year-old son's face, I thought of Kaline.

In my drinking days, .340 was a self-administered sobriety test (warning: this is not admissible in court). It will probably be my last volitional thought before sinking into Alzheimer's.

There was no way to explain this to Kaline, especially not at the front of a line of strangers under a blistering August sun. Besides, I didn't want to take the chance that he wouldn't be in the least interested.

The Freeman's Journal is Cooperstown's weekly newspaper. It was founded in 1808 by the father of James Fenimore Cooper. On Induction Weekend, with the national press assembled in the village, the *Journal* has an opportunity to express its thoughts on the state of baseball. The paper is independently owned, but it often publishes Hall of Fame press releases verbatim, has an unfailingly admiring view of Hall chairwoman Jane Forbes Clark, and is generally regarded as a reliable reflection of the Cooperstown establishment's point of view.* The subject of 2007's editorial was steroids—and what to do about Barry Bonds.

> *While 60,000 fans honor Ripken and Gwynn—both men symbolize hard work and fair play—in baseball's mecca, on the West Coast a tainted Barry Bonds is passing Hank Aaron's career home-run record of 755. It's widely believed that Bonds would not be where he is without long-term use of steroids . . .*
>
> *This isn't academic. Cooperstown depends on a healthy Hall of Fame, which depends on a healthy sport, which depends on the public's affection for the National Game.*

* The material on the Clark family is based largely on *The Clarks of Cooperstown*, by Nicholas Fox Weber. Jane Forbes Clark made it clear that she does not hold the book in high regard. As an antidote, she sent me *Cooperstown*, by Louis C. Jones, originally published by the Otsego County Historical Society. Unsurprisingly, the book contains a highly sanitized view of the Clarks and their beneficence.

> *Five years from now when he becomes eligible—and every year thereafter—the Baseball Writers' Association of America should categorically reject Barry Bonds for Hall of Fame enshrinement. MLB should crack down on steroid use definitively and with finality. The players' union should be just as adamant.*

The Cooperstown establishment was tacking up a message on its clubhouse door for the rest of baseball—including the BBWAA, whose members serve as an electoral college at the discretion of the Hall's board of directors—to see and absorb: No Cheaters Allowed.

On Sunday afternoon, a vast crowd gathered on the shadeless lawn of the Clark Sports Center to witness the enshrinement of Tony Gwynn and Cal Ripken, two "good guys" who had never been suspected (or at least publicly accused) of using any performance enhancer stronger than Wheaties.

Fifty-three of the sixty-one living Hall of Fame players were on stage, under a canopy that protected them from the blistering sun. The most notable absentee was Hank Aaron, who was maintaining radio silence during Bonds's run at his record. He had been a friend and competitor of Bonds's father, Bobby, and of Willie Mays, Barry Bonds's godfather, and Aaron didn't want to get stampeded by the establishment into saying something derogatory.

The Hall of Famers were introduced. Naturally, the Baltimore crowd gave loud, hometown ovations to Brooks Robinson, Frank Robinson, Eddie Murray, Earl Weaver, and Jim Palmer. Willie Mays, Yogi Berra, and Reggie Jackson drew huge cheers, too. The biggest applause of the day went to the elusive Sandy Koufax, one of the only Hall of Famers who hadn't spent the weekend signing autographs. Koufax is the Greta Garbo of baseball—short career, great charisma.

Sam Abbott, the rector of Christ Church in town, rose to render an Episcopalian baseball prayer. He assured the crowd that there were no losers there that day, only winners. He thanked the Lord for the inductees ("Have you ever created a man more effective with the bat than Tony Gwynn? Have you ever created a man more persevering in suiting up and playing hard despite nagging injuries, losing seasons, and mathematical elimination than Cal Ripken?"). He ended by thanking God for Stephen C. Clark, whose "vision and generosity" had enabled the founding of the Baseball Hall of Fame.

Jane Forbes Clark, Stephen's granddaughter, rose to greet the crowd. A handsome woman in her early fifties, she wore a simple white dress and a strand of pearls. "The men behind me," she said with aristocratic serenity, "define Hall of Fame character, integrity, sportsmanship, and incredible baseball careers." The crowd cheered, of course, but I couldn't help but wonder how much Ms. Clark actually knew about the men she had introduced with such sincerity. Many of them were, indeed, men of high character and unblemished reputation. But among them I counted a convicted drug dealer, a reformed cokehead who narrowly beat a lifetime suspension from baseball, a celebrated sex addict, an Elders of Zion conspiracy nut, a pitcher who wrote a book about how he cheated his way into the Hall, a well-known and highly arrested drunk driver, and a couple of nasty beanball artists. They had been washed clean by the magical powers of Cooperstown, HoF certified.

Tony Gwynn was the first inductee to speak. The Hall of Fame helps its new members prepare by sending them speeches from years past, but it doesn't do much good. In the old days, the players were mercifully brief. At the first ceremony, in 1939, Walter Johnson stood up, said "I'm very proud to have my name enrolled in the Hall of Fame. And I'm very happy to have my name enrolled with these men," and sat back down again. Gywnn said approximately the same thing in fifteen minutes. He thanked his parents, his brothers, his wife, his children (his son is a ballplayer; his daughter, a singer, had just performed the national anthem), his managers, coaches, teammates, opponents, friends, and fans. Then—totally oblivious to the tens of thousands of people baking on the lawn before him—he delivered a quotidian account of his long career. Presumably, San Diego fans found it interesting.

Cal Ripken came up next and gave an iron-man oratorical performance that made Gwynn's ramble seem like the Gettysburg Address. On a few memorable occasions in Cooperstown history, inductees have used their speeches to say something important. In 1995, Mike Schmidt called on baseball to reinstate Pete Rose. A year later, Jim Bunning, a congressman at the time, issued a stern warning to a baseball establishment that was stumbling through a series of strikes and scandals. "Get your house in order. Stop going to the players and asking them to foot the bill. And get a commissioner—a real commissioner [an allusion to the fact that Milwaukee owner Bud Selig was "acting commissioner" at the time]. Come up with a way to share the revenues . . . Find a rudder before Congress gives up on you and intervenes."

Bunning's warning was scoffed at by the press, but he proved prescient. In the years since his induction, Congress has become increasingly involved in baseball issues. A lot of lawmakers looked at Barry Bonds's expanding hatband and saw themselves on C-SPAN.

The most important induction speech in the Hall's history was delivered by Ted Williams in 1966. It came, appropriately, out of left field. "Inside the building are plaques to baseball men of all generations. I'm proud to join them. Baseball gives every American boy a chance to excel. Not just to be as good as someone else, but to be better than someone else. That is the nature of man and the nature of the game. And I've been a very lucky guy to have worn a baseball uniform, and I hope some day the names of Satchel Paige and Josh Gibson in some way can be added as a symbol of the great

Negro players who are not here only because they weren't given a chance."

Ripken was not planning to do a Bunning or a Williams. He began with the customary life list of thank-yous and then turned philosophical. "Did you ever stop to think about how your life would unfold or imagine how you would like your life to turn out? One of those reflective pauses happened in my life when I was around eighteen years old. I thought I had it all figured out: I would play big-league baseball until about forty-five and then worry about the rest of my life after that. It took me a little while, but I did come to realize that baseball was just one part of my life—with the possible exception of this weekend, of course. This was never more clear to me than when we had children. I realized that the secret of life is life."

The crowd cheered and cheered. They loved Ripken, a regular guy who said what they would have said. They loved Cooperstown, too; a place that looked like America was meant to look. They loved the Hall of Fame, a magical shrine with the power to freeze time and let heroes live forever. Eventually they stopped cheering and clapping and began to file out in the direction of the closest cold beer and the chartered buses that would take them back to Baltimore and the America that really is.

TWO . . . *Paternity Suit*

The Baseball Hall of Fame—like many great American institutions—was founded by a fortune and a fiction. Its story begins before the Civil War and, at first, it had nothing to do with baseball.

In 1851, a mad machinist named Isaac Merritt Singer patented a sewing machine. Singer was a man of huge physical size and appetites, husband and consort to multiple women, the father of at least twenty children.

To help patent his various inventions, Singer turned to a New York attorney named Ambrose Jordan. But Jordan found him so unbearably vulgar that he palmed him off on his son-in-law and junior law partner, a buttoned-down gentleman by the name of Edward Clark.

Together, Clark, the son of a well-to-do Hudson Valley family, and the scandalous Singer fought a prolonged legal battle with other sewing machine inventors and patent attorneys over the rights to the new machine. Finally, they reached an agreement that made everyone happy. Singer and Clark wound up as partners in the IM Singer Sewing Machine Company, and soon the two of them were among the richest men in America.

Singer used his money to acquire a mansion on Fifth Avenue and proceeded to scandalize polite New York society with orgies and excesses. Eventually he was arrested for bigamy. (Since he had three wives at the time, the charge probably should have been trigamy, or mass marriage—a fourth wife was discovered after he fled.) He escaped to Europe, where he remained in exile, with a new, French wife. Eventually he landed in England, where he built a 115-room mansion and populated it with many of the children from his five baby mamas. When he died, in 1875, chaos over the inheritance ensued.

Edward Clark spent his money in more genteel fashion. A staid Episcopalian and family man, he moved his newly wealthy family to Cooperstown in 1854 and embarked on the life of an American aristocrat. Clark picked Cooperstown because the beauty of the area charmed him and, mostly, because his wife had been raised there.

The village itself had been founded about 1800 by William Cooper, a hot-tempered New York Federalist who sided with Aaron Burr against Alexander Hamilton. Like Hamilton, Cooper got himself killed over politics, purportedly sustaining a fatal knock in the head during a heated political argument in Albany in 1809. Cooper left behind a passel of children, including his twenty-year-old son, James Fenimore Cooper.

The younger Cooper, of course, became a famous writer and a civic booster. In 1838, he predicted a fine future for his village. "We shall have no mushroom city but there is little doubt that in the course of time, as the population of the country fills up this spot will contain a provincial town of importance," he wrote.

Like his father before him, Cooper was the leading citizen of Cooperstown. And, like his father, he was a contentious fellow. His neighbors mostly hated him, especially after he refused to let them use the village picnic grounds, which he legally owned. He died in 1851, and two years later his grand house, Otsego Hall, burned down. When Edward Clark moved to Cooperstown the following year, the villagers were more than ready for a new squire.

The Clarks have now dominated Cooperstown and the region around it for five generations. They own just about everything, starting with the grand Otesaga Hotel, where Hall of Famers are put up during Induction Week. The family holdings include about ten thousand acres in and around the village. The family founded and controls the local hospital, donated the land for the public schools, and built the Clark Sports Center. The Clark Foundation supplies villagers with scholarships and grants, decorates the town for the holidays, and more or less takes care of whatever civic emergencies arise. And, of course, the Clarks control the Hall of Fame.

For Cooperstown, the regency of the Clarks has been, by and large, pleasant and prosperous. The family's excesses and eccentricities have been largely enacted away from home. Edward Clark built the Dakota, one of Manhattan's first luxury apartment buildings and now a cherished landmark, though at the time it was derided as "Clark's Folly." His son Alfred was the very model of a Victorian husband and father at home—and led a secret homosexual life in Europe. Alfred had four children, all boys, of which the two most interesting were Sterling and Stephen. They were fellow art collectors but bitter rivals. Sterling scandalized his (ostensibly) staid family by marrying a French actress. After the death of their mother, in 1909, Sterling, Stephen, and their two brothers were among the richest people in the world.

Sterling Clark was a nasty piece of work. He turned a fight over the inheritance into a long-running tabloid sensation. At one point he denounced his youngest brother, Stephen, as "that swine and treacherous sneak."

Sterling had nothing to do with the Baseball Hall of Fame, but he does merit an asterisk in the annals of American political scandal. Sterling despised Franklin Roosevelt, to whom he always referred as "Rosenfart," as a traitor to his class. In November 1934, the *New York Times* reported that a retired Marine Corps major general, Smedley Darlington Butler, had informed a committee of the House of Representatives that Sterling Clark had approached him with a plan to overthrow the government and replace Roosevelt with a military dictator, General Hugh S. Johnson. Both Johnson and Clark denied it, and a House investigation was inconclusive. But a member of that inquiry, John McCormack of Massachusetts, described the attempted putsch as "a threat to our very way of government by a bunch of rich men who wanted Fascism."

In 1936, Sterling decided to pack up and leave Cooperstown to his brothers. In a departing gesture of animosity, he refused to sell them his property, donating it instead to a children's home. It was only three years later that Sterling's brother Stephen would create the Baseball Hall of Fame in Cooperstown. This is where forgery and fiction enter the story.

To understand how this happened, you have to dial back to a clash of baseball titans in 1903. Henry Chadwick was the first great baseball journalist and statistician—the Bill James of the nineteenth century. Born in England, he came to America as a young man and for forty years was baseball's foremost historian and reporter. He edited the *Beadle's Dime Base Ball Player*, the sport's first publication, and created the game's essential statistical measures, such as batting average and earned run average. He also expanded the box score and was the first to compile running totals of home runs, games played, and other foundational numbers. Without Chadwick and his stats, generations of American kids would have been left with nothing to memorize.

In 1903, at the age of eighty, Chadwick published an article on the origins of baseball, in which he took a Darwinian view. The game, he argued, had its roots in the two-century-old English game of rounders, which in the new world had gradually morphed into town ball; the first organized team was the Olympic Town Ball Club of Philadelphia, circa 1833. Town ball had, he concluded, evolved into baseball as it was at the turn of the twentieth century.

This was not exactly news. Chadwick had been asserting this evolutionary doctrine of baseball's origins for twenty-five years. But the spirit of the times had changed. America was in the midst of the biggest and, to many, the most disconcerting wave of immigration in its history. In 1892, Ellis Island opened America's front door, and in the next two decades almost thirteen million people—almost a quarter of the entire pre-1890 population—came in. These new immigrants were not Protestant immigrants from northern Europe but Jews, Italian Catholics, and other exotic breeds. A lot of Americans worried that they would change the national character. President Theodore Roosevelt was among the concerned. He welcomed newcomers on condition that they learn English and blend into the American culture; the U.S., he warned, had no place for hyphenated citizens.*

Chadwick, the man who labeled baseball a foreign import, was himself hyphenated.

Someone had to challenge Chadwick's account. That man was A. G. Spalding.

If Henry Chadwick was known as the Father of Baseball, Spalding was its first superstar. He broke in as a pitcher with the Boston Red Stockings in 1871 and led the National Association in wins for five straight years. Twice he won 50 games in a season. In 1875, his record was 55–5. The following year, he moved to the newly formed National League, where the Chicago team paid him a salary and 25 percent of the gate in return for his services. He led the NL with 47 wins that year. Spalding retired after the next season with a lifetime 253–65 won–lost record and a 2.14 ERA. He was twenty-six years old.

The same keen business instinct that prompted Spalding to cut himself in on the Chicago gate receipts led him to found A. G. Spalding and Brothers, which turned into the first great American sporting goods empire. In 1878, he founded *Spalding's Official Base Ball Guide and Official League Book*, the most important baseball journal of its time. To edit it, he hired Henry Chadwick himself. A decade later, figuring that his fortunes were neatly tied up with the American

* Roosevelt didn't personally like baseball; he considered it a sport for sissies. But he often praised the game as "typically American."

game, he organized a baseball exhibition tour of Australia, New Zealand, Ceylon (now Sri Lanka), Italy, France, and England. The entire United States followed his exploits; in Egypt, according to legend, he used the pyramids as a backstop.

Spalding returned to great acclaim from his round-the-world tour, and by the turn of the twentieth century, A. G. Spalding was a very rich and prominent man. In 1900, President McKinley appointed him commissioner of the American Olympic Committee. The *Boston Herald*, with only slight exaggeration, called Spalding the most famous American after Lincoln and Washington. His name, the *Herald* reported, "has been blazing forth on the cover of guides to all sorts of sports, upon bats and gloves for many years. Young America gets its knowledge of the past in the world of athletics from something that has 'Al Spalding' on it in big black letters, and for that reason, as much as any other, he is one of the national figures of our time."

Spalding, a proud nationalist in the Teddy Roosevelt mold, was offended by Chadwick's notion that baseball had evolved from an Old World game. But Chadwick was his friend as well as his employee, and he loved the old guy. Besides, not even A. G. Spalding had the stature to challenge Chadwick's authority as a historian. What Spalding needed was an alternative creation myth, one backed up by evidence. To get it, he devised the Mills Commission.

Despite its official-sounding name, the commission was not a publicly appointed body. Its members were handpicked by Spalding. For a chairman, he selected Abraham G. Mills of New York, a businessman and former president of the National League who shared Spalding's nativist views of baseball. Other members included U.S. senators Morgan G. Bulkeley of Connecticut (another former president of the National League) and Arthur Pue Gorman of Maryland, along with the secretary of the Amateur Athletic Union and two former ballplayers turned businessmen.

For evidence, Spalding furnished chairman Mills with a sort of baseball Book of Mormon: an eyewitness account of the origins of the game, written by one Abner Graves, a retired mining engineer living in Colorado. In the letter, Graves, who grew up in Cooperstown, described how one day in 1839 a local chap named Abner Doubleday had laid out four bases in the shape of a diamond, divided the boys of Cooperstown into two teams, and brought order out of a chaotic town scrum. In Spalding's interpretation, this made Doubleday the architect and creator of baseball.

Doubleday was an excellent choice. He was a Civil War hero, an officer who fired the first shot at Fort Sumter, was wounded at the Second Battle of Bull Run, rose to the rank of major general, and commanded a division at the battles of Chancellorsville and Gettysburg, where a statue stands in his honor. After leaving the army, Doubleday moved to San Francisco, where he founded the first cable car company. He was also a prolific writer of memoirs and essays, none of which, oddly, ever mentioned playing baseball, let alone inventing it. And, when he died in 1893, none of his obituaries said anything about baseball, either.

But this didn't bother Spalding, and it certainly didn't matter to Mills, who like Doubleday was a Union veteran and a New Yorker. On December 30, 1907, he reported that after due consideration, the committee had concluded that Abner Doubleday had, indeed, invented baseball on the green in Cooperstown in 1839. Only one member demurred.

Mills was no fool. He knew his report was not a model of investigative rectitude. Asked directly in 1926 if he had any actual proof, he admitted that he had "none at all as far as the actual origin of the game of baseball is concerned." The commission, he said, had merely reported that the first actual baseball diamond was laid out in Cooperstown. "They were honorable men . . . if our search had been for a typical American village, a village that could stand as a counterpart of all villages where baseball might have been originated and developed—Cooperstown would best fit the bill."

But by the time Mills made this admission, Spalding and Chadwick were both long gone and their controversy over the game's origins considered a settled matter. Cooperstown was officially recognized by baseball as the site of its nativity and Abner Doubleday was its recognized father. According to myth, Abraham Lincoln himself had summoned General Doubleday to his deathbed and pleaded with him to keep the game alive. Lincoln was, in fact, a baseball fan. He even built a diamond on the grounds of the White House. But it seems extremely unlikely that, lying mortally wounded, the Great Emancipator would have had the future of baseball on his mind.

At first, the villagers of Cooperstown were bemused by the discovery that they were living in the Bethlehem of baseball. It had been almost eighty years since Abner Doubleday had been in town—if he ever was in town—and nobody remembered him. But it gradually began to dawn on folks that there might be money in the baseball connection. In 1917, five villagers kicked in a quarter of a dollar apiece to set up a Doubleday Memorial Fund. Their idea was to establish a "national baseball field" and a players' retirement home, which would attract tourism to the town. The Cooperstown Chamber of Commerce sent a delegation to New York City to ask the blessing of Major League Baseball, and National League president John Heydler promised his support. By 1919, a little cash was raised, enough to begin—but not complete—the construction of Doubleday Field in a swampy area on the exact spot Abner Graves had cited in his letter. The project might never have come to fruition if it hadn't caught the attention of the Clark family.

The years after World War I were tough on Cooperstown. A blight destroyed much of the hops crop, the agricultural mainstay of the area. Young people began leaving for the city, as they were doing all across small-town America. The depression hit hard. Cooperstown had once been a summer destination for wealthy New Yorkers, but with the economy in shambles, fewer and fewer could afford the excursion.

By the early thirties, the war between the Clark brothers had come to a close. Sterling was preparing to pack up and leave his stodgy younger brother and the village of Cooperstown to each other. Stephen, it seems, had won the war, and Cooperstown seemed to have gotten the better end of the stick, too. The younger Clark was a generous and civic-minded man and felt a sense of noblesse oblige toward his village. If Cooperstown was to fulfill the prophecy of James Fenimore Cooper and become a substantial town, it had to find a reliable source of income.

It was Alexander Cleland, one of Clark's senior executives, who came up with the idea of cashing in on baseball. Cleland had immigrated to the U.S. from Scotland at the age of twenty-six, and he neither knew nor cared much about his adopted country's national pastime. But he saw that Cooperstown's claim to be the birthplace of baseball was worth something. In 1934, he wrote Clark a letter proposing to establish a baseball museum that would draw fans. "Hundreds of visitors would be attracted to the shopping district right in the heart of Cooperstown, each year," he predicted.

The idea appealed to Clark. He didn't care much for baseball, either, but he saw the possibilities of tourist attraction. In the spring of 1934, he dispatched Cleland to New York City to discuss the matter with Ford Frick, newly installed as the president of the National League.

Frick was a former baseball writer and publicist, a man who thought big. As far as he was concerned, if Cooperstown got some tourists, fine, but the real goal was to build baseball's brand with something that would engage the imagination of fans everywhere, even the ones who didn't have the money to reach a museum way out in the sticks. What about a place that celebrated the players themselves—a baseball hall of fame? And what better place to build it than alongside the baseball museum in the hometown of Abner Doubleday?

Frick's hall of fame idea wasn't original. It was inspired by a recent visit to the Hall of Fame for Great Americans, founded in New York City in 1900 by Henry Mitchell MacCracken, chancellor of New York University. Its goal was to celebrate the eminent men and women of the world's ascending economic and cultural colossus. The constitution of the hall specified the sort of people who would be eligible: authors and poets, educators, men of the cloth, missionaries, social reformers, scientists, engineers and architects, physicians, inventors, captains of industry, military figures, statesmen, lawyers and judges, artists and musicians.

The Hall of Fame for Great Americans no longer adds members or draws many visitors. It's still open for business, though, on the grounds of what is now the Bronx Community College in New York. (The campus once belonged to NYU.) It commands a high bluff overlooking the Harlem River, and its main feature is a 630-foot open-air colonnade designed by the great American architect Stanford White. Bronze busts of the immortals are placed in niches along a walkway. Some of the likenesses were produced by Daniel Chester French, sculptor of the Lincoln Memorial. Lincoln was among the hall's first class of inductees, along with George Washington, Thomas Jefferson, John Adams, U. S. Grant, Benjamin Franklin, Robert E. Lee, Ralph Waldo Emerson, and a cast of now-forgotten jurists and ministers of the gospel. In 1910, the hall inducted Cooperstown's favorite son, James Fenimore Cooper.

"By happy chance," Frick writes in his autobiography, "I had visited the National Hall of Fame at New York University a few days before [his meeting with Cleland]. I was much impressed and had the notion that a Baseball Hall of Fame would be great for the game."

By 1935, Clark and Frick had a plan for a Cooperstown baseball multiplex—Doubleday Field, where construction, which had been going on in a desultory fashion since 1919, was now being completed by the WPA; a museum; and a hall of fame. Now all they needed were artifacts to put in the museum, a game to play on the field, and some players to enshrine in the hall.

Stephen Clark had a solution for the first problem, and it only cost him five bucks. Abner Graves's old home in nearby Fly Creek was being prepared for demolition and, in the process, an old trunk was found in the attic. It contained a small, weather-beaten ball stuffed with cloth. Walter Littell, editor of the local *Otsego Farmer*, decided that this must be a ball that had belonged to Graves. Perhaps it had been used by Doubleday himself. In fact, it might be the *very first baseball.*

Stephen Clark, one of America's great art collectors, understood the value of such a relic. He paid the farmer who owned the ball five dollars, put the ball on display in the Cooperstown Village Building, and sent out word that the new museum would be glad to accept donations to its collection.

The timing was perfect. Baseball was due to celebrate its centennial in 1939, just a few years hence. Frick went to the commissioner of baseball, Judge Kenesaw Mountain Landis, and proposed that the birthday be celebrated in Cooperstown with an all-star game on Doubleday Field.

Judge Landis was an imperious and vain man whose main qualification for the job of commissioner of baseball was cosmetic; he looked like an actor playing a figure of judicial rectitude. He didn't much care for ideas that originated with subordinates, but this one was too good to turn down. Clark would take care of building the museum. Washington, courtesy of the WPA, was providing the stadium. The Hall of Fame was a publicity bonanza for baseball, and it wouldn't cost him or his bosses, the team owners, a cent. It had been generally accepted that the centennial festivities would take place in Washington, D.C. But Cooperstown would make an even better venue for the commissioner; no elected officials would be able to crowd him off center stage. And so he gave the entire enterprise his blessing, which is when things really took off.

Stephen Clark appointed himself chairman, president, and CEO of the Hall of Fame, in which capacities he served until his death in 1960. This was an act of civic responsibility on his part. Clark was in his early fifties and art, not baseball, was his passion. Actually, passion might be the wrong word. Even his admiring biographer, Nicholas Fox Weber, concedes that Clark was seen by the world as a prim, cold, taciturn fellow. At the Museum of Modern Art in New York City, where he was president and chairman of the board between 1939 and 1946, some people referred to him as "the mortician." Clark ran his businesses and philanthropies with a high hand, but no one questioned his rectitude. "He was formal and aloof," writes Weber, "but he was driven by his morality, his perpetual wish to do what was best, to advance a good cause and to serve others."

When it came to modern art, Clark was no dilettante: he was a true expert, and he put the stamp of his collector's taste and judgment on the museum he led. Baseball was a different story. He lacked the expertise—and the desire—to act as a super curator.

What he did do was to make sure that the new museum to be built on Main Street next to Doubleday Field—a two-story, colonial red-brick edifice—would be a tasteful and elegant addition to the village. The museum had 1,200 square feet of exhibition space, large enough to house an initial collection that included a baseball from Cy Young's 500th win, one of Christy Mathewson's gloves, a uniform donated by Ty Cobb, and a pair of Babe Ruth's shoes, as well as the centerpiece Doubleday Baseball, a lopsided icon stitched from poor rags and a very rich imagination.

On June 12, 1939, the Hall of Fame held its grand opening. Frick had done a tremendous job of public relations. Special trains were engaged in New York City to bring fifteen thousand fans to Cooperstown. Baseball heroes roamed the town signing autographs (nobody dreamed at the time of charging for them) and chatting with the crowd. Babe Ruth bought cigars at the village drugstore and stopped at the local barbershop for a shave, but was too impatient to wait his turn. Over at the post office, a team of seventy, led by James Farley, the postmaster general of the United States, sold three-cent stamps commemorating baseball's hundredth birthday. Microphones for a national radio hookup stood on a high platform in front of the museum door. At the stroke of noon, Charles J. Doyle, president of the Baseball Writers' Association of America, opened the proceedings: "Today in Cooperstown, New York, home of baseball, we gather in reverence to the game's immortals—living and dead . . ."

A famous photo captured ten of the eleven living players inducted into the Hall of Fame that day: Eddie Collins, Babe Ruth, Cy Young, Honus Wagner, Grover Cleveland Alexander, Tris Speaker, Napoleon Lajoie, George Sisler, and Walter Johnson. Ty Cobb arrived late and missed getting into the picture. Christy Mathewson and Wee Willie Keeler were dead. Connie Mack was in the photo, too; he was one of thirteen foundational figures inducted.*

Naturally, Henry Chadwick and A. G. Spalding were among them. Their dispute, more than thirty years earlier, was responsible for Cooperstown's selection as the venue of baseball's nativity. Alexander Cartwright was selected, too. This was a matter of some delicacy for the Hall. Everyone knew that Cartwright had been the founder of one of the earliest formal baseball teams, the New York Knickerbockers, in the 1840s—reason enough to include him in the Hall. But in the run-up to the centennial celebration, Commissioner Landis received a letter from Cartwright's grandson Bruce, pointing out that his

* The players were all inducted at the same time, but they weren't all members of the inaugural class. The BBWAA began holding elections in 1936, when it chose Cobb, Ruth, Wagner, Mathewson, and Johnson. The others were elected in 1937 (Lajoie, Speaker, and Young), 1938 (Alexander), and 1939 (Collins and Keeler).

grandfather had written the rules for baseball in 1845, and he had diagrams and written notes to prove it. This came under the heading of news Landis couldn't use; he already had his creation story, and he was sticking to it. Landis kept the story hushed up and tried to pacify the Cartwright camp by making sure their candidate was among the earliest inductees. But even this might not have been enough to prevent a scandal at the ceremony itself had Cartwright's grandson and loudest booster not died three months before the Hall's dedication. Oddly, Doubleday himself was not inducted in 1939, and never has been.

Over the years, the implausibility of the Doubleday scenario became obvious. In 1953, Cooperstown skeptics convinced Congress to officially cite Alexander Cartwright as the founder of baseball. Like most efforts to legislate history, this was not entirely convincing, either. The best assessment is found on the Web site of the Hall of Fame circa 2008: "We may never know exactly where baseball was invented, and it's possible it was not invented in any one place, but rather evolved in several areas over several years. We do know that some of the earliest forms of organized baseball that we are aware of took place in settings similar to that of Cooperstown. In that sense, the village serves as a fitting representation of the heritage of the game, and a fitting home to the Baseball Hall of Fame."

No such agnosticism was in evidence in Cooperstown on June 12, 1939. Ken Smith, who covered the first induction ceremony for the *New York Mirror* (and later wound up running the Hall), gave a fair account of the general feeling. "Cooperstown . . . now a bustling little village and a shrine to the pioneering spirit of one Abner Doubleday, whose ingenuity conceived the first game of baseball on a pasture, only a few yards from where the remains of the author, [James Fenimore] Cooper, were to be laid years later . . .

"For while the pioneering Cooper may have created a greater

thing, his literary inventions reached fewer people. The product of Abner Doubleday's fertile brain was embraced by millions, accelerating through generations, creating national heroes, wealth, industries, careers and unprecedented recreation."

Earlier that year, the New York Yankees and Washington Senators had kicked off baseball's centennial at Arlington National Cemetery, by attending a memorial service at the graveside of Major General Abner Doubleday. Representative James Shanley, a Connecticut Democrat, introduced a bill making June 12 National Baseball Day. President Franklin Roosevelt sent a letter to Stephen Clark in which he declared it "most fitting that the history of our perennially popular sport should be immortalized . . . where the game originated and where the first diamond was devised a hundred years ago." Given FDR's mischievous sense of humor, it is not impossible that he got a smile out of sending this public blessing to the estranged brother of his would-be nemesis. But he had a serious purpose, too. The United States, in 1939, was preparing itself for a world war. The nation would be called upon to rally around the symbols of its own best self. Thirty years earlier, in the age of Theodore Roosevelt, A. G. Spalding, and the Mills Commission, baseball had been given a forged birth certificate and a war hero for a father, and invited millions of immigrants to learn real American values at the ballpark. Now the sons of the immigrants were preparing to go to war. Nations at war need a sense of shared history, sacred shrines, and heroic symbols. Cooperstown fit the bill perfectly.

The inductees spoke in turn. Nobody said anything particularly memorable.

Babe Ruth was given the final slot, and he used it to hit a rhetorical pop-up. "They started something here," he said, "and the kids are keeping the ball rolling. I hope some of you kids will be in the Hall of Fame. I'm very glad that in my day I was able to earn my place. And I hope that the youngsters of today have the same opportunity to experience such a feeling."

"I now declare the National Baseball Museum and the Baseball Hall of Fame in Cooperstown, New York—home of baseball—open!" boomed Judge Landis. The crowd cheered and headed for Doubleday Field to see a choose-up all-star game between teams captained by Honus Wagner and Eddie Collins. "Each of the major league teams had sent two representatives," wrote Ken Smith.

> *The selection of the two delegates from the New York Yankees had produced a whimsical observation from the loquacious Lefty Gomez. "Leave it to the Yankees to be represented by a couple of foreigners."*
>
> *But his humor only cloaked a deeper realization, that baseball, being a truly American game, reflects the heterogeneity that makes America unique among the nations of the world. The Yankees were represented by Norwegian Arndt Jorgens, a catcher, and outfielder George Selkirk, a citizen of Canada. Cincinnati sent Ernie Lombardi, a California Italian. The New York Giants sent Mel Ott, native of the Louisiana bayou country. Bill Herman of the Cubs and Charlie Gehringer of the Tigers were of German extraction. Morris Arnovich of the Phillies, Moe Berg of the Red Sox and Hank Greenberg of the Tigers were of Jewish parentage. Johnny Vander Meer was of Dutch descent. Pepper Martin and Dizzy Dean of the Cardinals, Lloyd Waner of the Pirates and Carl Hubbell of the Giants, sprang from Southwestern prairie stock . . . And so it went, kaleidoscopic representation welded into a unified purpose: the glorification of baseball's birth.*

Smith wrote these words of praise for the melting pot without noticing that there had been no black players on the field at Cooperstown that day (later that summer, on Fireman's Day, an exhibition contest was held between the Mohawk Colored Giants and the Havana Cubans). The all-star game ended as a tie, called after six innings to allow the assembled dignitaries to make their train back to New York City. It had been a great party and people went home happy. Clark and Cleland had the tourist attraction they wanted. By the end of the summer, almost thirty thousand paying customers visited the Hall—a far cry from the "hundreds" Cleland had predicted only a few years earlier. Ford Frick had put baseball at the very heart of the American narrative and, in the process, created a perpetual public relations machine. Baseball's greatest players had been granted immortality. And somewhere up in heaven, A. G. Spalding, entrepreneur and patriot, was smiling.

THREE . . . *James and the Vets*

If Stephen Clark had been more of a baseball fan, he might have insisted that there be some professional criteria for membership in the Hall. But he wasn't, and he didn't. Instead he farmed out the job of choosing to the BBWAA, which was delighted to have it. In 1938, Tom Swope, head of the organization, cut a deal with Landis by which the writers would get permanent control over twentieth-century players. A committee of veterans could continue to pick through the nineteenth century. Clark, who was nominally in charge of the Hall, waved the system through.

The idea for an external electoral college was borrowed from the Hall of Fame for Great Americans; but the credentials of the electors were not quite the same. The Great American voters were themselves distinguished men and women, whose ranks, over time, included professor Jonas Salk, nuclear physicist Robert Oppenheimer, anthropologist Margaret Mead, *Time* magazine founder Henry Luce, future Supreme Court Justice Thurgood Marshall, theologian Reinhold Niebuhr, and Ambassador Ralph Bunche. By contrast, to vote for the Baseball Hall of Fame, all you needed was a job covering a major-league team for a daily newspaper.

The Hall gave its voters almost no guidelines. They were free to vote for active as well as retired players, and there were no minimum statistical standards. Luckily for the writers, they had a comparatively easy job. They were working virgin territory, and the history of organized ball stretched back seventy years or so; it wasn't hard for

75 percent of them (the electoral minimum) to agree on the best players of all time. There had been no real surprises in 1939. Rogers Hornsby, Rube Waddell, and other near runners-up, it was assumed (correctly), would be chosen in subsequent elections. No one knew when elections would be held, though; the Hall left that up to the BBWAA.

In addition to the thirteen players elected by the writers in 1939, Commissioner Landis and a committee of baseball executives and insiders chose thirteen "pioneers" and "builders of baseball." They included Spalding, Chadwick, and Cartwright; former National League president Morgan G. Bulkeley (who had also been a member of the Mills Commission) and former American League president Ban Johnson; managers Connie Mack and John McGraw; George Wright, star shortstop of the first all-professional team, the Cincinnati Red Stockings (his brother, Harry, was inducted as a manager in 1953); Charlie Comiskey (later the owner of the Chicago White Sox), Cap Anson, Buck Ewing, Candy Cummings (often credited with inventing the curve ball), and Hoss Radbourn, a pitcher who once won 60 games in a single season (and who later died of syphilis).

So, from the beginning there were two gates to the Hall of Fame, one guarded by the writers, the other by a committee of insiders appointed by the Hall's board of directors. This two-track system is still in place, and so is the requirement that candidates receive 75 percent of the relevant votes.

In the winter of 1939, the writers held a special election for the purpose of inducting Lou Gehrig, who had fallen fatally ill. They didn't vote again until 1942, when they selected Rogers Hornsby, then took World War II off. Between 1946 and 1950, they chose seven more: Carl Hubbell, Frankie Frisch, Lefty Grove, Mickey Cochrane, Herb Pennock, Pie Traynor, and Charlie Gehringer. All these BBWAA picks were obvious, except perhaps Pennock, who benefited—as Lefty Gomez and other Yankees would later—from the publicity that comes from playing in New York. On the whole, the BBWAA did its part in keeping Cooperstown an exclusive and prestigious club.*

The same can't be said for the Veterans Committee. In the summer of 1944, Commissioner Landis expanded it to six members and then proceeded to die. At his funeral, the assembled committee members voted Landis into Cooperstown, installing him in the baseball firmament while he was still standing in line at the pearly gates. In the commissioner's (corporeal) absence, Connie Mack, a baseball elder whose managerial prowess and great dignity made him one of the Hall's first elected members, became the dominant voice on the committee. The following year, he and his colleagues went on a spree, choosing ten old-timers, and followed with eleven more in 1946. More than half of these inductees were, as it turned out, Irish: Bresnahan, Collins, Jennings, Delahanty, Duffy, Kelly, O'Rourke, Brouthers, Robinson, Clarke, McCarthy, and McGinnity—the new immortals sounded like a roll call at a meeting of the Ancient Order of Hibernians.

This wasn't simple ethnic favoritism. Irish players dominated the nineteenth-century game as Latinos rule today, for many of the same economic and cultural reasons. But it also didn't hurt that Connie Mack's real name was Cornelius Alexander McGillicuddy.

The dump of 1945–46 changed the balance of the Hall. In a stroke, it became less exclusive, less familiar to modern fans (al-

* Over the years, this appointed committee has had several names: the Centennial Committee, the Old-Timers' Committee, the Permanent Committee, and the Veterans Committee. Its composition has shifted over the years, and so has its purview. These days it is composed of all the former Hall of Fame players, meeting as a committee of the whole. It now has the power to elect players whose fifteen years of BBWAA eligibility have passed, regardless of whether they played in the twentieth century or, soon, the twenty-first. The committee, in all its iterations, has experienced rule changes "more often than a hooker's underwear," in the words of Bill James.

most no one had ever actually seen the old-timers play), and less logical.*

Connie Mack was one of the great baseball men of all time. Lawrence Ritter was an academic economist without any real baseball experience. But in the sixties and early seventies, Ritter's influence over the Veterans Committee's choices was almost as great as Mack's had been.

In 1966, Ritter published *The Glory of Their Times*, an oral history of baseball. He took a tape recorder, put it in front of twenty-two men who had played in the majors between 1898 and 1945, and asked them to talk about their lives and times. The old-timers reminisced about their teammates and rivals in mostly warm-hearted but refreshingly realistic terms. Here, for example, is Sam Crawford on player-manager relations at the turn of the twentieth century: "'Those old Baltimore Orioles didn't pay any more attention to Ned Hanlon, their manager, than they did to the batboy . . . He was a bench manager in civilian clothes. When things would get a little tough in a game he would sit there on the bench and wring his hands and start telling some of the old-timers what to do. They'd look at him and say, 'For Christ's sake, just keep quiet and leave us alone. We'll win this ballgame if you only shut up.' "

Fans, used to the formulaic writing of the sports pages and the corny, sanitized anecdotes of team announcers, were charmed by the sound of authentic voices from the past. Suddenly a cast of forgotten players came to life. In the next five years, four—outfielders Goose Goslin and Harry Hooper and pitchers Stan Coveleski and Rube

* In 1946, the Hall instituted another unfamiliar feature: the Honor Rolls of Baseball, an honor granted to 39 nonplayers—5 managers, 11 umpires, 11 executives, and 12 sportswriters. Eight of these men were later inducted into the Hall of Fame, but the Honor Rolls were never made concrete at the Hall and were subsequently discontinued. A complete list can be found in appendix 3.

Marquard—were tapped by the Hall's Veterans Committee. Goslin probably should have been there already; he hit a lifetime .317—impressive even in an era of high averages. Hooper, though, hit only .281 in an era of even *higher* averages. He was a fine fielder, but so were a lot of guys who didn't get into Cooperstown. Stan Coveleski had a distinguished career as a spitball pitcher for the Cleveland Indians and was a plausible if not obvious choice; but Marquard, who bounced from team to team and won only 201 games in eighteen seasons, was not.

In 1967, the Veterans Committee dynamic changed again when Frankie Frisch joined. In his prime, in the 1920s and '30s, Frisch had been a superstar for the Giants and Cards. He was a Gold Glove second baseman with remarkable range, an aggressive baserunner, a lifetime .316 batter, and a natural leader, whose teams won eight pennants. Frisch, known as the Fordham Flash in honor of his Jesuit alma mater, was better educated than most baseball people; he was also opinionated, articulate, and persuasive, and he very quickly became the dominant personality on the committee. Frisch thought modern players paled in comparison with the studs he had played with and against. And in 1971, Bill Terry, who had been Frisch's teammate with the Giants, was added to the committee and seconded Frisch's picks. Together they engineered a player dump of old teammates—pitcher Jesse Haines, shortstops Travis Jackson and Dave Bancroft, outfielders Chick Hafey and Ross Youngs, first basemen Jim Bottomley and George Kelly, and third baseman Fred Lindstrom—for the Hall. Many of these guys had no business on the same wall with Ty Cobb and Walter Johnson.

Nobody made this clearer than Bill James. In his 1995 classic *Whatever Happened to the Hall of Fame?* James called the Frisch and Terry choices "simply appalling" and "absurd."

"The selection of this group of eight men . . . is the absolute nadir of the Veterans Committee's performance . . . The selections of

Hafey, Kelly, Haines, Lindstrom and Ross Youngs are just absurd, absolutely beyond any logical defense."

James dubbed George Kelly "the worst player in the Hall of Fame." "George Kelly was a good ballplayer," he wrote. "So were Chris Chambliss, Bill Buckner, George McQuinn and Eddie Robinson. He wasn't a Hall of Famer on the best day of his life."

Nobody else in the baseball world could make this sort of ex-cathedra pronouncement and be taken seriously. But nobody, at least since Henry Chadwick, has known as much about the game of baseball.

Bill James never played pro ball. He never coached or managed, never reported on the game for a newspaper or broadcast one on the radio. He was just a fan and an amateur student of the sport. In 1975, he was in his mid-twenties, working as a night watchman in a Kansas bean factory, when he started mimeographing a self-published baseball newsletter. Two years later, he produced an annual in book form. It sold seventy-five copies.

James's early readers were members of the Society for American Baseball Research (SABR), which was founded in 1971 by Bob Davids, a Washington, D.C., baseball maven. James joined the group in the mid-seventies and soon became its most influential member. In fact, he coined the term for the particular way the society applied statistical methods to baseball questions: "sabermetrics." Led by James, sabermetrics became a subversive movement. Baseball, as generations of players and fans knew it, was full of unexamined axioms: *Never walk the first hitter. Pitching is 75 percent of the game. The weakest hitter should bat last. Runs batted in tell you all you need to know about a hitter's ability to produce under pressure. Earned runs are the best measure of pitching excellence. Hitting .300 is the gold standard for batters.* Such truisms formed the catechism of front-office decisions, on-field strategy, and what passed for expert analysis.

James and his disciples challenged the experts. Using statistical analysis, looking for variables where none had been perceived, reworking well-known numbers to find hidden meanings, they called everything rudely into question. Is the sacrifice bunt really a worthy offensive tool? Prove it. Does the category of "earned run" actually make sense? Defend the idea. Are left-handed pitchers really more effective against left-handed batters? How big is the home-field advantage? Do runners really steal on the pitcher, not the catcher? Show me the numbers. Sometimes James found that the conventional wisdom was actually wise, and said so. More often, he punched holes in it.

In May 1981, Daniel Okrent introduced Bill James to the nation in a *Sports Illustrated* article titled "He Does It by the Numbers." Okrent compared James to another baseball revolutionary. "As with Babe Ruth," he wrote, "when James hits one it's a beauty, and even when he strikes out it's worth watching."

For a year, *Sports Illustrated* had refused to publish Okrent's article. The editors simply didn't believe that some guy in Kansas had figured so many counterintuitive truths just sitting in his bedroom. Predictably, the baseball establishment reacted with ridicule. Who the hell was Bill James and where did he get off telling lifelong baseball men how baseball worked? The brotherhood of the BBWAA was especially hostile. If James was right, they had had spent their careers misunderstanding and misreporting the game they were paid to cover.*

But James was right, with intimidating frequency, and after a while smart baseball people stopped arguing. In 2006, *Time* named him

* Dan Okrent, who is not a member of the BBWAA, took a lot of abuse, but he handled it with aplomb (as befits a Detroit boy). Okrent made his journalistic bones as an editor at *Esquire* and *Time* and later as editor in chief of *Life* magazine and the first public editor of the *New York Times*—not a job for the faint-hearted. His baseball credentials come from two very good books he has written on the game and a gig as a talking head in Ken Burns's PBS documentary series *Baseball*. He is also the inventor, along with some friends, of the fantasy game Rotisserie Baseball, so named because his Doubleday Field was a table at La Rotisserie Française restaurant in Manhattan.

one of the hundred most influential people in the world. The Boston Red Sox hired him in 2003 as a senior adviser, and the following year they won their first World Championship since 1918 (and repeated in 2007). The Sox used sabermetrics, which by then was available in some form to every team in baseball, and James's expertise, which was not. You can't attribute those two world championships solely to Bill James, but having him on your side didn't hurt.

James has a reputation for being distant and difficult. In a book called *How Bill James Changed Our View of Baseball,* edited by Gregory F. Augustine Pierce, historian Ron Shandler describes his first encounter with the great man. Shandler had rented a table at a baseball convention and was trying to sell copies of his *Baseball Forecaster.*

> *Bill James was browsing the exhibition hall and came upon my table. I greeted him and introduced myself; he whispered a coarse "hello" under his breath as he picked up one of my books. And then he stood there, silently thumbing back and forth through the book for at least two or three minutes. It felt like two or three hours . . .*
>
> *[He] opened up to one page, leaned over the table to me and pointed to a single number amidst an ocean of data. And he said, "This is wrong." Then, without another word, he closed the book, placed it back on the stack, and moved on to the next table.*
>
> *After he was out of view, I reopened the book to the data point in question. It was the batting average of then Atlanta Braves prospect Andy Tomberlin. In those days of data entry by hand, I had mistyped Tomberlin's total at-bats; his batting average in the book was wrong.*

Yikes.

Still, when I began the research for this book I wanted to contact

James in the name of due diligence. A friend of his gave me the e-mail address and a tip. "Ask him a question. A *specific* question. If it interests him, he'll answer."

"What if it doesn't interest him?"

"You won't hear back," said the friend.

I labored over my question for several days. Finally I settled on: "Whose performance do performance-enhancers enhance more? Pitchers or hitters? Hitters or fielders? Major-league vets trying to hold on or minor-league players trying to move up? Or does it come out in the wash?"

Twenty-three hours later, I received a reply:

"That's a really good question. A minor league player once told me that, on the teams he was on, all the people who used steroids were the pitchers. Pitchers used to come back quicker from injury. People ASSUME that the hitting explosion of the last 15 years is caused by steroids, but there is very little real evidence that this is true."

I was elated. I had asked Bill James not just a good question but a *really good* question. Even better, he invited me to ask more. In the next few months, we exchanged dozens of messages about the Hall of Fame, how it works, and who belongs there. James responded to every one of my queries, let me bounce ideas off him (the bad ones didn't bounce far), and never minced words ("If you believe that you are as dumb as a bag of hammers," he wrote on one memorable occasion). These cyber-conversations made me feel like a man chatting with Newton about apples.

Cooperstown is the one place in baseball where James is not highly regarded. In fact, the Hall's bookstore doesn't even stock *The Politics of Glory*. Former president of the Hall Dale Petrosky admitted glancing through the book but failing to find it interesting.

The current president, Jeff Idelson, who knows everybody in baseball, pointedly told me he has never met or spoken to James. Jane Forbes Clark assured me that she has never read a word of the book.

But James's critique on the favoritism and random nature of Veterans Committee selections, which reverberated throughout baseball, did not go unheeded by Cooperstown. In 2001, the Hall ended the practice of allowing an appointed fifteen-member body to do the veteran voting in secret. Instead, it turned the process over to a larger electorate composed of all living Hall of Fame players, writers who had won the Hall's J. G. Taylor Spink Award, and broadcasters who had received the Ford C. Frick Award. Candidates—players whose fifteen-year eligibility for election by the BBWAA had expired—would need 75 percent of the vote.

Expanding the committee limited the possibility of a Connie Mack or Frankie Frisch slipping cronies into Cooperstown. But the new system had a flaw, too. In the first election, in 2003, nobody got in. This result was repeated in 2005.

In 2007, baseball insiders were sure that the new Veterans Committee would choose at least one new Hall of Famer. The odds were on Ron Santo, the old Cubs third baseman. Santo had lobbied hard, even enlisting Illinois senior senator Dick Durbin, who sent a letter to committee members making Santo's case.

"Beyond the numbers, there are other reasons why Ron Santo deserves to be in Cooperstown," Durbin wrote. "The first is his courageous struggle with diabetes and his tireless efforts to help others who suffer from this disease.

"Since 2001, Ron Santo has lost the lower portions of both legs to diabetes. He has also survived a bout of cancer and endured more than twenty three surgeries. Walking on prosthetic legs has slowed his gait, but not his charitable work."

The Veterans Committee, unmoved by this appeal, chose nobody for the third time in a row. Frustrated, Jane Forbes Clark announced that in 2008 the voting would be limited to Hall of Fame players, not writers or broadcasters (players who broke in before 1943 would be picked by a special committee). But the rule change didn't alter the outcome: another electoral shutout.

What accounts for this exclusivity? Some of the Hall of Famers, led by the most senior member, Bob Feller, have a low opinion of the players who followed them. Others believe that if you weren't good enough to be picked by the writers, you don't deserve to be enshrined.

But there is also an economic explanation. The Hall of Fame produces and markets its own line of memorabilia. For many years, members got nothing; but since 1995, the pot has been split three ways: 30 percent for the Hall, 40 percent for MLB, and the remaining 30 percent split evenly among the living Hall of Famers. Red Schoendienst gets the same cut as Nolan Ryan. So far, about $6 million has been divvied up.

Of course, the money that comes from the Hall directly is only a small part of the income generated by membership in the Hall; an HoF after your name means speaking engagements, endorsements, and memorabilia sales.

"Adding new people dilutes the total," Marvin Miller, who founded the baseball players' union, told me. "Recently I broached this question to one of the veterans. I asked if this was the single most important reason nobody gets picked. He said it had never occurred to him. But his tone told me I got it exactly right."

In December 2008, the Veterans Committee voted once again. There were ten players on the ballot: Dick Allen, Gil Hodges, Jim Kaat, Tony Oliva, Al Oliver, Vada Pinson, Luis Tiant, Joe Torre, Maury Wills, and poor Ron Santo. None was elected.

The Vets kept their perfect record: 0 for the twenty-first century.*

* Bill Mazeroski was elected by the old, appointed Veterans Committee in 1999. So was nineteenth-century second baseman Bid McPhee.

FOUR . . . *A Question of Character*

The rules for induction were infinitely contestible. It is probably more fun that way. And it is certainly closer to what Stephen Clark and Judge Landis envisioned. Clark, after all, was a great patron of the arts, and Landis was a lifelong moralizer. Together they created a Hall of Fame without statistical criteria of any kind. The only criterion they insisted upon was that the members of the new Hall be men of integrity, virtue, and character.

In the beginning, this went without saying. It got said in 1944, in Rule 5 of the Hall's election requirements: "Voting shall be based upon the player's record, playing ability, *integrity, sportsmanship, character and contributions to the team(s) on which the player played*" [italics added].

Known as the "Character Clause," Rule 5 is the *only* condition imposed by the Hall on its electors. There is a Kantian moral self-assurance to the formula. It assumes that sportswriters, Veterans Committee members, and the general public will share a common understanding of what constitutes integrity, sportsmanship, and character. This is the sort of thing that a man like Stephen Clark might well have believed in 1944. For all I know, men like him believe it today. But, in an age of moral relativism and cultural diversity, character evaluation isn't always clear-cut. And in no age would sportswriters be regarded as qualified arbiters of virtue.

Cooperstown is the model for hundreds of halls of fame around the country, but very few of them have insisted on virtue as a qualification. It is impossible to imagine the Rock 'n' Roll Hall of Fame or the Boxing Hall of Fame insisting on such a thing. In the fall of 2007, the Idaho Hall of Fame inducted Senator Larry Craig into its ranks. Only months earlier, Craig had been arrested in a Minneapolis airport men's room for attempting to play inter-stall footsie with an undercover vice cop. Some hardliners, such as Kootenai County Republican precinct chairman Phil Thompson, wondered if Craig deserved to be honored in the same institution as Boise State football coach Chris Peterson or hospitality magnate Duane Hagadone. But Craig had done his job in Washington, D.C., bringing home billions in pork over a twenty-year career. And, for the Idaho Hall of Fame, that's what counted.

But baseball isn't boxing or rock 'n' roll, or even the U.S. Senate. Cooperstown celebrates not just a game but the National Pastime, and its immortals are supposed to represent the country's best, most wholesome moral values. In the early days of the Hall, Commissioner Landis even proposed enshrining "Harvard" Eddie Grant, an outfielder of modest ability who died in combat in World War I. Grant didn't make it. Ty Cobb did. And this posed a problem that the Hall still wrestles with today—what to do when great things happen to terrible people, and when ideals bump up against reality.

For most of the Hall's history, reality has suffered, starting with the first inductee, Ty Cobb.

Nobody disputes that Ty Cobb was a transcendent baseball player. His lifetime .366 batting average, compiled over more than two decades, is a measure of professional greatness that will last as long as baseball. As kids in Detroit, we grew up on Cobb's legend as a fierce competitor. We were told that he sharpened his spikes to intimidate infielders, and we emulated him by filing down our own rubber cleats. We were also aware that he sometimes got into fights on the field, a form of trying hard that our coaches admired. What we didn't know—or care about—was that Cobb was a sociopath, a nasty drunk, a raving racist, and maybe a murderer.

In August 1912, newspapers in Detroit reported that Cobb had been accosted by three men and defended himself. He told one reporter that he had knocked a mugger down and caused two others to flee. He told another that he beat one of his attackers until the man fell to his knees and begged for forgiveness.

In 1959, in an authorized biography, Cobb told Al Stump that he had beaten one of his attackers bloody and, using the sight on the barrel of a Belgian Luger as a blade, slashed another and drove him away.

Then, in 1994, Stump published an *un*authorized biography, revealing the rest of what the long-dead Cobb had told him about the incident. "[I] lashed away until the man was faceless. Left him there, not breathing, in his own rotten blood." It isn't clear if this version is accurate. Perhaps it was only Cobb's after-the-fact embellishment. Baseball historian Doug Roberts combed through the Detroit Medical Examiner's autopsy reports for that period, found no corpse that matched the description, and concluded that there had been no murder. Even if Roberts is right, though, the story illustrates something fundamental about the first Hall of Famer—in old age, Cobb was still the sort of man who would have been proud to take credit for a murder.

In the parlance of a later time, Cobb was a hater. His teammate Sam Crawford said he never stopped fighting the Civil War. Early in his career, Cobb was convicted for assault and battery for slapping a black construction worker in Detroit. At Cleveland's Euclid Hotel, he slapped the black elevator operator and slashed the black night manager, George Stansfield, with a knife (to be fair, Stansfield hit Cobb with a nightstick). That fight resulted in criminal charges and an arrest warrant that forced Cobb to travel to the 1909 World Series in Pittsburgh by way of Canada. In New York, three years later, Cobb went into the stands after a heckler named Claude Lueker who called him "half a nigger." Cobb beat the man bloody with little resistance; Lueker, it turned out, had lost a hand in an industrial accident, and was missing three fingers on the other. Ban Johnson, the president of the American League, suspended Cobb indefinitely, but Cobb was unremorseful. "When a spectator calls me a half nigger, I think it's about time to fight," he told the *Detroit Free Press.*

At the end of the 1926 season, Cobb suddenly announced his retirement as player-manager of the Tigers. Shortly thereafter, Hall of Fame center fielder Tris Speaker quit as player-manager of the Cleveland Indians. Speaker, the only man to interrupt Cobb's streak of twelve American League batting championships, was voted into the Hall in 1937. He, too, was a racist, a sheet-carrying member of the Ku Klux Klan. There were lots of bigots in baseball (and in America) in those days, but most didn't go all the way to the KKK, and few fans would have thought of membership as representing integrity, sportsmanship, and character.

Cobb and Speaker had more in common than a hatred of black people. They shared a secret. The story began in late September 1919, when Cleveland had already clinched second place and the Tigers were fighting for third. According to Detroit pitcher Dutch Leonard, he met with Cobb, Speaker, and outfielder Joe Wood to discuss an illicit gambling deal. "Don't worry about tomorrow's game," Speaker allegedly told the others. "We have second place clinched and you will win tomorrow." With the fix in, the four of them planned to make wised-up bets on the next day's game.

Leonard confessed all this in a letter to American League president Ban Johnson at the end of the 1926 season. He also produced letters from Cobb and Wood that seemed to verify his claim. Cobb was late getting his money down and made nothing from the fixed game, but Wood won six hundred dollars, which he divided with Speaker and Leonard (by check!), minus thirty bucks to the clubhouse boy who actually placed the bet.

Ban Johnson reacted to this information by buying the incriminating letters from Leonard for $20,000, suspending Cobb and Speaker, and trying to force them into retirement. But Landis, who saw Johnson as a rival, reversed the decision.

"These players have not been, nor are they now, found guilty of fixing a ball game," Landis ruled. This, of course, was technically true; there had been no trial. (In the Black Sox case—which *had* gone to trial—Joe Jackson was acquitted, but that didn't stop Landis from banning him for life.) In the Cobb–Speaker case, Cobb and Speaker were reinstated in time for Connie Mack to sign them for the 1927 season.

Ty Cobb and Tris Speaker were both in Cooperstown in 1939 for the grand opening of the Hall. So was Babe Ruth.

Ruth was, of course, the greatest role model in baseball history. He visited sick kids in the hospital, the legend said. He handed out autographs to waifs outside the ballpark. He cautioned little children to stay in school and obey their parents and teachers. Some of this actually happened. Some was the creation of a pack of journalists and PR men whose job it was to keep Ruth's less-virtuous acts out of the newspaper. Almost the entire corps of baseball writers was complicit in this. Some of the scribes even took part in Ruth's orgies, joined his wild (and, during Prohibition, illegal) pub crawls, accepted his money, and even became his silent partners in business deals or his employees as ghost writers. Ford Frick himself worked for Ruth, when Frick was still on the payroll of the *New York American*.*

So did Marshall Hunt, a sportswriter for the *New York Daily News* who sometimes did Ruth the favor of forging his signature

* The Frick–Ruth connection didn't end there, either. In 1961, as commissioner of baseball, Frick ruled that Roger Maris's 61 season home runs should go into the record books with a tainting asterisk. Frick's effort was intended to protect the status of his former employer, Ruth, as the "real" record-holder. (The ruling was never enforced.)

on baseballs, accompanied him on binges, introduced him to women, and generally covered up for his bad behavior. Once he was asked why he didn't write a book on Ruth. "I just have to wait a while and let nature do a few things before I'd write that book because I might run into a suit," he replied. "Several things happened up in the Babe's farmhouse outside of Boston that are worth a couple of thousand words. That's never been touched, never been used. But I want to wait until that female is out of the way."

Even with all this protection, the public was not unaware that Ruth was a bad boy off the field and even on it. In 1923, he got caught using a corked bat. He was suspended from baseball for seven weeks by Commissioner Landis in 1922 for going on an illegal barnstorming tour after the previous World Series (why this should have been illegal is an open question). He was sometimes absent from games with "bellyaches" which his pals the beat writers knew perfectly well were alcohol-related. His behavior became so erratic that the mayor of New York, James J. Walker, staged a public (and highly humiliating) intervention. Speaking at an Elks Club dinner in Manhattan in November 1922, with Ruth sitting nearby on the dais, Walker said:

> *Babe Ruth is not only a great athlete, but also a great fool. His employer, Col. Jacob Ruppert, makes millions of gallons of beer, and Ruth is of the opinion that he can drink it faster than the Colonel and his large corps of brew masters can make it. Well . . . you can't. Nobody can.*
>
> *You are making a bigger salary than anyone ever received as a ballplayer. But the bigger the salary, the bigger the fool you have become. Here sit some forty sportswriters and big officials of baseball, our national sport. These men, your friends, know what you have done, even if you don't . . . You have let them down.*
>
> *But worst of all, you have let down the kids of America . . . You*

*carouse and abuse your great body and it is exactly as though Santa Claus himself suddenly were to take off his beard to reveal the features of a villain.**

Alas, it was not to be. That very night, Ruth was served with a paternity suit filed by a nineteen-year-old Bronx waitress named Dolores Dixon. "He said he didn't know the girl, but the way he said it, you knew he was lying," said Marshall Hunt. "He knew that girl. I said, 'Okay, Babe, that what's you say. That's what I'll put in the paper.'" Ruth's lawyers made the lawsuit go away, and nothing more was heard about the matter.

"Ruth was not unique," observed Bill Veeck. "Wake up the echoes at the Hall of Fame and you will find that baseball's immortals were a rowdy and raucous group of men who would climb down off their plaques and go rampaging through Cooperstown, taking spoils, like the Third Army busting through Germany. Deplore it if you will, but Grover Cleveland Alexander drunk was a better pitcher than Grover Cleveland Alexander sober."

Grover Cleveland Alexander was inducted into the Hall of Fame in 1939.

Ronald Reagan played him as a falling-down drunk in the 1952 movie *The Winning Team.* After Alexander retired, he became an itinerant barnstormer, chronically broke and occasionally jailed for public drunkenness. There was no big payoff for ex-ballplayers in those days. He barely had the money to make it to Cooperstown for the induction ceremony and remarked acidly that he couldn't eat the plaque he was awarded. The Hall got the hint and offered

* This was a bit much coming from Walker, who had a reputation of his own. He had famous affairs with chorus girls, protected illegal casinos, and was investigated for corruption. Walker was pressured into resigning in 1932 by his fellow New York Democrats and skipped the country to avoid prosecution, taking Betty Compton, one of his girlfriends, with him into exile.

him a job—as a security guard. Alexander turned it down and hit the road, drifting until he died.

Cap Anson was another charter member of the Hall of Fame, chosen by the Veterans Committee in 1939. His plaque reads: "Greatest hitter and greatest National League player-manager of 19th century. Started with Chicagos in National League's first year 1876. Chicago manager from 1879 to 1897, winning 5 pennants. Was .300 class hitter 20 years, batting champion 4 times."

Missing from this resume is Anson's crucial role in keeping organized baseball racially segregated. In 1883, Cap Anson declared that his team would not take the field against the Toledo Blue Stockings if Toledo's African American catcher, Moses Fleetwood Walker, suited up. (Contrary to popular belief, the first known black player in organized baseball was Walker, not Jackie Robinson.) Four years later, Anson threatened to cancel a White Stockings exhibition game against the Newark Giants if they used black players. Anson was a man of great influence. In the wake of his boycott, the International League voted to refuse contracts to blacks in the future. (The American Association and National League never took such a vote. They simply used a "gentleman's agreement" to keep baseball white.) Anson wound up his life managing a pool hall, but he always took pride in his role in preserving the racial purity of the national pastime.

Cobb, Ruth, Anson, Speaker, and Alexander were all inducted before the Character Clause was formally instituted. So was Rogers Hornsby, elected in 1942. Known as the Rajah, Hornsby was one of the greatest hitters in National League history. His lifetime average, .358, is second only to Cobb's.

Like Cobb, Hornsby was widely disliked around the league. He didn't bother to attend his own mother's funeral. He brawled with opponents on the field, ignored his own teammates, and, as a manager, was generally hated by his players. Like Tris Speaker, Hornsby was a member of the Ku Klux Klan. Bill James ranks him as perhaps the biggest "horse's ass" in baseball history, ahead even of Cobb.

Hornsby was famous for never going to the movies with the other guys on the team. A legend developed that he was trying to preserve his batting eye. In fact, he didn't give a damn about movies or teammates. Asked once what he did in the off-season back in Texas, he said that he sat by the window and waited for the next baseball season to start. His one great diversion was racetrack gambling. Commissioner Landis warned him a number of times that this was unacceptable; baseball couldn't afford any more gambling scandals. Hornsby ignored the warnings and Landis finally went public, telling the *Sporting News* that Hornsby's betting "has gotten him into one scrape after another, cost him a fortune and several jobs, and he still hasn't got enough sense to stop it." Hornsby responded by charging that Landis himself had recklessly gambled away baseball's money in the 1929 stock market crash.

Not all the early members of the Hall of Fame were rogues or racists. Many were great players and model citizens. Christy Mathewson was a college graduate and an officer in World War I who was gassed in a training exercise, later contracted tuberculosis, and died at the age of forty-five. Honus Wagner was beloved in Pittsburgh. Walter Johnson was known throughout baseball for his unwillingness to throw at batters, and he retained his good reputation even after retiring and entering politics. Connie Mack reached great old age without a serious blemish on his record. Henry Chadwick was a saintly figure, and his rival A. G. Spalding was a highly respectable citizen who, if he perpetuated a lie about the origins of the game, did it for unselfish, even patriotic reasons. The early Hall of Famers were probably neither better nor worse human beings than other players of their day, or any cross-section of red-blooded young men with money in their pockets and time on their hands. There is no evidence that they were deluded about their own level of sportsmanship, integrity, and character. That was Cooperstown's standard, not theirs.

Cooperstown has been aided and abetted in the public relations sham of the Character Clause by its appointed electoral college, the BBWAA. The Hall of Fame's own newspaper archive reveals the extent to which the national pastime was (and to some extent remains) sanitized by the journalists who cover it. Long before the Hall opened its doors, reporters were complicit in image building and preservation. The ethos of the press box in the early days was summed up by Abe Kemp, a San Francisco baseball writer (and horse-racing reporter) whose career spanned sixty-two years, from 1907 to 1969. "When I broke in . . . the only advice [the sports editor] gave me was, 'Abe, I'm not telling you to do this, but if you can't write something nice about a ballplayer, don't mention his name.'"

Writers were a part of the team. Not only did they travel with the players, they sometimes roomed with them on the road, at the team's expense. Writers and players socialized and kept each other's secrets. When the public somehow did learn about Babe Ruth's whoring, Grover Cleveland Alexander pitching drunk, or Tris Speaker betting on games, these lapses were spun by reporters as harmless and even charming examples of the sporting mentality.

Why did the writers protect ballplayers? Start with self-preservation. In most cities, there was a close relationship between the local team and the local newspapers. Whatever journalistic ethics applied elsewhere in the paper didn't seem relevant to the toy department. Disillusioning the public about its heroes wasn't good business. If writers got too cranky, teams would simply deny them access and that was the end of them.

For some, though, it was less a professional instinct than a personal one. Grantland Rice, the most famous sportswriter of the twenties, once told a colleague, "When athletes are no longer heroes to you anymore, it's time to stop writing sports." This is exactly the right approach for a public relations shill or a team-employed baseball announcer, and precisely the wrong one for a self-respecting reporter, in any field, in Rice's time or today.

Great rewards were in store for compliant writers. When they went out with players, they drank and ate on the house, and they sometimes benefited from the surplus of enthusiastic Baseball Annies. They got to spend their afternoons watching baseball, a plum job on any newspaper, and travel in major-league style. Many writers took their relationship with players—and major-league teams—beyond hero-worship and revelry into something closer to partnership. They served as ghostwriters for players they were supposedly covering, or even took part in salary negotiations by writing puff pieces about their friends at contract time or tamping down a player's value on behalf of management.* The most avaricious, like Marshall Hunt, worked both sides. He actually brokered at least one of Ruth's salary negotiations, closing the deal with Yankees owner Jacob Ruppert in a steam bath.

Not everything was about money. Jimmy Cannon worked for the *New York Post* and the *New York Journal-American* between 1940 and 1960. A lot of people considered him the best sportswriter of his era. He was capable of tough judgments, but not about Joe DiMaggio. "It's one of the great boasts of all journalists, and especially baseball writers, that they are not influenced by their relationships with people off

* John Drebinger of the *New York Times*, for example, ghosted for Giants manager John McGraw. Ford Frick, during his baseball-writing days, worked simultaneously for Babe Ruth and the Hearst newspaper chain. These weren't isolated incidents by any means, nor were they regarded as flagrant violations of the prevailing journalistic ethics. Drebinger was considered a man of outstanding character by his colleagues. Frick went on to help found the Hall of Fame and wound up as commissioner of baseball.

the field. This is an absolute myth. I always considered myself a fair and neutral man, and yet how could I not be for Joe DiMaggio, who lived in the same hotel with me? We went on vacations together. We were great friends."

Buddy-buddy journalism was not invented by baseball writers. White House correspondents covered up Roosevelt's wheelchair when they could. World War II war correspondents didn't bust Dwight Eisenhower for tooling around London with his mistress. The Washington press corps turned a blind eye to John F. Kennedy's drug abuse and his ties with organized crime. The legendary Ben Bradlee, the editor of the *Washington Post* who broke the Watergate story that brought down President Richard Nixon, socialized with JFK and kept his secrets. Today's "serious" journalists are not really much different. They form mutually beneficial social friendships with the political and economic figures they cover and, people being people, this often blossoms into a sort of love affair (which is rarely mutual, and almost always ends when the journalists are no longer useful).

The close friendship that Jimmy Cannon and Joe DiMaggio enjoyed is less common today. Money is the main reason. Before the advent of the players' union in 1966, writers and baseball players were more or less in the same economic and social class.* Most major-leaguers were paid so little that a lot of them had off-season jobs, often in professions even less prestigious than journalism. The superstars made bigger money, but even they weren't stratospherically rich. Writers, a little older and more worldly than the players, often assumed the role of consigliere. These days, major-leaguers are surrounded by personal managers, agents, and public relations specialists; press availability is carefully managed, and it is a weapon in the hands of astute media advisers. Today, as always, a beat reporter who gets cut off from a key player or an angry locker room is going

* A union had been created for the players in 1954 to settle contract disputes, but it was dominated by owners and didn't become a true labor union until Marvin Miller came on in 1966.

to have a hard time keeping his job. That is increasingly true of the print reporters who comprise the membership of the BBWAA. In the Internet age, they are a vulnerable and diminishing breed.

As the gap widened between players and writers, feelings got hurt. Players' union executive director Marvin Miller remembers standing with Dick Young near the players' entrance to Shea Stadium as a visiting team filed off the bus for a game against the Mets. The players were quickly surrounded by a crowd of attractive women.

"Look at that," Young said to Miller. "I've been covering baseball for all these years. Some people say I'm the premier writer in the game. And these Baseball Annies make fools of themselves over these players."

After World War II, the writers and the Veterans Committee continued to honor Rule 5 mostly in the breach. Lefty Grove, perhaps the greatest pitcher between Johnson and Koufax, was hated throughout the American League for throwing at hitters, feuding with other players (he held a lifelong grudge against teammate and fellow Hall of Famer Al Simmons for letting him down by taking a day off), and staging epic fits of temper on and off the field. "He was a tantrum thrower like me, but smarter," said Ted Williams. "When he punched a locker, he always did it with his right hand. He was a careful tantrum thrower."

Jimmie Foxx, another Williams teammate who made the Hall of Fame (class of '51), was a degenerate drunk who often went to bat with a flask in his pocket. (Foxx served as the model for the alcoholic manager played by Tom Hanks in *A League of Their Own.*)

In fact, the roster of Hall of Famers who were also hall of fame–quality boozers is long and distinguished. King Kelly, the Babe Ruth of the nineteenth century, drank during games. Outfielder Paul Waner was praised by Casey Stengel as a very graceful player because "he could slide without breaking the bottle on his hip." Shortstop Rabbit

Maranville was beloved by baseball writers for his drunken antics. So was Tigers outfielder Harry Heilmann, who once drove a small automobile directly down the stairs of a speakeasy as a joke. Manager Joe McCarthy drank himself out of a job and retired for "health reasons." A's pitcher Rube Waddell was once the victim of a mock trial, staged by manager Connie Mack, meant to frighten him away from the bottle (it worked, but not for long). The great John McGraw was arrested as a result of a drunken brawl during Prohibition (a sympathetic New York jury acquitted him). Cubs slugger Hack Wilson played outfield, but Chicago columnist Mike Royko once suggested moving him to first base so that "he wouldn't have so far to stagger to the dugout." Mickey Mantle more or less drank himself to death. In all, it is quite a roster of public drunks (and a partial one, at that) for an institution that supposedly immortalizes only models of high morals and good character.

The Cardinals Dizzy Dean, HoF '53, liked a drink as much as the next guy (and the next guy on the Gashouse Gang team of the thirties liked a drink), but his real weakness was gambling. In 1934, at the height of Dean's career, National League president John Heydler hired detectives to shadow the pitcher. When this news leaked out, Heydler implausibly called it a "routine precaution."

Dizzy Dean was never caught gambling during his career (as far as we know), but in 1970, when he was a Cardinals announcer, he got swept up in a federal gambling raid and named a coconspirator along with some mobsters. "I won't say I haven't done some foolish things in my life," Dean told a press conference in Phoenix. "But I'll assure you of one thing: I have nothing to do with big-time gambling—never did and never will. I want to tell you exactly how I became involved in this thing. It was through a friend who asked me to make wagers for him, and I did. I was told there was no harm in it. Later on I was told it was the wrong thing to do, and I stopped it." According to *Time* magazine, the incident "cast black shadows on the national game—and all professional athletes."

Leo Durocher, HoF '94, a teammate of Dean's, cast a similar shadow. Leo the Lip was a flamboyant and contentious character who managed the Brooklyn Dodgers in the forties.

In 1946, the new commissioner of baseball, Happy Chandler, confronted Durocher about his gambling and his associates, who included Bugsy Siegel, gunman, gambler, and Vegas casino visionary; Joe Adonis, a notorious Mafia hit man who, at the time, was running the National Crime Syndicate on behalf of the exiled Lucky Luciano; bookie Memphis Engelberg; and George Raft, a mobbed-up Hollywood movie star. Chandler, who had been the governor of Kentucky before he moved to baseball, told Durocher that he was giving baseball a bad name and ordered him to stop hanging around racetracks and socializing with organized crime figures.

Durocher considered Chandler a lightweight—who ever heard of a commissioner nicknamed Happy?—and ignored the warning. But Durocher had misjudged his man. Chandler was a politician. He knew public opinion, and he saw that it was against Leo the Lip. Durocher had recently, and very publicly, "stolen" an actress named Laraine Day from her husband. Today such a theft would be considered a social misdemeanor, but in 1947 it was a real problem. A lot of World War II veterans had been on the receiving end of "Dear John" letters from faithless spouses and sweethearts, and they considered wife-rustling to be a hanging offense. The Church didn't approve of divorce, either. The Catholic Youth Organization of Brooklyn denounced Durocher as "a powerful force for undermining the moral and spiritual training of our boys" and withdrew its fifty thousand members from the Dodgers Knothole Gang fan club. Durocher was suspended without pay for a season. (His pal Bugsy Siegel had an even worse 1947. On June 20, he was shot to death in a gangland hit in Los Angeles.) Durocher came back and managed various teams for the next quarter century, but he was seldom anything but nasty. He called his autobiography *Nice Guys Finish Last.* None of this prevented the Hall of Fame Veterans Committee from putting him in Cooperstown in 1994.

Hornsby, Durocher, and Dean were all known to be men of somewhat dubious character. Hank Greenberg, on the other hand, was regarded as a model citizen. He was one of the first players to join the military, even before the United States joined World War II. After the war, he was among the few stars to stick up for Jackie Robinson. A generation later, he went to Congress to testify on behalf of Curt Flood, who was challenging the right of owners to keep players under lifetime contracts—a highly controversial demand at the time. But despite his many virtues, Greenberg was a man of his time and place. When he broke in with the Tigers, Prohibition-era Detroit was a wide-open city, handily located on the Canadian border. Organized crime in the city was still dominated by the Purple Gang, a collection of Jewish rumrunners, gunmen, and thugs. The Purples were active in the sporting life of the city, and of course they made a point of befriending the new Jewish first baseman. Nothing much was written about this at the time, although his connections were an open secret in the delis of Detroit.

Greenberg joined the army in 1941 and was sent to Fort Custer, Michigan, for infantry training. His officers naturally wanted him to play ball for the fort team, but Greenberg declined. "I left a $55,000 contract, $11,000 a month, to sign up for the army for $21 a month and I'm not going to waste [my free time] playing baseball," he later explained.

Greenberg waived his no-free-baseball policy only once—after receiving an offer he felt he couldn't refuse. "I got a special request, an unusual request," he writes in his autobiography.

> *I was asked by a friend of mine in Detroit named Abe Bernstein, to play in a game. Bernstein, I had been told, was head of the Purple Gang . . .*

Well, it seems that Abe Bernstein's brother Joe was convicted of killing someone; he was given a life sentence and sent up to Jackson Prison. And he was spending his off-time training canaries. So Abe asked me, as a special favor, if I would play an exhibition game between the Fort Custer team and the prison team. He prevailed upon me because he said the warden was a great baseball fan and if I played he thought he would help his brother. So I consented.

Greenberg played for the prison team against his army buddies that day and went three for three. The Bernstein brothers had delivered a future Hall of Famer to the warden. Presumably, everybody was happy.

Joe DiMaggio was the other great ethnic baseball hero of the thirties and forties. His connections to the Sicilian Mafia were a matter of New York gossip and speculation for decades. In 2000, biographer Richard Ben Cramer took them public. According to Cramer, mobster Joe Adonis—Leo Durocher's pal—regularly supplied DiMaggio with hookers in every American League city (there was no interleague play in those days).

"No writer wanted to put that kind of thing in the paper," writes Cramer. "You'd be finished—washed up with DiMag, probably non grata with the rest of the Yanks—and maybe with the mob, too."

Cramer reports that Frank Costello—a head of the National Crime Syndicate who was forced into retirement after surviving a botched assassination attempt in 1956—was a particular friend of the Yankee Clipper. Costello set up a secret mob-financed trust fund for DiMaggio at New York's Bowery Bank. There is no evidence that he had to throw ballgames or do anything illegal for the money. All he had to do was frequent nightclubs owned by Costello and his associates and let other wise guys draw their own conclusions.

"Joe let those thousands and tens of thousands pile up, untouched and for the most part unmonitored," writes Cramer. "He didn't want to know more than he needed to . . . he could have men sit with him, take him around, buy for him, do for him . . . he could have any woman he fancied—fresh or famous—and no questions asked . . . he could have all the money he needed, and a tidy pile left over, growing in a dark place. He understood: we would give him anything—if he would always be the hero we required."

There is an argument to be made that the world needs heroes. Are the kids of America better off knowing that Major League Baseball players (or other athletes) drive drunk, abuse drugs, cheat on their wives, consort with gamblers, and generally act like other rich young men their age? And, if the Character Clause is a deception, isn't it a gentle one? After all, it hasn't kept most of the rogues out of Cooperstown. There were bad popes, too, but they don't keep their likenesses out of the Vatican gallery.

There *is* something to be said for hypocrisy: at the very least, it implies standards. A lot of the conventions of any society are based on unspoken and unacknowledged truths. If we could go back and unlearn that George Washington owned slaves, or that Henry Ford was a fascist, or that Winston Churchill fought World War II drunk, maybe we'd be happier for it.

But I doubt we would be better off.

Waking up is painful. For many years, the fans of the Minnesota Twins loved Kirby Puckett. He was a hometown hero—until he left the game and the worshipful local sports media, and became the focus of attention of reporters whose beat includes the police blotter.

Puckett is in the Hall of Fame, and he belongs there. He was a terrific center fielder who won six Gold Gloves, hit .318 lifetime, and led the Minnesota Twins, a small-market underdog, to two World Series championships in twelve years. And he did it with a smile. He founded charitable organizations. He was polite to the fans. He even made writers feel important. "When you talked to Kirby, he gave you the feeling that he knew there was a real person sitting across the table from him," a defender of Puckett's said. "He knew your name and what you said to him the last time you met. He cared what you thought, too. Not a lot of superstars are like that, even the ones who try to be nice."

In the spring of 1996, Kirby Puckett woke up blind in his right eye. He had glaucoma, and there was nothing that could cure it. He was forced to retire at the peak of his career. "Kirby Puckett's going to be all right," he said (of himself). "Don't worry about me. I'll show up and I'll have a smile on my face." When he was inducted into the Hall of Fame, in 2001, he seemed to be the very embodiment of the Character Clause.

In March 2003, *Sports Illustrated* ran a cover story entitled "The Secret Life of Kirby Puckett." The magazine reported that Puckett had been arrested for sexually assaulting a woman in a suburban Minneapolis restaurant (he was eventually acquitted), calling the charge "the latest in a pattern of alleged sexual indiscretions and violent acts."

A woman named Laura Nygren told *SI* that she had been Puckett's mistress before his storybook marriage, and again, later, after it ended. Puckett, she said, had cheated on her as well as on his wife. Not only that: she had obtained a temporary restraining order against him after he threatened her.

The magazine also reported that shortly before Puckett was inducted into the Hall of Fame, a Twins employee threatened to file a sexual harassment suit naming Puckett (among others). The suit was settled out of court.

It got worse. Puckett's ex-wife, Tonya, had reported him to the police for threatening her life. She claimed he had once tried to strangle her with an electrical cord, locked her in the basement, and put a cocked gun to her head while she was holding their young daughter.

Kirby Puckett was not only a member of the Baseball Hall of Fame; he was also a member of something called the World Sports

Humanitarian Hall of Fame. But his mistress told *SI* that his good deeds were a sham. She recalled an incident when Puckett had to leave for the hospital to visit a sick child. "You get to make the kid's day, that must make you feel good," she said.

"I don't give a shit," he replied. "It's just another kid who's sick."

Minneapolis is basically a small town. The reporters who covered the Twins weren't shocked by these revelations, especially after Puckett's name had begun showing up on the police blotter. But it took a national publication to make the story public.

There are a few crimes that journalists will not forgive, and one is being made to look ridiculous. Kirby Puckett was already in the Hall of Fame when the story of his secret life hit, and it is lucky for him that Cooperstown has no mechanism for removing and re-mortalizing its members.

Steve Garvey wasn't so lucky. Like Puckett, he was an imperfect man who made fools of a lot of writers. Unlike Puckett, he got caught when the writers could still do something about it.

I met Garvey in Cooperstown during Induction Week 2007. He was there to cheer on his former teammate Tony Gwynn and to do some campaigning for himself. His fifteen years of BBWAA eligibility were up, but he still hoped that he might have a shot with the Veterans Committee, and he knew Gwynn, who would be joining that committee, would lobby for him.

Once Garvey was considered a BBWAA shoo-in. In 1986, the *Sporting News* asked major-league managers, "Which players in your league, if they were to retire tomorrow, already have accomplished enough to merit selection to the Hall of Fame?" The managers selected ten. One of them was Steve Garvey. But it didn't work out that way.

Garvey thinks he has been unjustly excluded and, over Saturday morning coffee and muffins at Schneider's Bakery on Main Street, he made the case. "In my first year of eligibility the Dodgers were so sure I'd get in that they were going to hold a luncheon for me at Cooperstown," he said. "But the writers only gave me forty percent. I guess you could argue that I didn't have first-ballot stats, but my career stacks up pretty well against some of the guys who did get in. If you look at my numbers, nobody's out who's done what I've done."

That's true. Garvey's career matches up against that of a number of Hall of Famers. He was a superb defensive first baseman who once played a record 193 games without an error. Ten times in his nineteen-year career he was chosen for the National League All-Star team. In 1974, he was the National League's Most Valuable Player. Garvey hit a lifetime .294. Five times he drove in more than 100 runs in a season. And he was even better when it counted most. In 222 postseason at-bats, he hit .338, including a .417 performance against the Yankees in the 1981 World Series.

Not only that: Garvey, a former Dodgers spring training batboy, was famous for playing the game "the right way." He set a National League record by playing 1,207 consecutive games. He won the Roberto Clemente Award for combining good play with strong service to the community. He won the Lou Gehrig Memorial Award, which goes to the player who best exemplifies character and integrity on and off the field. He served on charitable boards, raised money to fight diseases, went to mass on Sunday, and was generally a happy warrior. When he was traded by the Dodgers to the San Diego Padres in 1983, he took out a full-page newspaper ad to thank the Los Angeles fans for their support. In 1985, in the midst of a cocaine scandal that "shook" baseball (don't they all), Garvey pushed for a one-strike-and-you're-out policy. "I'm most concerned about influencing the next generation of fans. If we allow players to take drugs and then come back, what does that tell the kids?"

Admiring teammates nicknamed him "The Senator," and Garvey sometimes seemed like a movie star playing a baseball star. His wife

Cyndy was a beautiful and glamorous Los Angeles television celebrity. If there had been a Hall of Fame for people who looked like they belong in a Hall of Fame, Garvey would have been a first-ballot choice.

But the press-perfect Senator had a weakness. Garvey, it turned out, wasn't the ideal husband. In fact, he got hit with two paternity suits by two different women who weren't his wife. Cyndy divorced him and wrote a book about it, a vindictive account in which she characterized Garvey as a "sociopath" and said that she had to get psychological help because of all the suffering he had put her through. In San Diego, fans put mocking bumper stickers on their cars: STEVE GARVEY IS NOT MY PADRE.

Who knows what goes on in celebrity marriage, or any marriage for that matter? Babe Ruth, Ty Cobb, Ted Williams, Joe DiMaggio—Cooperstown is full of guys who were hard on their wives and wound up in divorce court. But Garvey was different. The writers had bought and burnished his Mr. Clean act, and they felt like suckers. The Hall of Fame vote offered them a shot at payback.

At sixty, Steve Garvey still looks like a senator—square-jawed, clear-eyed, and coiffed, John Edwards with shoulders. He has spent many years trying to rehabilitate his image (Garvey's, that is; Edwards is a lost cause). As we spoke, two teenage boys came up to our table and asked for autographs. This is bad form during Induction Weekend, and Garvey would have been within his rights to refuse. Instead, he picked up a pen and signed. As the kids were leaving he said, "Those boys could sell those autographs right now. But I'm not going to turn down kids. I have to assume that they're doing it because they like me."

A few minutes later, a pretty woman walked into Schneider's and gaily waved at Garvey. "That's Wade Boggs's wife, Debbie," he said in what sounded like a wistful tone. About the same time Garvey was being hit with paternity suits, Boggs had been sued by his former mistress, Margo Adams, for palimony. Adams was with Boggs for two years or four, depending on whose story you believed. She traveled with the Red Sox on the road, sometimes at team expense, while Boggs kept his lawful wife at home with the kids. When the affair broke apart, Adams filed a multi million-dollar lawsuit and peddled her tale of adultery and betrayal on *The Phil Donahue Show* and in *Penthouse* magazine.

The scandal didn't cost Boggs his place in the Hall of Fame. For one thing, he had never presented himself as a beacon of rectitude. For another, he was smart enough to go on TV and confess to Barbara Walters that he was suffering from something called "sex addiction," and Debbie stood by him all the way. After all, how much can a voter hold adultery against a guy like Boggs if his own wife takes him back? Cooperstown's real character rule: don't get caught. And if you do, at least get a note from your wife.

FIVE . . . *The Monks*

Cooperstown is a seasonal village. In summer, it is full of visitors to the Hall of Fame, the Fenimore Museum, the Glimmerglass Opera festival, and the other attractions of the scenic Leatherstocking region. In winter, the town empties out; the baseball memorabilia stores along Main Street close down and the bed-and-breakfast owners head to Florida. The town's lone stoplight continues to signal, but there aren't enough cars around to bestow it a sense of authority.

Even in good weather there is no such thing as drop-in traffic. "If you get to Cooperstown by mistake, that means you've been lost for at least forty-five minutes," Ted Spencer told me. But in December 2007, the village experienced an epic snowfall, and I got caught in it. For several days I was practically the only guest at the Cooper Inn. The only visitors to the Hall I encountered were a Japanese couple and three boisterous college boys.

The arctic weather and near isolation made the Hall of Fame a cozy place, and when I first arrived the staff welcomed me into its hot stove league. They struck me as an order of baseball monks, a brotherhood of arcane scholars and pure-hearted lovers of the game. They weren't naïve. They were aware that many of the players enshrined in the great hall of plaques were not embodiments of the Character Clause and that baseball had a checkered past. The Mitchell Report on the use of performance-enhancing drugs was due that week, and they were bracing for that, too.

But they didn't confuse historical failings or contemporary controversies with the essence of the game. They talked baseball all day long, but the conversation was mostly swapping historical anecdotes, testing one another with obscure trivia questions, or fondly contemplating the sacred relics of the game on display in the museum or secured in its underground vaults.

One of the first monks I met was Gabriel Schechter. On the day we met, he was supposed to have been on his way to Hollywood to appear on *Jeopardy*, but just as he had been about to leave the house, word came that host Alex Trebek had suffered a heart attack, and his trip was postponed.* Schechter seemed disappointed but sanguine. Born in New Jersey, he taught English at the University of Montana before drifting down to Las Vegas in 1980, where he worked in casinos and wrote freelance stories. Five times he was a dealer in the World Series of Poker. He knows that there are always winners and losers.

In 2002, Schechter came east to Cooperstown to research a book. A few months later he was offered a job, and he's been there ever since. Among his tasks is fielding questions from fans around the world. The Hall gets an estimated sixty thousand each year, and the monks spend a significant part of their day trying to answer the questions of baseball fans who range from the idly curious to the obsessed. Nothing is too obscure to be researched seriously.

"Once," Schechter told me, "two graphic designers called to settle an argument over which of two fonts was used for the numbers on the backs of New York Yankee uniforms in the 1970s. The answer was, the Yankees created their own font, so they both lost.

"Another time a woman called from Florida. Her boss, she said,

* Schechter's appearance on the show was rescheduled for February 2008, taped, and aired in April. He won $20,000, and his fellow monks threw him a party in the Hall's Grandstand Theater, where the show was screened and coffee and cake served.

had bought four baseballs at an auction, each signed by a Hall of Famer. The boss was getting ready to mount them and he wanted some information about the players.

"I asked who he had and she said: Bob Feller, Yogi Berra, Stan Musial, and Jose Alvarez. I told her there was no such player as Jose Alvarez. Later she called me back and said oh, it was *Jesus* Alvarez, as if that made a difference. The only Jesus Alvarez we could find played high school baseball in Texas."

Although he never existed, Alvarez has attained a kind of immortality in the Hall of Fame archives. "Whenever we come across a photo of an unidentified player, we call him 'Jose Alvarez,'" Schechter told me.

Freddy Berowski is another of the research monks. He was born in Brooklyn, so I naturally turned to him to solve the mystery of another son of the borough, Lipman Pike, and his phantom Cooperstown vote.

Lip Pike was reputedly the first man to play baseball for money. When he first broke in, around the end of the Civil War, baseball was supposedly an amateur sport, played for fun and exercise and the delight of the occasional crowd. Unmarried ladies, at that time, were regarded as virgins, too, unless proven otherwise, and bankers were generally regarded as models of probity if they were not actually in prison. In short, it was a credulous era, and it is possible that players before Pike were paid under the table. But Lip, the son of a Jewish haberdasher, was reported to take his money up front, like any honest workingman. In 1866, the Athletics of Philadelphia got busted for paying him twenty dollars a week.

It was a bargain at twice the price. Pike was one of the best players of the prehistoric era. A left-handed second baseman, he led the league in home runs three straight years, hit .321 between 1871 and 1881, and starred in Brooklyn, Philadelphia, Hartford, Atlantic City, St. Louis, and other venues. His career ended ignominiously in 1881, when he was banned from the National League for suspicious "underperformance."* Despite this, Pike remained a very popular fellow in Brooklyn, where he eventually opened his own haberdashery. Thousands attended his funeral service at Temple Israel in 1893.

A lot of baseball sources say that Lip Pike got one vote in the 1936 balloting for the Hall of Fame. But the Web site of the Hall itself doesn't list him among the fourteen players who were mentioned on at least one ballot that year.

It took Freddy less than a day to get back with an explanation. It turns out that in the early days of the Hall, Veterans Committee members were allowed to vote along with the BBWAA. But those votes were only counted and made public once, in the 1936 election.

"So," I asked Freddy, "is it correct or incorrect to say that Pike got one vote?"

"Can't say for sure. He might have gotten votes from the veterans in other years, but those were secret ballots. And they're still sealed."

So we may never know how many votes Lipman Pike got. Like I said, there are mysteries in every shrine.

Tim Wiles is the director of research at the National Baseball Hall of Fame library, but he is a literary man at heart, the editor of a book of baseball poetry, *Line Drives*, who performs dramatic readings of "Casey at the Bat." Wiles is a connoisseur of Cooperstown whimsy. He told me, for example, that there are restaurants in town owned by men called DiMaggio and Yastrzemski, neither of whom is related to his Hall of Fame namesake.

"The Hall of Fame players are great, but the guys I really love meeting are the ones who only played a year or two," he says. "The big stars, a lot of times their profession is being themselves. But some of the other guys are great characters. Pumpsie Green, for

* In his book *Great Jews in Sports*, Robert Slater attributes this punishment to Pike's manager, who made him a "scapegoat" for the team's poor play. Some other scholars believe that Pike was guilty of not trying his hardest in contests on which money was being wagered.

example. Or Spook Jacobs, who has the world's biggest collection of baseballs. And I really loved Clete Boyer. He used to come up here and sit on a bench on Main Street and sign autographs at ten dollars a pop, just for the fun of it. I remember meeting Lou Limmer, too; he brought his grandkids up here and he was more excited than they were."

Wiles presides over a vast quantity of information. The Hall has a file on every man who has played major-league baseball since 1871—more than seventeen thousand in all.

The chief librarian of the Hall, Jim Gates, came to the Hall of Fame in 1995 from the University of Florida and began putting order into what had been a huge, unorganized pile of material. Gates took me on a tour of the museum's lower level, which contains an estimated twenty thousand books about baseball and a vast number of artifacts. The best are kept in a small, vault-like room designed to preserve and protect fragile treasures. There is a handwritten manuscript of "Take Me Out to the Ballgame" composed in 1908 (by two guys who had never been to a ballgame). The original promissory note for the sale of Babe Ruth to the New York Yankees is there, as is Judge Landis's first contract. The papers of the Mills Commission, which proclaimed baseball's Cooperstown paternity, are carefully guarded. So are the scorecards of the first perfect game (pitched by J. Lee Richmond in June 1880) and the scoresheet kept by broadcasters Ernie Harwell and Russ Hodges of the final game of the 1951 season, when Bobby Thomson's "shot heard round the world" home run sent the Giants to the World Series. Among the most treasured books are a first edition of Sol White's *The History of Colored Base Ball*, published in 1907; and the *Eagle Base Ball Club Rule Book*, circa 1854.

Experts put the value of the Hall's memorabilia at upward of $100 million. Only a tiny fraction is ever on public display. How it is shown is up to Ted Spencer, whose job as head curator makes him a Cooperstown abbot.

As a boy growing up in Boston, Spencer rooted for the Red Sox and dreamed of becoming an artist. The combination of art and baseball has been helpful in trying to blend Cooperstown's traditional Norman Rockwell portrait of American baseball with the United Colors of Benetton realities of the modern age.

The monks work intently at the Hall of Fame, even in the off-season. Teams and players send in material that has to be read and cataloged. Hundreds of old boxes of team rosters, scouting reports, financial statements, notes of director's meetings and fan club proceedings, attendance slips and ticket stubs, contracts and scorecards—the curatorial staff can't keep up with it all. Thousands of calls come into the research center (every baseball fan has his own personal Lip Pike). Still, there is always time for a cup of coffee and an intense discussion about their favorite topic: baseball. One morning, the talk turned to favorite books.

Tim Wiles was enthusiastic about *The Great American Baseball Card Flipping, Trading and Bubble Gum Book*, by Brendan C. Boyd and Fred Harris. It is a look at life and baseball in the 1970s through the trading card explosion of the time; people of a certain age and sensibility find it magical. Lenny Di Franza, a one-time punk rocker who works in the research department, picked *The Boys of Summer*, Roger Kahn's elegiac retrospective of the 1950s Brooklyn Dodgers. Kahn has come to Cooperstown for years to work on his projects and is a house favorite. Gabriel Schechter chose Lawrence Ritter's *The Glory of Their Times*, which appealed to his sense of nostalgia. Ted Spencer liked Darryl Brock's *If I Never Get Back*, a fable about traveling with the 1869 Cincinnati Red Stockings. And everyone kept coming back to Harold Seymour's three-volume history of the game, written between 1971 and 1991. The monks venerate Seymour not only as the Herodotus of baseball but as a member of the brotherhood, so devout that when he died his ashes were scattered near first base at Doubleday Field.

There is also a lot of collaborative work that gets done just for the fun of it. One such project was the story of Walla Tonka. On the wall of his office, Ted Spencer had hung a framed copy of an old newspaper article, the account of a brush with the executioner's noose on the part of one William Goings in 1897. Gradually, the other staffers began wondering who Goings was and why he merited a framed article. They started to dig.

Goings, they discovered, was a Choctaw Indian who lived in the Oklahoma Territory, and around the turn of the century he was considered a five-skill player and a bona fide star. He also had a temper. One day in 1897, he took it into his head that a woman was trying to work witchcraft on him, and he murdered her. A tribal judge sentenced him to death.

This sentence greatly perturbed the local sporting crowd, coming as it did in the middle of the 1897 baseball season. The judge bowed to public sentiment and commuted the term of William Goings's execution until the end of the pennant race. He was allowed not only to play at home, but to travel with the team. This decision raised questions in some judicial circles. Some speculated that Goings, whose Choctaw name was Walla Tonka, would go on a road trip and never return.

This must have generated some widespread discussion in the turn-of-the-century press. Not long after the Walla Tonka project began, a member of Spencer's staff discovered another clue: a letter in a Chicago newspaper written by Buffalo Bill Cody. Buffalo Bill said that, while he hadn't met Walla Tonka personally, he was well acquainted with the Choctaw character and would vouch for the fact that a brave like Walla Tonka would show up as the law required. (Cody added that he would never give such a character reference to an Apache.)

Buffalo Bill was right about Walla Tonka. He showed up for the final game of the season, which was on a Friday, fully expecting to be hanged the next day. The game, however, was rained out and rescheduled for Monday. A furious legal argument broke out over the disposition of his sentence, which was interrupted when a writ of habeas corpus arrived from a federal judge. The *New York Times* reported that Walla Tonka, roused from bed to be handed the writ, received this reprieve with "true Indian stoicism." He said, "Maybe me play more ball now," and went back to sleep.

Two years of legal dithering ensued. The feds claimed that an Indian tribal court could not carry out a death sentence. The Choctaw judge begged to differ. In 1899, the argument came to a head. Just as a government posse was on the way to rescue Walla Tonka from tribal justice, the judge ordered him shot. Four bullets didn't do the job, so a hose was forced down his throat and he drowned. It was the last capital sentence ever carried out by an Indian tribal court.*

"That's not the end of the story, though," Spencer told me. "One day, one of the curators walked in with a ten-minute silent film called *His Last Game*, from 1909. It was based on Walla Tonka—one of the first baseball movies ever made."

After twenty-eight years on the job, Spencer is still excited when fragments come together like this to form a bigger picture. "After World War II, the War Department gave permission for returning [ballplayer] veterans to wear a special patch on their [baseball]

* Spencer says that the Hall of Fame is contemplating an exhibit of some kind on Native Americans in baseball. According to *The Baseball Almanac*, forty-seven full-blooded Indians have played in the majors. The first was Louis Sockalexis, a Penobscot who played for the Cleveland Spiders.

The most famous Indian baseball player was Jim Thorpe, who won both the decathlon and the pentathlon in the 1912 Olympics but was stripped of his medals because he had played semipro baseball in 1909–10. Thorpe was a great football player but only an average outfielder in a six-year major-league career.

There are two full-blooded Indians in the Hall of Fame: left fielder Zack Wheat (Cherokee) and pitcher Charles Albert "Chief" Bender (Ojibwa). In the good old days, baseball writers referred to Indians as "Chief" in the same automatic way that Jewish players were dubbed "Moe." Other Hall of Famers who claim some Indian ancestry are Johnny Bench, Early Wynn, and Willie Stargell.

uniforms," he told me. "A circle with an eagle in the center. A few guys wore it, but most of them didn't, and I never knew why. Then one day one of our staff people up here was going through a big box of National League material, just randomly, and discovered the minutes of a meeting on the veterans' patch.

"Turns out, the owners were against it. See, a lot of players had baseball injuries that kept them out of the army, and the owners thought it would be unfair to them. The public might think they had been draft dodgers or slackers. The league didn't prohibit the patches, but it definitely discouraged them."

One of Spencer's great curatorial successes was sparked by an article he came across in the *Los Angeles Times* in 1986. Written by Janice Mall, it was the story of the nearly forgotten All-American Girls Professional Baseball League. The AAGPBL was established during World War II by Phil Wrigley, the owner of the Chicago Cubs. American men were serving in the army, and women were taking their places in factories and farms and other parts of the economy. Baseball, without its stars, was slumping at the box office. Wrigley thought there might be a profit in a baseball version of Rosie the Riveter.

The AAGPBL started out as a softball league, with underhand pitching and eighty-five-foot base paths. Soon it changed to hardball, and adopted most of the standard rules of baseball—on the diamond. Off the field, it was a different story. Girl players were required to wear skirts and lipstick at all times and to keep their hair long enough that they didn't raise uncomfortable questions about their extracurricular lives. They were strictly chaperoned on the road. Even at home, they were forbidden to drive a car beyond city limits without permission from their (male) managers. If al Qaeda ever starts a ladies' baseball league, the AAGPBL rulebook will come in handy.

Women's baseball was a good idea whose time never fully arrived. The league limped along for a decade in midwestern cities like Muskegon, Peoria, Kalamazoo, and Rockford. When it folded in

1954, few noticed, and no bona fide successor has arisen. Girls who want to play ball don't have to wear skirts and lipstick any more, but they better be able to pitch underhand.

When the *Los Angeles Times* article ran, Spencer was looking for ways to delve into unexplored corners of baseball history. The Hall wanted to attract female visitors (and make wives and mothers more willing to accompany the menfolk to Cooperstown). The story about the lost ladies' league seemed to fit. He reached out to AAGPBL alumnae and offered to host a reunion in conjunction with an exhibit. Hollywood producer Penny Marshall attended and filmed scenes from the event, some of which were used in *A League of their Own.*

The film came out in 1992. Starring Madonna, Rosie O'Donnell, Geena Davis, and Tom Hanks, it remains the biggest-grossing baseball movie of all time. It also had a very powerful effect on Cooperstown. "We usually get ten, twelve letters when we put up a new exhibit," says Spencer. "This was completely different. I stopped counting the letters after two hundred, and that was just in the first month." Mothers came to Cooperstown with their daughters. And in the wake of the women fans came women ballplayers.

I met a couple of these Girls of Summer at Induction Weekend, 2007. I found them sitting in the back of a Main Street memorabilia emporium selling autographs at five dollars a pop and fending off an elderly gent with a bottle of Budweiser in his hand who, it appeared, was some sort of geriatric groupie. He focused his attention mostly on Ruth Richard, who was played in *A League of Their Own* by Geena Davis.*

"Ruth was always the glamour puss," said Alice Pollitt Deschaine. She said it in the bantering tone that ballplayers of every time and gender use in lieu of actual communication.

* I later learned that the derivation of the characters in the film is a matter of some dispute. According to Alice "Lefty" Hohlmayer, Geena Davis's role was modeled on Lavonne "Pepper" Paire Davis.

"Aw, nothin' of the sort," said Richard. "I never went in for that stuff." Richard was one of the great players in the AAGPBL, a catcher who made the all-star team six times as a Rockland Peach.

Pollitt was a slugger. When she was with the Racine Belles, in 1951, she tied for the home run crown. That year she got married. Her son was born in 1954, just as the league folded, and she spent the rest of her life as wife and mother until the Hall of Fame rediscovered her. "Rosie O'Donnell played me," she said.

"You were both something," the old guy with the Bud said. "Still are."

Pollitt brushed the flattery away. She had money on her mind. "I heard Madonna's uniform from the movie is worth fourteen thousand bucks," said Alice.

"Really?" said Ruth. "I didn't hear that. I should have saved my old uniforms, I guess."

"I bet you looked better than Madonna," the groupie said. What's the male equivalent of a Baseball Annie, I wondered? A Baseball Andy?

A young man approached the signing table and bought an autograph. Both women appended "HoF" to their signatures. Only members of the Hall are allowed that honorific. Women ballplayers might have an exhibit in the museum, but you won't find any in the plaque room. When I pointed this out, I got a couple of hard looks in return.

"That's how we sign," said Alice. "That's it." I tried, and failed, to imagine her as a young woman asking a manager's permission to drive her car beyond the city limits.

The following summer, Dottie Collins died at age eighty-four. She was the Bob Feller of the AAGBPL, a 20-game winner in four straight seasons who, in the underhand pitching era of the league, struck out 293 batters in one season. Collins was instrumental in setting up the league's alumnae association, and she collaborated with Spencer in trying to collect AAGBPL memorabilia for the Hall of Fame (despite their efforts, most of the good stuff, including MVP trophies, has wound up at the Northern Indiana Historical Museum in South Bend). Collins was devoted to the Hall. "Being accepted at Cooperstown was the greatest thing that happened to any of us," she told a reporter in 1992. But she was never really a member. The *New York Times* gave her a long send-off, but it didn't include a statement by the Hall of Fame. Brad Horn, the spokesman, told me that the Hall only says official good-byes to certified HoF inductees and members of the board of directors, such as Tim Russert, who died two months before Collins.

Dottie Collins was a second-class citizen of baseball, ineligible for a plaque. But that could change some day. Once nobody dreamed about Negro leaguers in Cooperstown, either. The Hall deals with ethnicity, race, and gender when group pressure creates a cultural moment. No one wants to talk about it at the Hall of Fame, but even after women get their due, there is still at least one big locker left to open.

Americans of my generation, and Spencer's, could no more have imagined a gay baseball player than a gay archbishop. We now know better. Some percentage of big-league players, like some percentage of the population, were, and are, homosexual. In an era of gay pride, gay marriages, and gay identity politics, homosexuality has become both a political cause and, for many, an identity. Sooner or later, gay parents will want to use the Hall to connect generations, just as straight parents do. It has been widely rumored that at least two of Hall of Famers are gay, and there is speculation about at least one player who will be a first ballot choice. Maybe one or more of these guys will step forward, or others will on their behalf; one way or another, it seems likely that something about gay ballplayers will wind up on YouTube.

This is one parade the Hall of Fame does not intend to lead. "It's a subject we don't discuss," Spencer told me. "If it gets to be an issue, if it reaches a certain point, we'll have to deal with it." He said this with the sangfroid of a man due to retire within a few months. On his watch, he dealt with blacks and women. New claimants to a portion of the baseball heritage will be somebody else's problem.

SIX . . . *The Haul of Fame*

In January 2008, Jane Forbes Clark and the BBWAA convened a press conference at the Waldorf, in Manhattan, to introduce the only player who had been elected that year: journeyman relief pitcher Goose Gossage.

In his prime, Gossage threw a hundred miles an hour, clocked. He made a career out of intimidating brave men and, at fifty-six, some of that swagger was still there. When I got to the Waldorf, there were TV trucks parked outside, and a crowd of writers, baseball officials, and hangers-on filled the Empire Room. As always at these Hall of Fame events, almost everyone was white, male, and middle-aged. People milled around, trading offseason gossip.

Jack O'Connor, as secretary of the BBWAA, called the proceedings to order and read the election results. Five hundred and forty three writers had voted and Gossage had been mentioned on 85.8 percent of the ballots, easily clearing the 75 percent hurdle. It had been a long slog—this was Gossage's fifteenth and last year of eligibility. In his first year, he had gotten only 33.3 percent—and he had grown increasingly, audibly, impatient over time. Now, though, he was at ease, and he thanked all present in their native language, Baseball Cliché. He was "totally in awe" of being picked. It had been "special" to pitch in New York with its wonderful fans. He was only sorry that his mother hadn't lived long enough to see this moment.

A short Q&A session followed. A reporter asked Gossage what he thought of players who used steroids. "Their records mean nothing," he snapped. "I don't think you guys are going to vote them in." Later, when an intrepid journalist (okay, it was me) asked Gossage if he, himself, had ever used amphetamines, Goose denied it with strenuous sincerity.

Overall, the steroid issue made Jeff Idelson, president of the Hall, nervous, but there was a silver lining. "At least they didn't ask about Pete Rose," he said. "This is the first time they haven't asked about him."

After the press conference, Gossage, accompanied by an entourage of Hall of Fame officials and business agents, hopped into a black Escalade and headed for the studio of MLB.com. Everybody had a cell phone and they were all going off at once. Gossage was talking to Joe Torre, who had called from Hawaii with congratulations, as we stopped at a light on the corner of Fifth Avenue and Twenty-seventh, across the street from the Museum of Sex.

"Wonder what the curator does there?" said Idelson, who spends a fair amount of time on the road, chasing memorabilia.

"Maybe he collects famous G-strings," someone said, and we all laughed."*

Idelson's phone rang. "Brett wants to talk to you," he said, handing Gossage his BlackBerry.

"Hey, George, I was just talking about your tired ass," Gossage roared. "I was telling some people that you were the greatest hitter I ever faced. I should have hit you in the neck a couple times."

Gossage laughed. Presumably Brett was laughing on the other end. The agents and officials chuckled, too, third parties to some

* Just for the record: The Museum of Sex has fifteen thousand artifacts, most of them donated. The largest single donor was Ralph Wittington, a librarian at the Library of Congress, who gave the museum between eight and nine hundred boxes of pornography. According to Sarah Jacobs, the curator, many items are donated by children and grandchildren of departed loved ones; usually these artifacts are discovered postmortem. The museum also has exhibits. When we drove by, it was featuring "Kink: Geography of the Erotic Imagination."

genuine Hall of Fame banter. When he hung up, Gossage shook his head and said, "I really should have hit that motherfucker in the neck, I ain't lying." The agents laughed more loudly. This was great. A big personality, like Gossage's, would be salable, along with his walrus moustache and his cool, old-timey nickname. An HoF membership is a get-rich-quick card and an annuity. The Goose had laid a golden egg.

Idelson said, "Gary Carter called again while you were on the other phone. He's called ten times already, to congratulate you. And Paul Molitor wants to say hello. I'm just telling everyone you'll get back to them."

On the street in front of the MLB studio, people called Gossage's name and waved. The staff looked up from their computers when he walked in and gave him a round of applause. It had been many years since the Goose had elicited this much excitement in the big city, and he was beaming.

The MLB.com newsroom is a cyber-age facility built as a monument to baseball's recent discovery of modern business and marketing. For decades, most teams, and MLB itself, had the attitude (common in monopolies) that their product would sell itself—and if the public didn't like it, tough. Illustrative of this high-handed approach was the refusal of onetime Yankees general manager George Weiss to hold a free hat day at the Stadium. He explained that he didn't want to cheapen his brand by having kids walk around town wearing Yankees caps. This sort of marketing acumen didn't keep Weiss out of the executive wing of the Hall of Fame.

In those days, baseball was run as a collection of family fiefdoms—the Griffiths, the Yawkeys, the Wrigleys, the Macks, and so on. These barons were capable of collusion, as demonstrated in the gentleman's agreement that kept blacks out of the game, but rarely cooperation. Their old-fashioned rivalries and backward understanding of business ended up costing them a lot of money and, ultimately, their franchises.

After a post–World War II jump, baseball attendance dipped. The teams made terrible television deals, refused to share revenue, did nothing to encourage competitive balance, and failed to grasp the most basic principles of modern marketing. In the mid-sixties, when New York Jets owner Sonny Werblin gave rookie quarterback Joe Namath a $400,000 contract, baseball people laughed. How many games would the young quarterback win? Werblin was going to wind up paying, what, $50,000 a victory? Who was worth that? They didn't understand that paying more than necessary was an investment in public relations that would be returned manyfold in the glamour that sells tickets and builds television ratings.

The arrival of younger, hipper owners changed the attitude, but slowly. In 1975, shortly after buying the Atlanta Braves, Ted Turner tried to explain the realities of the media age to his counterparts. "Gentlemen," he told them, "we have the only legal monopoly in the country and we're fucking it up." Turner was a promoter of the Sonny Werblin variety; he gave Andy Messersmith a three-year contract for $1 million and then suggested that his pitcher adopt the nickname "Channel" and wear number 17, to promote Turner's Atlanta-based TV station.

The arrival of young owners like Turner and George Steinbrenner, who bought the Yankees in 1973, ushered in a new consciousness—baseball did, indeed, enjoy a monopoly. Teams might be rivals on the field, but they were partners in business. It was this realization that eventually led to the creation of MLB.com, a joint entity that broadcasts games and streams them over the Internet and developed a dedicated baseball network that started in 2009. It is also the biggest source of MLB gear. These days, the Yankees *want* kids to wear their caps; and if they buy them online via MLB.com, all the teams get an equal portion of the proceeds.

Gossage waved at the staff and huddled with two broadcasters, Billy Sample and Harold Reynolds, both former major-leaguers. They swapped anecdotes while the agents, BlackBerries in hand, gathered in a nearby conference room and fielded offers and business opportunities. Before his election, Gossage's speaking fee had been between $7,500 and $10,000. Andrew Levy, Gossage's agent, was hearing new numbers now. "Goose is getting offers that are triple his rate," he told me happily, between calls. "Twenty, twenty-five thousand. For the first year at least, everything will triple."

Jeff Idelson's phone rang. Jim Rice was on the line. Rice almost got in this year, and he was now entering his final year of eligibility. "Damn, buddy, fuck this," Gossage told him encouragingly. "You'll make it next year for sure."

Gossage hung up and shook his head. "Rice ought to be in the damn Hall, and so should Bert Blyleven. Bert was *filthy*," he said in admiration. "And I'll tell you who else. Rickey Henderson. He'll go in on the first ballot. He was the best leadoff hitter ever. Nobody even came close."

Everyone nodded, even the agents. (Gossage was right, of course; Henderson and Rice were inducted in 2009.)

"But tell you what," Gossage said. "I didn't *like* his ass."

Gossage finished an interview with MLB and headed for the Letterman show where he was scheduled to read a top-ten-reasons list of why he should be in the Hall of Fame. He shook hands with Sample and Reynolds and headed for the Escalade.

At the door, he paused with a final thought about Henderson.

"Tell you one thing about Rickey," he said. "He was great, but I really hated that motherfucker."

Even in this knowing age, many baseball fans don't want to think about the monetary aspect of getting elected to the Hall of Fame. Virtue is supposed to be its own reward.

But like everything else in Major League Baseball, the Hall of Fame is a business opportunity. The days when Grover Cleveland Alexander ruefully said that you can't eat a plaque are long gone.

There are four basic ways that retired baseball stars make post-career money: speaking engagements, memorabilia signings, products endorsements, and public relations gigs. An HoF after your name is a major economic-force multiplier for every one of them.

Not all Hall of Fame members are equally commercial. Tier one superstars—Willie Mays, Stan Musial, Hank Aaron, Sandy Koufax, Yogi Berra—will cash in with or without an HoF. But for the less obvious choices, it can be a life-changer.

"Take a guy like Robin Roberts," an executive at Steiner Memorabilia in New York told me. "He had a great career, but it was a long time ago, and it wasn't in a major market. But because he's in the Hall, his annual baseball income, not counting his pension, is probably in the low six figures, counting his signings, his regional corporate gigs in Philadelphia, and whatever else. That's not bad money."

"Guys like Cal Ripken and Tony Gwynn, superstars who played not so long ago, had lots of speaking engagements before they got inducted," says Jonathan Wexler of Playing Field Promotions, a Denver-based speaker and endorsement company. "But after making the Hall, their fees went up thirty to forty percent, and they were expensive to begin with. Gwynn was getting about thirty thousand dollars for a speech. Now it'll be fifty. And he'll have many, many more engagements."

Gossage was closer to the Robin Roberts model than the Ripken/Gwynn first tier. The Goose was a nine-time All-Star, but he also played for nine teams in his twenty-two-year career. Transcendent stars don't usually move around that much.

Plus, Gossage was almost exclusively a relief pitcher. Only once in his career did he pitch more than two hundred innings in a season—for the White Sox in 1976*—and his record that year was 9–17 for the last-place Sox. It's not that Gossage doesn't belong in the Hall of Fame. It's just that he doesn't necessarily *have* to be there. Neither do Jim Bunning or Bill Mazeroski or quite a few other guys. Jim Bunning, for example, was a fine pitcher for the Tigers of my youth, and later on for the Phillies. But he wasn't really much better than his 1963 Detroit teammate Mickey Lolich. Their careers were similar. Bunning pitched a no-hit game, but Lolich won 3 games in a World Series, a much rarer and more important achievement.

The difference was that Mickey Lolich was an overweight, happy-go-lucky guy who rode his motorcycle to Tiger Stadium and hung out with the fans. His motto was "The only thing running and exercising can do for you is make you healthy." After he retired, he opened a donut shop in suburban Detroit, and he sometimes went into the kitchen to bake his own batches. Bunning was an intense, ambitious college graduate who retired from baseball at age thirty-nine, went home to Kentucky, and entered politics. When he was elected to the Hall of Fame in 1996, he was already a five-term Republican Congressman with an eye on the Senate. The Hall of Fame credential didn't hurt him with Kentucky voters. And having a man on Capitol Hill was a lot better for baseball than having a guy in a donut shop in Detroit.†

If Bunning's induction stemmed at least partly from political interest in the establishment, the election of Bill Mazeroski was a labor of love, the result of a years-long push by a single fan named John T. Bird. Mazeroski was a second baseman for the Pittsburgh

* Gossage was tried as a starter in 1976. He started 29 games that year—he had started a total of 8 games in his four previous seasons—and he never started another game in his remaining seventeen years in the big leagues.

† Bunning was passed over by the writers and chosen by the Veterans Committee. In those days, that meant being chosen by a committee handpicked by the Hall itself.

Pirates, a great fielder and an unassuming guy who averaged .260 at the plate. His great moment of glory came in the 1960 World Series, when his home run won the series for the Pirates. Beating the Yankees made him a working-class hero, but one great moment isn't usually enough for immortality. If it were, Don Larsen and Bobby Thomson would be in Cooperstown.

The writers never took Mazeroski seriously. His BBWAA vote peaked at 42.3 percent in 1992. That was before John T. Bird came along.

"I grew up near Forbes Field," Bird told me. "I loved watching Maz, and *I* thought he belonged in the Hall of Fame. One day I had an epiphany. I realized that if I didn't do something, he would never get in."

Bird is a literary gent, a Dartmouth graduate who now lives in Birmingham, Alabama. At one time, he was Warren Buffett's editor. He didn't know Mazeroski or anyone in baseball. For an outsider like him to be taken seriously, he would have to build a case.

Bird went to Cooperstown, sat in the library, and researched Mazeroski's career. Then he traveled the country, interviewing old players who admired Maz. In 1995, he wrote and self-published *The Bill Mazeroski Story*, a three-hundred-page brief for his candidate, and sent a copy to every committee member.

Bird used sabermetrics, and he got some top statistical historians to help him convince the electing public that Mazeroski was a good candidate—at least as good as his American League contemporary Nellie Fox of the White Sox, then seen as Maz's biggest rival for induction. After Fox beat out Mazeroski in 1997, Bird stepped up the pressure with a four-minute campaign video he made at his own expense. He also traveled to Tampa, Florida, where the old fifteen-member Veterans Committee met, to lobby for his man.

Mazeroski needed at least twelve votes from the fifteen-member committee, and in 2001 he finally got them. "Toward the end, the

Pirates got involved," Bird says modestly. "When Hank Aaron and Juan Marichal joined the committee, they were on our side. And, of course, Joe Brown, Maz's general manager with the Pirates, was the head of the committee that year, which was extremely helpful."

Bird's campaign paid off big-time—for Mazeroski. "Before Mazeroski made the Hall of Fame, he was really cheap," Wexler told me. "But he had a huge surge when he was elected, and it lasted. Because of being in Cooperstown, he'll always be valuable. For him, it's a long-term thing."

These days, few aspiring immortals are prepared to rely on the kindness of strangers like John T. Bird. They mount sophisticated campaign operations run by professionals with their eyes on the prize. This is a fairly new phenomenon. The convention is that you are not supposed to lobby for yourself. Thirty-five years ago, Cleveland pitcher Bob Lemon sent each member of the BBWAA a box containing a lemon, and purists still regard this as an example of the hard sell. Lobbyists tread carefully.

Bert Blyleven's effort is in the hands of Bill Hillsman, a top Minneapolis political consultant who worked for Senator Paul Wellstone and helped Jesse Ventura get elected governor of Minnesota. "Bert isn't paying me, and neither are the Twins," he told me over the phone. "The Twins are good for anything that doesn't cost money. But a group of sponsors got together and put up the money to help Bert."

Blyleven is a worthy candidate. He won almost 300 games for mediocre teams. Baseball-Reference.com compares him to Don Sutton, Gaylord Perry, Fergie Jenkins, Early Wynn, and other Hall of Famers. In 2007, he got 61.9 percent of the BBWAA votes. Hillsman felt that with a little push, he could go over the top.

"The BBWAA is a small universe," he says. "And it can be a very tough crowd. They don't want to be pushed. The trick is to get the information out there, keep the name in front of them, but not be seen to be trying too hard. That's unseemly."

If they had a spot for lobbyists in Cooperstown, Tim Gay would deserve one, with an asterisk. He is the Washington operator who put together the CITGO-Cooperstown partnership. Not coincidentally, he ran a Hall of Fame campaign for Hugo Chavez's favorite shortstop, Dave Concepcion.

Concepcion was a lot like Bill Mazeroski—good field, no hit. His lifetime average was .267, with only 101 home runs in nineteen seasons. Those puny numbers were reflected in the balloting of the BBWAA. Concepcion's first year of eligibility was 1994, and he got just 6.8 percent of the vote. By 2006, three years from the end of his eligibility, he had barely doubled that.

Concepcion is a national hero in Venezuela. Unlike a lot of Latin players who make it in the majors, he continued to go home each year and play winter ball. Concepcion grew rich, bought himself a large farm and a transportation company, and became a well-compensated spokesman for CITGO, which figured he'd be even more effective with an HoF after his name.

Gay took on the case and, like any smart campaigner, he began by mobilizing his base. He persuaded the Reds to hold a Davey Concepcion Day at the ballpark in Cincinnati and to publicly retire his number, 13. The Reds were happy to oblige. Cincinnati is a venerable baseball town—the Red Stockings, Lip Pike's old crew, were the first openly professional team and Cincinnati has been a major-league town since 1876 (with the exception of 1881). But the quality of Cincinnati baseball hasn't matched its longevity. The Reds still dine out on the glory of the Big Red Machine of the 1970s. Concepcion was the shortstop on that team, and getting him into Cooperstown would have excited the fans.

After Concepcion Day, Gay sent media kits to the members of the BBWAA. He got a couple of former teammates, Hall of Famers Johnny Bench and Joe Morgan, to vouch for him.

Another, Tony Perez, went down to the MLB winter meetings to talk to the writers in person. But despite all these efforts, the eligibility clock ran out on Concepcion without his being inducted. Now, his only chance is the Veterans Committee. Gay is not optimistic. "It's almost impossible," he told me. "They are a very exclusive group and they want to keep it that way."

The most famous exclusion from the Hall of Fame is, of course, Pete Rose. I ran into Rose during Induction Weekend. He was in the back room of Ballpark Collectibles, seated behind a plush rope, signing autographs for sixty-five dollars apiece.

Even nearing seventy, Rose is a hard-looking character and there was something pathetic about seeing him roped off, mugging for the crowd. A couple of college-aged guys pointed their cameras at him and hollered, "Hey, Pete, say cheese!" Rose complied—his living depends on being nice to the public—but to my eye he seemed to be seething behind the smile. I imagined him wishing he could climb over the rope and pound the punks to death with their own Nikons.

The battle between Pete Rose and the Hall of Fame goes back almost twenty years. He retired after the 1986 season, which made him eligible in 1991. But he never got to a ballot. In August 1989, Major League Baseball put him on its permanently ineligible list for gambling. Two years later, the Hall of Fame decided, at the urging of the Commissioner's Office, to formally exclude anyone on the permanently ineligible list. In the history of baseball, seventeen players have been banned for life, but only two were Hall of Fame quality stars. One, Joe Jackson, has been dead since 1951. The Hall's new rule was clearly directed against Rose.

There is no doubt that Pete Rose bet on baseball as a player and a manager. And there is no doubt that he lied about it to the commissioner. He didn't come clean until his book *My Prison Without Bars* was published in 2004. Even then, he might not have told the entire truth. Rose admitted that he had gambled but claimed that he had bet on *every* game, and always for his own team, giving gamblers no helpful hints or selective information.

The suspension hit Rose hard. Sure it was a mistake to gamble, but the Hall of Fame was full of gamblers, wasn't it? Players in other sports had done what he did. Hell, Paul Hornung and Alex Karras gambled in the NFL, and they got one-year suspensions, not the death penalty. It was wrong to lie to the commissioner, okay, but damn, Bill Clinton lied to the whole country and all he lost was his license to practice law.

A lot of players took Rose's side. In his book, he describes a visit he made with teammate and Hall of Famer Mike Schmidt to the office of baseball commissioner Bud Selig to ask for reinstatement. In the waiting room, Schmidt pointed to some photos of great players hanging on the wall. "Just about every Hall of Famer in baseball is hanging on these walls and Pete Rose has more hits than any of them. Mickey Mantle's dead, Jackie Robinson's dead, Joe DiMaggio, Ted Williams, Satchel Paige, and Babe Ruth—all gone. You're one of the last men standing from the old regime."*

Baseball's ongoing snub has made Rose alternately remorseful and defiant. In 1993, he first came to Cooperstown, to "Mickey's Place," and signed autographs during Induction Weekend, upstaging the official ceremony. "Apparently, my appearance didn't set too well with members of the Hall of Fame board of directors, either," he writes. "But since I was already banned for life, what could they do . . . ban me again?"

In 1995, Mike Schmidt used his induction speech to argue for Rose. "I join millions of fans around the world in hoping that, some day very soon, Pete Rose will be standing right here."

Schmidt's hope hasn't materialized. There is no sign that Bud

* Rose is the all-time leader in career hits; in 1985, he broke Ty Cobb's record and ended up with 4,256. He accomplished this by going to bat roughly 10 percent more often than any other hitter in the history of baseball. He wasn't the greatest hitter in baseball history, but he was the most frequent.

Selig will reinstate Rose and none that the Hall of Fame will act independently. But baseball occasionally sends Rose a hint of reconciliation. In 1999, he was chosen for the Major League Baseball All-Century Team, a promotion officially endorsed by MLB. The living members of the team were introduced at Turner Field in Atlanta, before the second game of the 1999 World Series, and Rose got a thundering ovation.

Bill James spoke for the many baseball people who feel Cooperstown is incomplete without Rose. "I don't see that the Hall of Fame is so full of wicked people that it needs to abandon the effort to elect people who meet some standards of decency," he says. "Neither do I see that its roster is so pure that it can't honor Mark McGwire or, for that matter, Barry Bonds. They don't ask me to vote, but if they did, I'd probably vote for Bonds, I think. I'd vote for Pete Rose."

Joe Jackson is another story. James says Shoeless Joe betrayed baseball by selling games. Marvin Miller sees it differently. "In my world, a man who is never convicted is innocent," Miller told me. "And Jackson was never convicted of anything."

Everyone knows that Joe Jackson was one of the greatest hitters of all time, and that he was banned for life for allegedly taking part in the 1919 plot to fix the World Series. Jackson always denied it, claiming that he knew about the plan but didn't participate (he offered his .375 batting average in the World Series as evidence). It is not so well remembered that Jackson, along with the rest of the "Black Sox," was tried and acquitted in a Chicago court in 1921.

Commissioner Landis saw this as an occasion for jury nullification. "Regardless of the verdict of juries," he ruled, "no player that throws a ballgame, no player that undertakes or promises to throw a ballgame, no player that sits in conference with a bunch of crooked players and gamblers where the ways and means of throwing games are planned and discussed, and does not promptly tell his club about it, will ever play professional baseball . . . regardless of the verdict of juries, baseball is entirely competent to protect itself against crooks, both inside and outside the game."

Jackson had already been convicted by public opinion. But it took a federal judge of Landis's arrogance to boldly set aside the presumption of innocence, the legal rights of the acquitted, and the validity and relevance of the jury system. Landis wanted to make an example of Shoeless Joe, and he did, sentencing him to a life without baseball (and, in the process, sentencing baseball fans to a life without Jackson). A precedent was set. Baseball was not only above the Constitution, it was also above the rulings of the criminal courts.

Joe Jackson slunk away and died in obscurity in 1951, at the age of sixty-three. But he has not been forgotten. On July 16, 2008, the official Shoeless Joe Jackson Web site published birthday wishes to its hero. He would have been 121 years old. These birthday greetings were not the work of hopeless baseball romantics. The site belongs to GMC, which owns Jackson's intellectual property rights. Right now, that amounts to his likeness, a couple of posters featuring his image, and a line of baseball bats. You want to use Shoeless Joe in a shoe commercial, for example, or work his picture into a baseball collage, you come to GMC Worldwide.

Jackson is a dependable earner, bringing in $75,000 in a good year, occasionally more. But making it to Cooperstown would be a great career move. "If Joe gets into the Hall of Fame, it would increase his annual revenue stream by a factor of five to ten times," a senior executive of the company told me. "A lot of corporations and companies like to make ad campaigns around a Hall of Famer. If he isn't reinstated, we can't sell him in uniform, we can't market him in major-league stadiums or in MLB's online stores, and mass marketers licensed by MLB won't take him."

GMC has tried various approaches to this problem. From time to time, it petitions Bud Selig on Jackson's behalf. (All requests for reinstatement remain, as they have since the Harding administration, "under consideration" by the Commissioner's Office.) There have been congressional lobbying efforts, which have garnered support from South Carolina senator Jim DeMint and others, but Congress has no authority in the matter. And there is the Virtual Joe Jackson Hall of Fame (and gift shop), whose goal is "to educate" the public to the "injustice" done to Jackson and offers fans the opportunity to contribute money to sustain the effort.

It is hard to imagine what Jackson himself would have made of all this. Once, the story goes, Ty Cobb ran into him working behind the counter of a liquor store in Greenville, South Carolina. "I know you, you're Joe Jackson," Cobb said. "Don't you know me, Joe?"

"I know you," Jackson supposedly replied, "but I wasn't sure you wanted to speak to me. A lot of them don't." Jackson died thinking he was worthless. He wouldn't have believed that his ghost would be making more than he ever did, and that there's a whole corporation out there, working to get him into Cooperstown.

Steve Verkman doesn't care if Joe Jackson gets into the Hall of Fame or not. Verkman is the president of Clean Sweep Auctions, a memorabilia dealership. He sells mostly autographs, and Jackson's is "golden."

"Jackson was illiterate, and his wife signed for him," Verkman explained. "He could scratch out his name, but there aren't more than twenty signatures extant. One of those is worth a fortune, Hall of Fame or not."

No one passing Verkman's nondescript premises, on a leafy side street in suburban Long Island, would imagine that it contains some of baseball's most valuable treasures. In the front of the building are a couple small offices. Behind it is a large work room strewn with signed memorabilia on its way out to customers. And, in the back, there is a windowless, two-thousand-square-foot space crammed with baseball history. Verkman's got the first baseball card ever made, featuring the 1869 Cincinnati Red Stockings and its two future Hall of Famers, George and Harry Wright. Two cinderblock walls hold approximately one thousand autographed baseballs, including one signed by the entire 1927 Yankees team. There are mountains of World Series programs going back to the start of the twentieth century, plastic boxes holding one of the biggest pre-1960 baseball card collections in the world, a bat used by Willie Mays (priced at $9,000), and even some boxing memorabilia for the eclectic.

People don't come to Verkman's place to browse. The Internet has made card shops passé. These days the autograph action is in cyberspace. Verkman is one of the dozen or so largest dealers in the country, and he stages about ten memorabilia auctions a year. He was in the midst of one when I visited.

On the block that day was a group of Pinkerton baseball cards featuring Walter Johnson, Nap Lajoie, Honus Wagner, and other legends of antiquity. "A real connoisseur's piece," he said lovingly. "This is the largest public sale of Pinkertons in ten years." There was also a scuffed Babe Ruth baseball, Mickey Mantle's signed rookie card, a handwritten note from Hall of Famer Johnny Evers, circa 1934, and hundreds of similar antiquarian items.

Verkman estimates that there are ten thousand collectors around the world who collect primarily HoF memorabilia, and even general collectors covet it. "HoF is the single best predictor of baseball price," he told me. "Especially when someone unexpected is chosen. When Bruce Sutter went in, for example, that changed everything for him. His rookie card went from a dollar to twenty dollars overnight. The demand for his autograph increased a thousandfold."

Autograph dealers and collectors invest in Hall of Fame futures. Obvious Cooperstown candidates are worth less than borderline cases. I asked Verkman how he saw the next twenty years. Jeter, Rivera, A-Rod, Joe Torre, and Manny Ramirez are locks," he said.

"Pedro Martinez, what's he got, three Cy Youngs? He'll get in. Randy Johnson will make it, Mike Piazza, Pudge Rodriguez, Frank Thomas, Ken Griffey Junior, Greg Maddux, Tom Glavine. Alomar, although he didn't finish very well. Biggio should get in. And I've got a feeling about Barry Larkin, too.

"Then you've got some question marks. Clemens and Bonds, with the steroid issue. Gary Sheffield and Tejada, too, although I'm not sure they'd make it anyway. Pujols, it's too early to say, but he's looking good. Smoltz and Thome are maybes. Ichiro will be interesting. Trevor Hoffman is in the borderline group. And Billy Wagner."

"Billy Wagner? The Mets reliever?"

"Hey, it could happen," Verkman said with a small grin. He was born and raised in Queens, and he has his sentimental favorites, just like everyone else.*

Sometimes even dealers get burned. "In the 1980s, Ruben Sierra was supposed to be an absolute lock," Verkman said. "A lot of people lost money on him. Same with Will Clark and Bo Jackson. Juan Gonzalez was supposed to be a sure thing. I hate to say this, but the biggest flop by far was Don Mattingly. A lot of guys start out great, but their careers die, they don't improve, they get hurt. And the steroids issue complicates calculations."

The changing cultural norms of Cooperstown also play a role. The mass induction of Negro-leagues players in 2006 opened a whole new market. "Bullet Joe Rogan died in 1968, and nobody even heard of him," said Verkman. "After he was inducted in 1998, I sold a softball signed by him for nine thousand dollars. A signed hardball, if I could find one, would go for forty to fifty thousand."

Lately Verkman told me he had been investing in Joe Gordon, a nine-time All-Star second baseman between 1938 and 1950. Gordon hit just .268, but he was a Yankee, and that counts for something.

* A few weeks later, Wagner was injured and missed the rest of the 2008 season. Verkman told me that, with sorrow, he was demoting Wagner to "unlikely."

Around 20 percent of Hall of Fame inductees played at least a large part of their careers in New York. It turned out to be a good move for Verkman. At the end of 2008, the special Hall of Fame committee for old-timers who broke in before 1943 selected Gordon. His memorabilia went way up, which was no particular use to him, since he had been dead since the Carter administration.

Verkman is now betting on Ed Reulbach, a right-handed pitcher who won 182 games between 1905 and 1917. Reulbach is best known, if he is known for anything at all, for jumping to the outlawed Federal League—an early and short-lived effort to break Major League Baseball's monopoly. Verkman isn't betting heavily on him, but he does own a signed Reulbach baseball, and, if Cooperstown lightning should strike, it would fetch around $20,000.

This may seem improbable, but Verkman has seen long shots come in before. George Davis was a shortstop for the Giants and White Sox around the turn of the century. He retired in 1909 and died without fanfare in 1940. Almost sixty years later, he was chosen by the Hall of Fame Veterans Committee, and Verkman, who happened to have thirty George Davis original tobacco cards circa 1909, cleaned up. He hit again when Billy Southworth was inducted in 2008, after a managerial career that ended in 1951. "I had some of his items, and they went up by a factor of ten," he says.

Before autographs became a commodity, in the sixties and seventies, a lot of great stars simply signed whatever was put in their hands or sent to them in the mail. Babe Ruth was famous for promiscuous signing (even through the actual work was sometimes done by an accommodating baseball writer or clubhouse man). Ty Cobb was a soft touch, too, at least in this area. The rarest—and most valuable—Hall of Famers are Eddie Plank, Addie Joss, and Ross Youngs. "These guys are ten times more expensive than Babe Ruth," said Verkman. "Ross Youngs on a piece of paper is worth ten thousand dollars. If he wasn't a Hall of Famer, he'd be worth a hundred bucks."

From a marketing point of view, death is an excellent career move. Dead players can't sign any more. It's even better if they die young, further limiting supply. Kirby Puckett, for example, was a fifty-dollar HoF signature until he passed on at the age of forty-five in 2006. Today, despite the unflattering revelations about his character, he goes for five times that and rising. "Kirby has great potential," Verkman says.

As we talked, Verkman's computer screen lit up with offers. There was action on a Chief Bender baseball card. A handwritten Cy Young postcard had four bids. A man in Colorado wanted the Johnny Evers letter. But the biggest hit of the day was a Hank Greenberg package: a signed baseball and a cancelled ten-dollar check, sent by the fan who had mailed Greenberg the ball, to pay for return postage. This fetched $4,500, making it the most expensive Greenberg ball of all time.

"Greenberg's Jewish," Verkman explained. "There's a premium for him and Koufax. Sandy used to be a good signer, but lately he doesn't do much. Cubans and Jews are the only ethnic groups that matter as far as their market is concerned. One reason that Ed Reulbach is so expensive—an autograph goes for five hundred dollars or more—is that a lot of collectors think he was Jewish."*

I laughed, and Verkman regarded me solemnly. "But you know what? The thing that made the Greenberg package so expensive isn't the Jewish part. It isn't the ball, either. It's the cancelled check. Collectors love a story. I know it sounds silly, but this

* Since long before my Uncle Pinchus mistook the Detroit Tigers for the Jewish People, there has been confusion among Jewish fans over who was, and wasn't, a member of the tribe.

Many believe that Johnny Kling, the old Cubs catcher, was Jewish. He wasn't, although his wife was, and Kling let people believe that he might be Jewish, too. Who knows—that may be what they told his wife's parents.

On the other hand, Jimmie Reese, Babe Ruth's Yankee roommate, is often mistaken for Irish, when his real name was James Hymie Solomon. Presumably the Babe was in on the joke.

business isn't only about money. Buying a Hall of Fame autograph? For a lot of people, it's a chance to own a millisecond of a hero's life."*

Steve Verkman told me that baseball card shows have been killed by the Internet, but I saw life after death on a Saturday afternoon in Secaucus in mid-January. It was Yankee Pride Day, and thousands of fans showed up at the Crowne Plaza Hotel to buy an autograph from a rotating cast of ninety-eight former Yankees. The star of the show was Goose Gossage in his first HoF autograph session. The ringmaster was promoter Molly Bracigliano of MAB Celebrity Service. Bracigliano started out as a fan and autograph hound herself, and, while the high rollers may buy their memorabilia from brokers, she caters to Everyfan. "I know how people feel, the dream of meeting their favorite players," she told me. We were sitting in a quiet niche of the Crowne, surrounded by controlled chaos. People formed long lines to buy an autograph or a photo, or pawed through a memorabilia bazaar searching for bargains. "I once stood in lines like these for hours."

In recent years, scholars of Jewish baseball have discovered that Lou Boudreau's mother was Jewish, although he was not raised Jewish and never publicly discussed it. That's more than enough, however, to get him on the Hall of Fame scrolls along with Greenberg and Koufax. Some also add Rod Carew, who married a Jewish woman and raised Jewish children but, despite much speculation, never took the final plunge himself. My friend and colleague Gary Rosenblatt calls Carew "the longest convert."

Strangely, there are more Jewish players in MLB today than at any time in history. Three played in the 2008 All-Star Game: Ian Kinsler of the Texas Rangers, Kevin Youkilis of the Red Sox (often mistaken for a Greek because of his nickname, "Euclis, the Greek God of Walks"), and Ryan Braun of the Brewers, known as the "Hebrew Hammer." Braun's mother is not Jewish, so according to Talmudic law he does not qualify as a Jew. It is my belief, however, that Talmudic law does not apply to Jewish baseball players who are kosher under the Lou Boudreau Exemption.

* A few months later, Verkman sold a ticket stub to Lou Gehrig Day, Yankee Stadium, July 4, 1939—the day Gehrig delivered his famous "luckiest man on the face of the earth" speech—for a record-setting $22,000.

Molly Bracigliano grew up as an intense baseball fan, thanks to her father and three brothers—"dolls weren't even an option"—and she still has a tendency to idolize her clients. In addition to putting on theme shows like "Yankee Pride," she is the exclusive speaking agent for Tom Seaver, Willie McCovey, Don Sutton, Tony Gwynn, Bruce Sutter, Carlton Fisk, and Rod Carew.

"Hall of Fame members are wonderful," she says. "Getting into Cooperstown is a sacred thing. It makes me feel special just to be involved with these men."

For her shows, Bracigliano pays the players a guarantee, and sells tickets at fixed prices, each one good for an autograph—your choice of the surface—and a personal moment.

The biggest draws are Hall of Famers. "Baseball's big three are Willie Mays and Hank Aaron—who get between two hundred and three hundred dollars per ticket—and Koufax, who doesn't even do public signings any more—the only sports figures in his league are Michael Jordan and Muhammad Ali," she says.

Stan Musial is a two-hundred-dollar signature, mostly because he rarely travels outside St. Louis. Yogi Berra is "the steal of the century," at seventy-nine dollars. Berra, an adopted son of New Jersey, was at the show, and she expected him to sell upward of two hundred tickets. "I love Yogi," she said. "He and Moose Skowron were scheduled to sign today at one o'clock, but Yogi showed up at ten in the morning. That's what a hard worker he is."

Bracigliano, like any impresario, is all about pleasing the public, and she prefers players who play ball with fans. "Willie Mays is a real gentleman, but he can't see very well and sometimes people think he's being grouchy," she said. "Jim Bunning is always well dressed, but he's stand-offish and *very* cautious. And as for Carl Yastrzemski . . ." She trails off graciously.

Yastrzemski is the Hall of Fame's most infamous living misanthrope. Collectors, dealers, and even baseball executives regard him as unfriendly and unpleasant. "I was at a show once, bought an autograph from him, and asked him who the best hitter he ever saw was," one collector told me. "He didn't even bother looking up, much less answer. That hurts. You pay good money for a signature, you expect a little courtesy."

According to Bracigliano, Tom Seaver, Johnny Bench, Don Sutton, and Berra are great to the fans. But the real Mister Congeniality is Cal Ripken. "He's the best I've ever seen," Bracigliano says. "He looks every person directly in the eye. He comments on the item he's being asked to sign. He'll pose for pictures. He gives the impression that he has all the time in the world."

Gary Carter is another favorite, enough so that Bracigliano is personally indignant that he was forced by Cooperstown to go into the Hall as a Montreal Expo rather than a New York Met. This was a financial, as well as sentimental, issue. Big-market teams sell better than small ones. "If Dave Winfield had gone in as a Yankee instead of a Padre, his price would be double," Bracigliano told me.

Traditionally, guys who played on more than one team could choose the logo on their plaques. Reggie Jackson, for example, picked the Yankees over the Oakland A's. And in 1999, Nolan Ryan went into the Hall wearing a Texas Rangers logo, despite the fact that he spent only five years with the team. It was rumored—but not confirmed—that the Rangers paid him $1 million to make the switch. There is considerable public relations value to having a Hall of Famer connected to a franchise; and there is money to be made selling Hall of Famer merchandise at the ballpark.

In 2001, following the Nolan Ryan rumors, the Hall of Fame changed its rules. Players would be consulted about their preference, but the final choice would be made by the Hall itself. Two years later, Gary Carter became the first player to be affected by the new ruling. He wanted to go in as a Met, and probably should have—there isn't even a team in Montreal any more. The Hall's decision has cost him (and Bracigliano) a lot of money.

By contrast, Goose Gossage's multiple teams turned out to be a lucky break for him. He didn't stay anywhere long enough to really belong to a single franchise, and he pitched in New York a little longer than Chicago or San Diego. He went in wearing a Yankees cap.

I saw Gossage in the crowd, Andrew Levy by his side, heading for a signing table. Not every Yankee is willing to do these events. The famously private Bernie Williams isn't comfortable doing shows, and Bracigliano told me that Scott Brosius won't sign for money. "He's very religious," she said in a hushed tone. A lot of younger players are so rich that they don't need to sign anything.

The big names were down in the ballroom meeting the public. Meanwhile, upstairs in the Diamond Room, away from the crowd, half a dozen players sat at long tables, signing their names to group photos and team posters (known in the trade as "flatware") and baseballs. Collectors like to buy full team items, and for that you need not just the stars, but the supporting cast—guys like Willie Banks, Shane Spencer, and Jim Bruske, all of whom were churning out product. Bruske, who only pitched 3 games for the Yankees, was there with his son.

Meanwhile, back downstairs, a paging system summoned customers airport-style: "Attention all Joe Girardi ticket holders, please go to the main ballroom." I settled in next to Chili Davis, "the Jamaican Sensation," who sat, pen in hand, receiving customers one at a time. Davis was a fine outfielder during his nineteen-year career, the last three of which he played in New York, and he had an easy way with the fans. "Enjoy," he said each time he handed back an autograph.

There were a surprising number of women among the collectors. A college student from Connecticut handed Davis a ball already signed by several players, including Roger Clemens. "I got him outside Yankee stadium when I was in the seventh grade," she said. Since the steroid scandal, the bottom has fallen out of Clemens autographs. A few months earlier, signed Clemens balls sold for

$299; now they were going for $50. "If he goes into the Hall, the price will go back up," Bracigliano told me later.

Davis signed, and the woman, whose name was Kristen, produced a second baseball from her purse. She had no ticket for this one. "You don't do charity signings, do you?" she asked hopefully.

Davis shook his head. "Sorry, but they won't let me," he said. For emphasis, he directed her gaze to a middle-aged woman sitting nearby, wearing an MAB shirt; the selling of baseball autographs is a trust-but-verify business.

Another fan approached with a baseball, and Davis signed it. She inspected the signature and said, "I bet you went to a Catholic school. You have very nice handwriting. Lou Piniella does, too. He went to a Catholic school." Davis smiled. "Enjoy," he said.

A middle-aged man came up to the table clutching two posters so crammed with signatures that Davis had to search for a spot to write his name. Davis read the names out loud—Hank Aaron, Pete Rose, Willie Mays. "These are worth some money," he said.

"Yep," said the man, "one is for me. The other one is putting my daughter through graduate school."

"Enjoy," said Davis, handing over the signed posters. As the man walked away, Davis turned to me and said, "That thing is worth a fortune." He knows the business from both sides of the table. "I've got a ball from David Wells's perfect game," he said. "Isn't that something?"

On the way out of the show, I stopped in the men's room, where I encountered Goose Gossage. He peered at me warily. "We met at the Waldorf," I reminded him. "I went with you to the Letterman show?"

"Right," he said, uncertainly.

"I was in the car when you told George Brett you were sorry you didn't hit him in the neck."

Gossage brightened. "Now I remember. Yeah. Tell you what,

buddy, I should have, too." He reached out and slapped me on the back in a moment of restroom camaraderie. "How you doin', buddy?"

"How are *you* doing? This is your first show as a Hall of Famer."

"Great, fantastic!" he said. "HoF!" He had the giddy tone of a man who had just discovered that he could print his own money.

SEVEN . . . *Bad, Bad Barry Bonds*

In August 2007, Barry Bonds hit his 756th home run, eclipsing Hank Aaron's record. The fan who caught it put the ball up for sale, and it was bought by fashion designer and businessman Marc Ecko.

Ecko was known for his lines of sportswear, his video-game company, his support for graffiti artists, and his work on behalf of the rhinoceros. He wasn't exactly publicity-averse, and he saw the Bonds ball as a public relations investment. Ecko announced that he would run an online election among fans about what to do with the ball: donate it to the Hall of Fame as is, mark it with an asterisk and send it to Cooperstown, or shoot it into space. Eventually he decided to deface the ball—purportedly as a protest against Bonds's alleged steroid use. Hall of Fame president Dale Petrosky accepted the offer, declaring that the Hall was "thrilled that we now have the opportunity to preserve [the ball] forever and to share it with everybody who wants to see it."

Bonds already had a fraught relationship with Cooperstown. In the past, he had accused the Hall of selling memorabilia it collected from him. It had been Jeff Idelson's task to reassure him that this wasn't true. ("Sometimes he believes me and sometimes he doesn't," Idelson told me.)

The notion of a marked ball on display in Cooperstown ignited Bonds's fury. He threatened a boycott, although he stopped just short of burning the bridge to Cooperstown. "I will never be in the Hall of

Fame. Never," he told a reporter. "Barry Bonds will not be there. That's my emotions now. That's how I feel now. When I decide to retire five years from now, we'll see where they are at that moment... and maybe I'll reconsider."

Ecko's publicity stunt fit in well with the campaign that baseball had been waging to delegitimize Bonds. The Hall of Fame had made its views known earlier that summer via an editorial in the *Freeman's Journal.* Writers across the country denounced Bonds as a cheater, unworthy of the record. Commissioner Selig was at the game in San Diego when Bonds tied Aaron, but he conspicuously refrained from applauding. After the game he went home to Milwaukee, enabling him to skip Bonds's record-breaker on August 7. He explained his behavior with a tepid statement: "While the issues which have swirled around this record will continue to work themselves toward resolution, today is a day for congratulations on a truly remarkable achievement."

Selig's attitude, like that of Petrosky and the Hall of Fame, was not a profile in courage. Bonds was extremely unpopular around baseball (outside of San Francisco), and disrespecting him in public was an assertion of the game's integrity and purity.

Black America didn't see it that way. They had seen this kind of thing before. In 1974, when Hank Aaron broke Babe Ruth's record, a large portion of white America was scandalized. "Dear Nigger" letters poured in, and Aaron was forced to travel with bodyguards. Some pundits argued that Aaron had come to bat four thousand times more than Ruth, and his record should therefore have an asterisk affixed to it. Commissioner Bowie Kuhn skipped Aaron's record-breaking game, a snub the usually mild-mannered star noted afterward with bitterness.

Aaron writes about this incident in his autobiography, *I Had a Hammer.*

Coauthor Lonnie Wheeler, who occasionally interrupts Aaron's narrative for comments of his own, makes a surprising observation—that Aaron and Ruth had little in common aside from the fact that they were both referred to "publicly and frequently as 'nigger,' although Aaron was black and Ruth wouldn't have been allowed to play big league ball if he had been."

"It angered [Aaron] that he could not go about his private quest without being compared, criticized, cross examined, and cussed out in the context of a *broad-nosed white man* he cared little about" [italics added].

There are many ways to describe Babe Ruth, but Wheeler (and Aaron) chose one with a coded meaning. All his life, Babe Ruth was "suspected" of being a black man passing for white. He had, as Wheeler notes, "certain facial features that some regarded as Negroid."

As a boy at St. Mary's Orphanage in Baltimore, Ruth's nickname was "nigger lips." Throughout his major-league career, bench jockeys called him "Nigger" and "Nig." According to Fred Lieb, Ruth's sometime ghostwriter, Ty Cobb once refused to share accommodations with Ruth at a hunting lodge in Georgia, saying, "I never have slept under the same roof with a nigger and I'm not going to start here." In the 1922 World Series, Ruth invaded the Giants clubhouse to challenge Johnny Rawlings, who had rained down a string of racial epithets on him during a game.

The stories that Ruth might be racially mixed were widely believed in the black community. According to Ruth's biographer, Robert Creamer, "Even players in the Negro Leagues that flourished then believed this and generally wished the Babe, whom they considered a secret brother, well in his conquest of white baseball." Hank Aaron, who himself came up in the Negro leagues, must have known this. What he probably didn't know is that Ruth placed a statue of Blessed Martín de Porres next to his death bed. De Porres, a sixteenth-century Peruvian mulatto, is known as the patron of blacks and biracial people.

White America eventually made peace with Aaron's conquest of

Babe Ruth's record. In fact, Aaron became a retrospective favorite of baseball writers, especially when they could contrast his nobility to Barry Bonds's Rule 5–busting self. Stephen Cannella, a *Sports Illustrated* writer, captured the love: "When I see the footage of Aaron's 715th home run, I'm still struck by the way he rounded the bases that night in Atlanta: quickly, purposefully, without a hint of self-congratulation, so focused and self-assured that he barely broke stride even when two fans hopped out of the stands to accost him as he headed for third base. Bonds caught Aaron, too, but in our hearts, the Hammer hasn't stopped running, and 755 is still greater than 762."

Despite the best efforts of the baseball media to whip up an Aaron–Bonds feud, the two men refused to go along. Aaron, who had played against Barry's father, congratulated him for breaking the record. Bonds responded by praising Aaron's prowess and generosity of spirit.

Whatever the motives of Bonds's critics, black America saw a black hero getting beat up by white America. Comedian Chris Rock appeared on the HBO show *Costas Now* and voiced a common feeling: "Ty Cobb's numbers are bullshit, and Babe Ruth's numbers are bullshit," he said.

A visibly surprised Bob Costas said, "Because of segregation—"

"Because they didn't play against black players," said Rock. "It's like saying I won the New York City Marathon but no Kenyans ran that year. Babe Ruth has 714 affirmative action home runs."

E. R. Shipp, a Pulitzer Prize–winning columnist and an African-American, explained that she was rooting for Bonds "because so many others—especially white people—are rooting against this man who lives by his own rules of media engagement. White sports journalists are not accustomed to this and have accentuated the negative. That has poisoned the history."

Some black ballplayers spoke up, too. "Whenever I go home, I hear people say all of the time, 'Baseball just doesn't like black people,'" said former All-Star outfielder Matt Lawton. "If Bonds were white, he'd be a poster boy in baseball, not an outcast."

Not more than fifteen or twenty of the five hundred-plus BBWAA voters across the country are African-American. Black ballplayers have English in common with the writers, but the two groups don't always communicate too well. There is a long history to this difficulty.

In 1946, after Jackie Robinson had been signed by Branch Rickey, the New York Baseball Writers' Association made this the subject of a skit at their annual winter dinner. "Commissioner Chandler" carried on a dialogue with a butler in blackface, dressed in a Montreal Royals uniform. The Royals were the farm team to which Robinson had been assigned by Branch Rickey. The show included this dialogue:

> *Chandler: (Claps hands and calls) Robbie-eee! Robbiee!*
>
> *Butler: Yassah, Massa. Here I is.*
>
> *Chandler: Ah! There you are, Jackie. Jackie, you ole wooly-headed rascal, how long have you been in the family?*
>
> *Butler: Long time, K'unl. Marty long time. Edder since Marse Rickey bought me from the Kansas City Monarchs.*
>
> *Chandler: To be sure, Jackie, to be sure. How could I forget that Massa Rickey brought you to our house. (Aside) Rickey—that no good carpetbagger. What could he have been thinking of?*

Wendell Smith, a sportswriter for the African-American *Pittsburgh Courier* (who had been turned down for membership by the BBWAA on the grounds that he didn't work for a mainstream newspaper), called it a "Nazi opera." But Arthur Daley defended the show in the *New York Times,* assuring readers that "no one's feelings were really hurt." The *Sporting News* gave the show a rave review, which wasn't a surprise. The "Bible of Baseball" had long opposed race-mixing; in a 1942 editorial, its editor opined that most blacks and whites wanted to keep the game segregated and that the issue was being raised by "agitators ever ready to seize an issue that will redound to their profit and self-aggrandizement." The publisher of the *Sporting News* at the time was J. G. Taylor Spink, for whom the Hall of Fame's writer awards are named.* Wendell Smith won a Spink Award in 1993. Posthumously.

Smith's protégé, Robinson, broke in with almost no media support. "The baseball writers at that time were very conservative," Smith said in an interview many years later. "Individually, a lot of them were wonderful. But as a group they never have been known to be overly liberal. As an organization, they didn't do much to advance our cause."

A lot of writers who didn't like Jackie Robinson were, like Spink, believers that baseball should hold the color line. Others, like Dick Young, were sympathetic to Robinson in his first, mostly passive season with the Dodgers; Branch Rickey had asked him to adopt a mild manner in his first couple of seasons, and Robinson went along. But by 1949, he felt well enough established to begin acting like himself, and writers like Young didn't care for the New Jackie at all. "Robinson has reached the stage where he says what he believes and says it without reservation, which is unfortunately a trait frowned on in most social circles," Young wrote. In a private conversation, Young made this even clearer. "I'm telling you as a friend that a lot of newspapermen are saying that Campy [Roy Campanella, the Dodgers catcher and a former Negro-leagues star] is the kind of guy they can

* Baseball scholars will note that although the winners of the Spink Award (for baseball writing) and the Frick Award (for baseball broadcasting) are honored during the Hall of Fame induction ceremonies and have their names listed in an exhibit in the museum, they don't receive plaques and aren't mentioned in the gallery itself. Wendell Smith, thus, is not a Hall of Famer in the same sense that Rickey Henderson is.

like but that your aggressiveness, your wearing your race on your sleeve, makes enemies."

Mainstream sportswriters in those days were used to dealing with accommodating black athletes like Joe Louis, Jesse Owens, and Campanella. But Robinson was outspoken even for a white player in an era when jocks were supposed to be seen and not heard. In 1952, he publicly accused the Yankees—the only New York team without black players—of racism. The *Sporting News* denounced him for this with headlines like "Robinson Should Be a Player, Not a Crusader."

In 1957, on the eve of Robinson's retirement from baseball, Dick Young published an interview with Campanella in which the Dodgers catcher accused his teammate of being insufficiently grateful to baseball for the chance it had given him to play in the majors. Campanella later said that the conversation had been off the record, but it made big news at the time and soured Robinson's exit from the game—as Young must have known it would.

In 1962, Jackie Robinson became eligible for the Hall of Fame. Dick Young endorsed his candidacy but added that Robinson didn't have many friends among the BBWAA voters. Robinson, one of the two or three greatest figures in the history of the game, barely got into Cooperstown. Of the ten players elected by the BBWAA in the sixties, only Lou Boudreau, the Cleveland manager-shortstop, got fewer votes.

Robinson was the first black member of the Hall of Fame, but for many years Cooperstown treated him with studied indifference. His plaque hung with the others but made no mention of his special role in baseball history. As far as the Hall of Fame was concerned, Jackie Robinson was just another All-Star ballplayer, no more significant than Gabby Hartnett or Rabbit Maranville.

Since 1962, Robinson has been followed to Cooperstown by more than twenty black players. A few, like Bob Gibson, Dave Winfield, and Frank Robinson, have been aggressive, Jackie Robinson–style guys. Most, however, have been more in the easygoing mold of Cam-

Cap Anson: The leader of the baseball segregationists, he was inducted into the Hall of Fame in 1939. (COURTESY OF CLEAN SWEEP AUCTIONS)

Ty Cobb: One of the first inductees, seen here with his best friend. (COURTESY OF CLEAN SWEEP AUCTIONS)

Babe Ruth: The Negro leaguers called him "the secret brother."

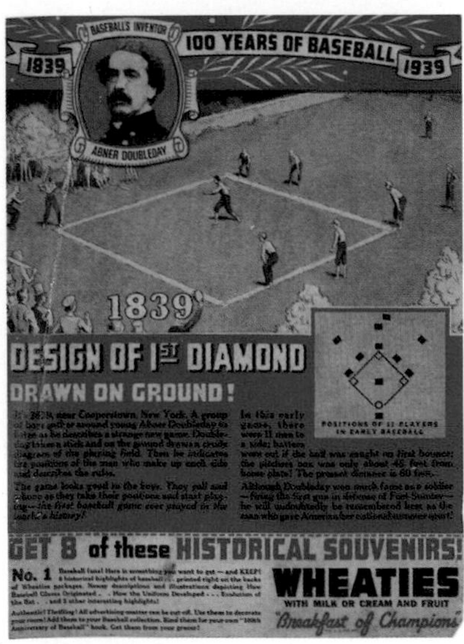

From a series of Wheaties centennial cards celebrating Abner Doubleday's invention of baseball—and baseball's invention of Abner Doubleday. (COURTESY OF CLEAN SWEEP AUCTIONS)

Dizzy Dean: He got a thrill from gambling, too. The president of the National League hired a private eye to find out how much of a thrill, but it took the Feds to finally bust him. (COURTESY OF CLEAN SWEEP AUCTIONS)

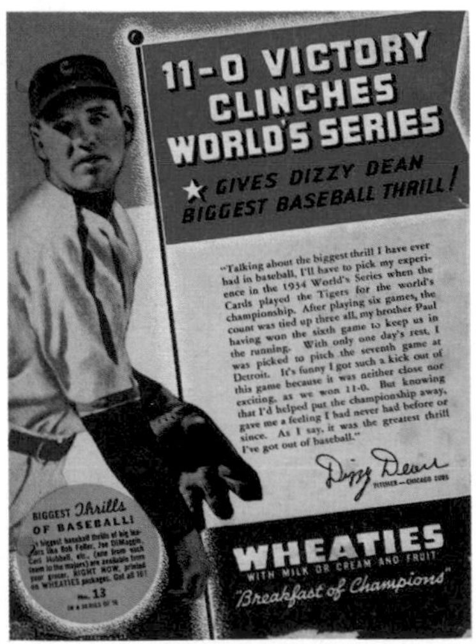

"Bob" Clemente: The first out-of-the-closet Hispanic in Cooperstown. When the Hall put up his plaque, it got his name backward. (COURTESY OF CLEAN SWEEP AUCTIONS)

Jackie Robinson: It took the Hall of Fame forty-five years to figure out why he was really there. (COURTESY OF CLEAN SWEEP AUCTIONS)

Hank Greenberg and **Joe DiMaggio:** Cooperstown heroes who also had good friends in less exalted institutions. (COURTESY OF CLEAN SWEEP AUCTIONS)

Mickey Mantle: The Mick and JFK shared a drug supplier, New York's notorious Doctor Feelgood, Max Jacobson. (COURTESY OF CLEAN SWEEP AUCTIONS)

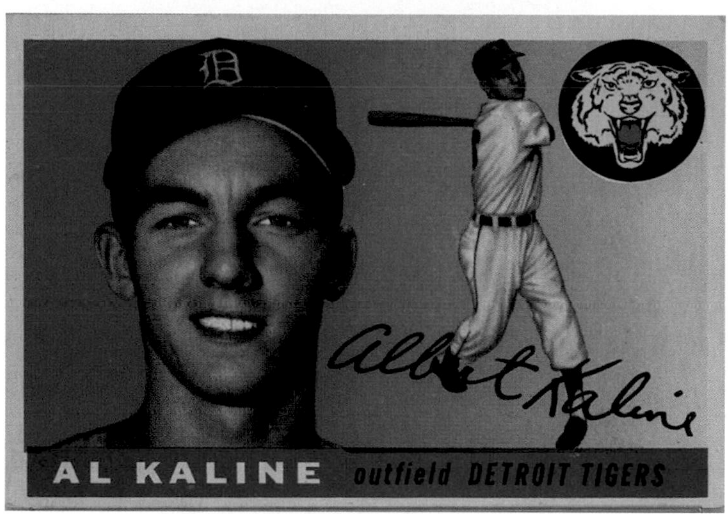

Al Kaline: My hero. We broke into baseball together. (COURTESY OF CLEAN SWEEP AUCTIONS)

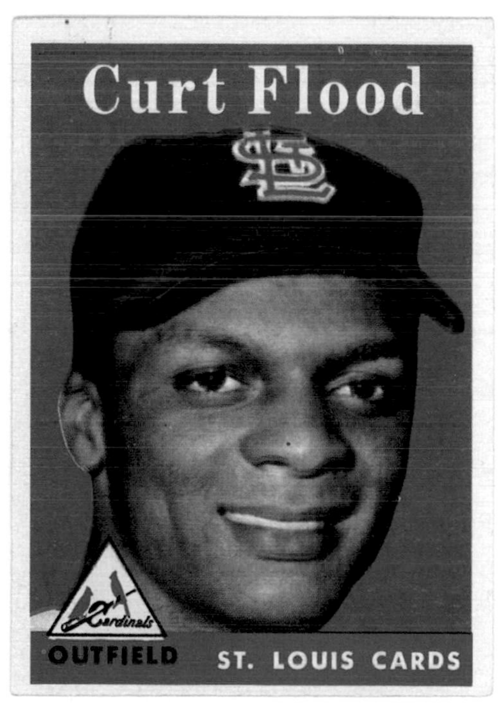

Curt Flood: He and Marvin Miller made the players rich and the owners furious. Neither is in the Hall of Fame. Lesson: Be careful who you hurt—and who you help. (COURTESY OF CLEAN SWEEP AUCTIONS)

Steve Garvey: His teammates called him "The Senator," and he looked like a lock for the Hall—until he got impeached by his wife on national television. (COURTESY OF CLEAN SWEEP AUCTIONS)

Pete Rose: A great player, but not good enough for the Hall of Fame.
(COURTESY OF CLEAN SWEEP AUCTIONS)

Goose Gossage's golden egg. The "HoF" next to his name tripled his prices overnight. (COURTESY OF STEINER SPORTS)

Cal Ripken Jr.: The biggest crowd in Hall of Fame history bused up from Baltimore to cheer a guy who played the game the right way (at least as far as we know). (COURTESY OF CLEAN SWEEP AUCTIONS)

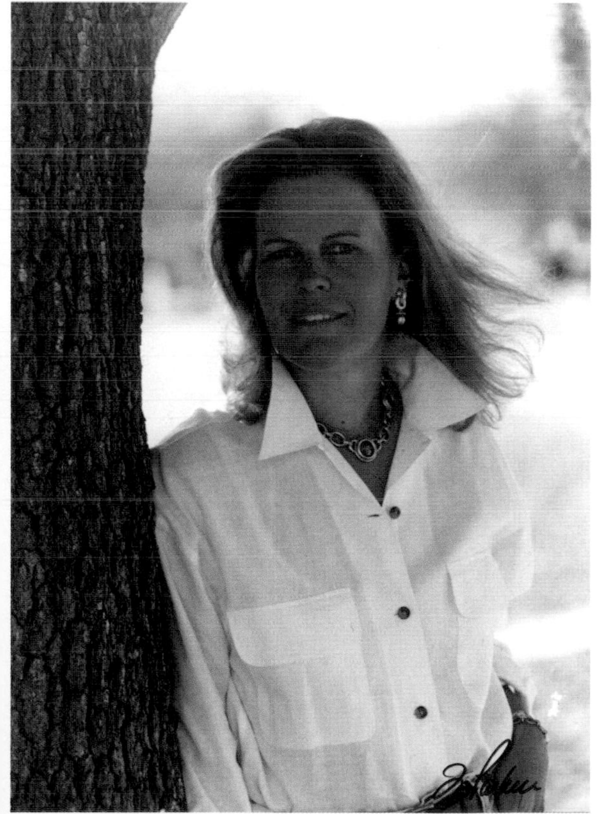

Jane Forbes Clark: The first lady of baseball. Her family has controlled the Hall of Fame for three generations. (COURTESY OF NATIONAL BASEBALL HALL OF FAME LIBRARY)

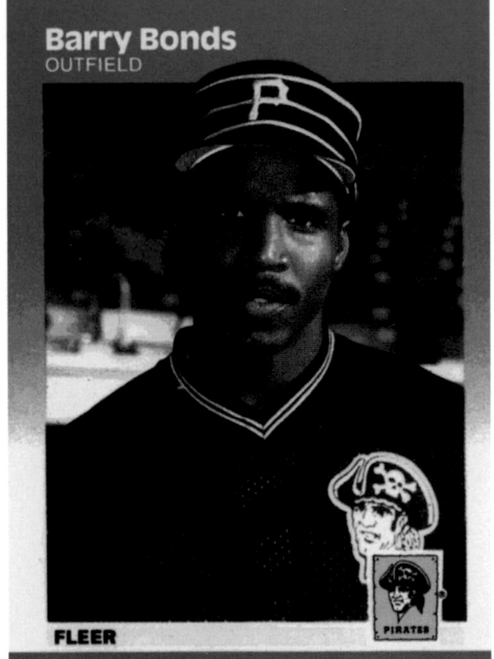

Alex Rodriguez, **Roger Clemens**, and **Barry Bonds** in more innocent times. Keeping them out of Cooperstown would be like excluding Cobb, Ruth, and Walter Johnson. (COURTESY OF CLEAN SWEEP AUCTIONS)

panella, players like Tony Gwynn, Kirby Puckett, and Willie Stargell, the sorts of black men with whom a white writer can share a joke or make a harmless little comment without whipping up a lot of static.

Dave Parker was definitely not in that mold. In his playing days he was 6'5", 230 pounds with a mouth to match—an intimidating figure to pitchers and writers alike. He broke in with the Pirates in 1973, replacing Roberto Clemente in right field (who had his own problems with baseball writers around the league, but was instantly sainted by the press when his plane, carrying relief supplies for the survivors of a Nicaraguan disaster, went down in 1972). Parker proved to be a worthy successor to Clemente: twice he led the National League in batting average, and he was MVP in 1981. Lawrence Ritter named him one of baseball's 100 all-time best players. But a lot of the Pirates beat writers found him sullen and uncooperative. Parker was a cocaine addict, which didn't improve his social graces. And he didn't use alone. The Pirates were the worst cokeheads in baseball. Even their mascot, the Pittsburgh Parrot, was using and dealing. Seven Pirates were suspended for a year by Commissioner Peter Ueberroth. Dave Parker was among them.*

By this time, Parker had left the Pirates and was playing in Cincinnati. He finished the season second in the MVP voting, with a career-high 125 runs batted in. In his nineteen-year career, Parker hit .290 with 339 home runs and appeared in seven All-Star Games.

Parker thinks this should be enough to get him to Cooperstown. "As a Christian, I try not to be bitter about not being in the Hall of Fame," he told me during a long conversation at the end of 2007. But he *is* bitter. "I was the best player in baseball between 1985 and 1990. Not just as a hitter, all around. Dave Winfield and I changed the entire concept of what an outfielder is. I love Gary

* Four other players were suspended for sixty days. In fact, none of the eleven suspended players actually missed a game. They were allowed to contribute part of their salaries to a drug program, submit to random testing, and do one hundred hours of community service.

Carter, but compare our numbers. Or Wade Boggs. If Boggs is in, I definitely should be in."

It's hard to compare Parker with Gary Carter, a catcher. As far as Boggs is concerned, he was a lifetime .328 hitter, with five batting titles and 3,010 hits. True, he didn't hit for power and barely cracked 1,000 lifetime RBIs, compared to Parker's nearly 1,500. But Parker's lifetime batting average is almost forty points lower than Boggs's. Still, there's a very good case to be made for Dave Parker. Bill James ranks him above Hall of Fame outfielder Harry Heilmann.

Parker's best shot at the Hall was in 1998, when he appeared on about 25 percent of the writers' ballots. Since then, he has gone downhill. He got 11.4 percent in 2007. Some writers, he believes, have ignored him because of his drug use. Others, he suspects, have different motives.

"When I was in Cincinnati, one guy, John Donovan, wrote bad things about me seven days a week. What kind of resentment is that? Is he white? Yeah, he's white. I hate to bring up racism, but just look around. Why isn't Lee Smith in the Hall of Fame? He was a great relief pitcher, but he's not in the Hall. Neither is Andre Dawson. You figure it out."

Today, Dave Parker is a successful businessman and community elder, the owner of several Popeye's restaurants around Cincinnati. He also understands what he didn't get as a younger man—that there is a Hall of Fame price to pay for stiffing baseball writers. "Some of them were jealous of my money and status," he says. "Some were just racist. But either way, it was hard for me to open up to them."

It would be nice to believe that Dave Parker's Cooperstown chances weren't ruined by the perception in the baseball establishment that he was a "Bad Negro." It would be nice to believe that about Dick Allen, too.

Allen broke into baseball via the Arkansas Travelers, the Phillies AAA team in Little Rock, in 1960, only three years after Governor

Orval Faubus had refused a federal order to integrate Central High School, prompting President Eisenhower to (reluctantly) send 101st Airborne troops to enforce the law. On opening day, Faubus threw out the first pitch and fans screamed racial insults from the stands. Allen stood in the field reciting the Twenty-third Psalm to himself. "I was scared, I don't mind saying it," he admitted later. After the game, he found a note on his windshield that summed up local sentiment: "Don't come back again, nigger."

In 1963, Allen went up to the Phillies. It wasn't that much of an improvement over Little Rock. The Phillies had been a notoriously racist franchise from the earliest days of integration. From the start, he rubbed a lot of people the wrong way. In 1965, he got into a fight with a white teammate, Frank Thomas, who hit Allen with a bat. Several teammates said that Thomas was the aggressor, but Philly wasn't a town where a black man hit a white man for any reason. The fans took to throwing garbage and batteries at Allen, and he responded by wearing his batting helmet in the field and saying unpleasant things about the city and its fans. "I can play anywhere," he once said, "first base, third base, left field, anywhere but Philadelphia."

Allen also clashed with the front office. On one occasion, Phillies owner Bob Carpenter, who inherited the team from his father, told Allen to "grow up."

"I am grown up," Allen snapped. "I grew up black and poor, you grew up white and rich. But we're both grown."

The Philadelphia writers sided with management. They branded Allen a head case, and the image stuck. Bill James, no racist, has come out against Allen's Hall of Fame candidacy on the grounds that he was "at war with the world" and that he did "more to keep his teams from winning than anybody else who ever played baseball."

A lot of Allen's teammates felt differently. In 1975, after retiring from the Chicago White Sox, a delegation of Phillies players led by Mike Schmidt talked him into coming back to Philadelphia, where he more or less finished his career. In subsequent interviews, all his living managers said good things about him. Does Dick Allen belong in the Hall of Fame? He hit .292 in a low-hitting era, with 351 career homers over fifteen seasons. He won an MVP. Twice he led the American League in home runs. He made seven All-Star teams. It's true that he wasn't much of a fielder, but that describes a lot of power hitters in Cooperstown. He could be nasty at times, but that describes a lot of Hall of Famers, too. It is possible that, on merit, Allen didn't deserve election to Cooperstown. But it is more than possible that his image as a Bad Negro accounts for the fact that in his first year of eligibility he got exactly fourteen votes, or 3.7 percent, from the members of the BBWAA.

Unlike Dick Allen, Albert Belle grew up black and middle-class. He was a Boy Scout, a member of the National Honor Society, and vice president of the Future Business Leaders of America. But the older he got, the less friendly he became, especially to the press, and eventually he refused to give any interviews at all. He let his game do the talking. Belle played twelve seasons, two more than required for membership in the Hall. He hit .295 with 381 homers. In his ten peak seasons, he averaged 37.3 home runs a season. My hero Al Kaline, a first-time selection, averaged a little more than half of that. Belle led the American League three times in runs batted in, once in homers, with 50, and in 1995 he was voted Major League Player of the Year. In the decade of the nineties, nobody had more runs batted in or extra-base hits.

Albert Belle was a Hall of Fame player by almost any standard. But not only did he have black skin, he had *thin* black skin. He once threw a baseball at a heckler. On another occasion, he chased trick-or-treaters who were egging his house and bumped them with his car. The Indians fined him thousands of dollars every year for damage to the clubhouse and team property. After a bad at-bat in Boston, he took a Louisville slugger to a teammate's boom box. He demanded that the locker room thermostat be kept at 60 degrees, which earned him the nickname "Mr. Freeze." When Belle retired in 2001, *New York Daily News* columnist Bill Madden was gleeful. "Sorry, there'll be no words of sympathy here for Albert Belle," Madden wrote.

"He was a surly jerk before he got hurt and now he's a hurt surly jerk . . . He was no credit to the game. Belle's boorish behavior should be remembered by every member of the Baseball Writers' Association when it comes time to consider him for the Hall of Fame."

Bob Lipsyte responded for the defense. "Madden is basically saying, 'He was not nice to me, so let's screw him.' Sportswriters anoint heroes in basically the same way you have crushes in junior high school . . . you've got someone like Albert Belle, who is somehow basically ungrateful for this enormous opportunity to play this game. If he's going to appear to us as a surly asshole, then we'll cover him that way. And then, of course, he's not gonna talk to us anymore—it's self-fulfilling."

Lipsyte's was a minority view; in 2006, Belle's first year of eligibility, only forty writers voted for him. The other 92.3 percent of the Cooperstown electors ignored him. In 2007, his total shrunk to nineteen votes, Dick Allen territory.

Jim Rice played his whole career, sixteen seasons, in Boston, where he hit .298 lifetime, with 382 home runs. He was an eight-time All-Star, led the league three times in home runs and twice in runs batted in. He was also among the league leaders in bad public relations. Fourteen years in a row he was up for Cooperstown, and fourteen years in a row he failed to make it.

In 2006, after Rice's thirteenth miss, *Boston Globe* columnist Dan Shaughnessy diagnosed the problem as Bad Negro Syndrome. "Is Rice coming up short because of his terrible relationship with baseball writers during the time he played? Is this petty payback for years of churlishness? Would Rice be in the Hall of Fame if he'd been as media-friendly as, say, Kevin Millar?"

Rice missed again in 2008. But, as Goose Gossage had predicted, Rice made it in 2009, in his last year of eligibility—barely. He got 76.4 percent of the vote. Rice was asked why it had taken so many years for him to be elected, and he replied with his customary candor: "If you look at my numbers [against] some of the numbers of guys who are in the Hall of Fame—my numbers are compatible. I don't know why. The only thing I'll say is I'm glad it's over with. I'm not going to badmouth any writers or what have you. I'm just looking forward to the days to come." Just to make sure the point was clear, he added that his numbers hadn't changed over the last fourteen years.

Gary Sheffield could very well be the new Jim Rice. When he broke into baseball in 1988, he was, at nineteen, the youngest player in the majors. In those days both leagues were still loaded with African-American talent. His career parallels the sharp decrease of black players. Sheffield doesn't buy baseball's feel-better theories about the lack of young black talent. Sure, there aren't many baseball diamonds in inner cities. And it's true that baseball equipment makes it an expensive game to play. But football also requires good facilities and lots of money, and somehow black players are flourishing at every level. Sheffield attributes the decline of African-American players to a combination of racial prejudice and the easy availability of cheap, pliable players from Latin America. In the middle of the 2007 season, he unburdened himself on the subject to a reporter from *GQ* magazine. "I called it years ago," he said.

> *What I called is that you're going to see more black faces, but there ain't no English going to be coming out . . . [It's about] being able to tell [Latin players] what to do—being able to control them.*
>
> *Where I'm from, you can't control us. You might get a guy to do it that way for a while because he wants to benefit, but in the end, he is going to go back to being who he is. And that's a person that you're going to talk to with respect, you're going to talk to like a man.*

These are the things my race demands. So, if you're equally good as this Latin player, guess who's going to get sent home? I know a lot of players that are home now can outplay a lot of these guys.

Predictably, this racial analysis antagonized the media who, in any event, didn't care much for Sheffield's blunt style. The prevailing opinion was expressed by a *New York Post* headline that called him "surly"—the kiss of death for black power hitters hoping for Hall of Fame entry.

I don't know if Sheffield belongs in the Hall of Fame. Over twenty-one seasons, he has been a .292 hitter, with an OBP of .394. At the start of the 2009 season, he was one home run short of 500. He has made nine All-Star teams, was MLB Player of the Year in 1992, and won a batting championship. But Sheffield is very much in the line of Dick Allen, Dave Parker, Albert Belle, and Jim Rice, a fact underscored by his outspoken remarks about Latino players and the beloved Joe Torre. A discerning reporter named Jesse Sanchez put the question to Sheffield directly: How was this going to affect his future immortality? "First ballot, second ballot, whatever," Sheffield replied breezily. If he really believes he isn't going to spend a long time in BBWAA purgatory for his "attitude" and off-the-field opinions, he belongs not only in Cooperstown but in the Optimists' Hall of Fame.

All this history helped explain why a CBS News/*New York Times* poll, published in July 2007, showed such a stark discrepancy between the way blacks and whites understood the Bonds controversy. The survey found that 54 percent of blacks—but only 29 percent of whites—were rooting for Bonds to break the home run record. Sixty-two percent of black baseball fans said that race was a major or minor factor in steroid charges against Bonds; just 14 percent of whites agreed. Asked if they had a favorable view of Bonds, black fans responded positively by an almost three-to-one margin; white fans were negative by nearly two to one. Twice as many whites as blacks said that it would be bad for baseball if Bonds broke the home run record.

After the 2007 season, Bonds was indicted on charges of perjury and obstruction of justice for lying to a grand jury about using steroids. An indictment is not a conviction. If a senior government official is indicted for such crimes, it might be seemly for him to step away from the job, at least temporarily. But Bonds was a forty-two-year-old baseball player. Time was running out on his career, and he wanted to play again in 2008. He filed for free agency after the World Series, and he had every reason to expect that he would be snapped up. He had a name that sells tickets in droves and draws more media attention than almost anyone in baseball. On the road, fans might come to boo, but in his home park he would be a hero, as he has been, and remains, in San Francisco.

Even more important, Bonds in 2007 was still one of the best players in baseball. He hit 28 home runs in just 340 at-bats, had a .565 slugging percentage, and led the National League in walks and in on-base percentage (OBP), with a colossal .480. Since 1950, only four players have bested that OBP—Bonds himself from 2001 through 2004, Ted Williams three times, Mickey Mantle twice, and the Tigers' Norm Cash in his unforgettable (and, sadly, unrepeated) 1961 season. It's true that Bonds was no longer one of the greatest defensive outfielders in the game, as he had been in his prime, but in most ballparks he would have been adequate, and he was perfect for the American League, where designated hitters don't need to field at all.

What lucky team signed baseball's best slugger in 2008? The answer is: none. Bonds didn't get a single serious offer.

The baseball press handled this with astonishing equanimity. Bonds's exile from the game—which is also his profession—was treated as a natural and positive development. He hadn't been convicted of anything. He hadn't confessed to anything. The evidence that he used steroids was anecdotal—he had grown bigger and stronger over time—but there were plenty of players in the game who had admitted to using steroids. But Bonds was guilty no matter what. It was back to the days of Judge Landis, when not even a jury acquittal mattered.

In the mid-eighties, MLB had lost a series of collusion suits against owners who had refused to compete to hire expensive players. Salaries had been rising drastically since the end of the reserve clause, and Commissioner of Baseball Peter Ueberroth and the owners decided to put a stop to it. Top players no longer got offers from other teams, and sure enough, salaries declined.

The only problem was that this was illegal. Baseball's collective bargaining agreement says: "Players shall not act in concert with other Players and Clubs shall not act in concert with other Clubs." When stars like Tim Raines, Kirk Gibson, Carlton Fisk, and Hall of Famer Phil Niekro couldn't get offers from other teams, it didn't take Sherlock Holmes to detect collusion on the part of franchises. MLB lost three straight cases and in 1990 agreed to pay $280 million in back wages to the players. This money was not awarded for damages; it is simply the amount the owners had swindled.

Marvin Miller, who founded the players' union and was the chief witness in the first collusion cases, looked at the Bonds situation and saw an open-and-shut case. "It's obvious," he told me in the spring of 2008. "If Bonds decides to pursue this, it will cost the owners a lot of money."

At the end of the 2008 season, with Bonds still unemployed, the Players Association came to a similar conclusion and announced that it had sufficient evidence for a grievance. The union agreed with Commissioner Selig's office to hold off on an actual filing, presumably to give the sides time to negotiate. A senior union official conceded that the owners had learned from the debacle of the mid-eighties not to put collusion agreements in writing or discuss them in meetings where notes are kept. But, like Miller, he thought that the failure of a single team to approach one of the best players in the game spoke for itself. He predicted a collusion finding that would cost baseball $62 million, roughly three times Bonds's last annual salary.

The cost to baseball in good will in the black community is likely to be much higher.

A great deal has been written about the estrangement of blacks from the game of baseball. The great gush of postwar black ballplayers has dried up. So has black rooter interest. In the early days of integration, black ballplayers with a flamboyant Negro-leagues style, like Jackie Robinson, Satchel Paige, and Willie Mays, threatened to change the game with their base-stealing and basket catches and jive talk. Baseball didn't want to be changed. Vic Power, a good-fielding first baseman with the Kansas City Athletics, was disparaged for catching balls one-handed (it didn't help Power's popularity with the establishment that he also openly dated white women). Hank Aaron was praised for his quiet, workmanlike excellence. "In baseball, if you are a showboat, they bust you up," said Dave Parker.

The National Basketball Association, which integrated after baseball, was far more open to black styles of showmanship and athleticism. So, after Jim Brown's reign as rushing king, was the National Football League. Both leagues cultivated and promoted great black talent and allowed the players a wide measure of self-expression. Baseball didn't. Its statistical obsessions, antique uniforms, and ancestor worship all look back to an idealized version of America that did not include blacks and that many blacks simply don't share.

Baseball's distance from black America is evident even in the names of its players. Football and basketball rosters are packed with LeBrons and Carmelos and Tayshawns. At the start of the 2007 season there were sixty-nine African-Americans in MLB. Only two, Dontrelle Willis and LaTroy Hawkins, had what could be NBA-worthy names.

Fewer and fewer black kids even give baseball a thought. Little League teams are rare in America's inner cities, and a lot of high schools have dropped the sport. On the college level, more than 40 percent of football players and about 60 percent of basketball players are black; for baseball, the figure hovers around 6 percent. Twenty-five years ago, almost a third of major-leaguers were African-American. Today it is less than 10 percent—3 percent for pitchers.

In most major-league ballparks, on most days, the number of black fans can be counted in three digits. The game is full of subtle and not-so-subtle cultural disincentives. Tattoos are frowned upon. Dreadlocks are, too. A home run hitter who bursts into a spontaneous end-zone-type dance is instantly denounced as a hot dog. Ballpark music tends toward "Take-me-out-to-the-ballgame" riffs and Queen-sized stadium rockers.

Jackie Robinson's last appearance on the diamond came at the second game of the 1972 World Series, where he was honored on the twenty-fifth anniversary of his first season. Robinson, who suffered from diabetes, was extremely sick. He was also angry. Like his fellow revolutionary Babe Ruth, Robinson found himself excluded from baseball after his playing career ended, denied a chance to manage a team. There were no black managers in 1972. And so Robinson took what baseball imagined would be a nostalgic celebration of its racial liberalism and turned it on its ear. He was pleased to be recognized, he told the crowd, "[but] I'm going to be tremendously more pleased and more proud when I look at that third base coaching line one day and see a black face managing in baseball."

Robinson died ten days later, at the age of fifty-three. It took three years before the Cleveland Indians hired Frank Robinson to manage. He did okay; over sixteen seasons, with four teams, he compiled a .475 winning percentage and never came in first. It is fair to say that he didn't establish a trend. At the start of the 2009 season, there were still only four black managers in the big leagues, up from just two in 2006.

On April 15, 1997, fifty years after integration, Major League Baseball held a "Jackie Robinson Day." His number, 42, was retired from the game forever. Seven years later, Commissioner Selig milked Robinson again, proclaiming that henceforth, April 15 would be Jackie Robinson Day. Selig and other major-league officials and players voiced the hope that this would help repair relations with blacks who had given up on the game.

Hostile relations between baseball and black America are a problem for the game—as Chris Rock said, it makes the game look like an exercise in reverse affirmative action. It also seems anachronistic. George W. Bush was a baseball man; but Barack Obama is not only the first African-American president but, not coincidentally, the first basketball player in the White House.

Playing racial catch-up has always been a problem for Cooperstown. In 1962, Bob Feller published an article in the *Saturday Evening Post* advocating a "niche in the Hall of Fame for Satchel Paige." Feller had barnstormed against Paige and, in the twilight of their careers, they were teammates on the Cleveland Indians.

Four years later, in his celebrated Hall of Fame speech, Ted Williams—nobody's idea of a flaming radical—made his own plea for including Negro leaguers in Cooperstown.

Commissioner Ford Frick, backed by a representative of the Clark family, Paul Kerr, adamantly opposed putting Negro-leagues players into the Hall of Fame. Frick argued that (1) this would water down the standards of the shrine; (2) it would violate the rule that candidates had to have played at least ten years in the majors; and (3) no reliable statistics were available to judge the Negro leaguers. Objections 2 and 3 were transparently circular. Negro-leagues players had been prevented from playing in the majors—how were they supposed to log ten years? Similarly, they couldn't have accumulated major-league-quality statistics. The first point—that the Negro-leagues players weren't good enough—was refuted by Feller, Dizzy Dean, Joe DiMaggio, and the other Hall of Famers who had barnstormed against them. If further proof were necessary, there was Paige's "rookie" season with the Cleveland Indians, 1948, when, well past the age of forty, he won 6 and lost 1, posting a 2.48 ERA. And, of course, Negro leaguers like Willie Mays, Hank Aaron, Ernie Banks, Roy Campanella, Don Newcombe, Jackie Robinson, and Larry Doby competed pretty well in the majors.

Three years after Williams's Hall of Fame speech, Cooperstown still had not moved. In 1969, the writers finally spoke up. The unpredictable Dick Young, by now the president of the Baseball Writers' Association of America, forcefully put the case at the annual Hall of Fame induction ceremony:

> *Until now, there has been one failing, and the baseball writers intend that this should be rectified. Nobody questions, certainly, the credentials of these great ballplayers on my right. They all belong. But we do ask the question, "Why should Waite Hoyt and Stanley Coveleski be in the Hall of Fame and not Satchel Paige? Why should Roy Campanella be in the Hall of Fame and not Josh Gibson?"*
>
> *There are other men, great ballplayers, who certainly have a place here in this shrine. They were not part of organized ball. When the rules were set up, one of the rules was that you should excel for a period of ten years, because time proves a man's worth. And it might be said that Satchel Paige did not play Major League ball for ten years and that Josh Gibson did not play Major League ball for ten years. But was that their fault, gentlemen? The answer, of course, is obvious.*

Bowie Kuhn, then commissioner of baseball, agreed with Young. But the Hall's board of directors was adamant in its refusal. A compromise was crafted: Cooperstown would establish a special display of Negro-leagues players, to be chosen at a rate of one per year by a committee of experts.

The announcement of this arrangement, at the start of 1971, caused a storm of outrage. "I was just as good as the white boys," said the far-from-militant Satchel Paige. "I ain't going in the back door to the Hall of Fame."

Ebony magazine, the organ of the black middle class, published a full-page editorial on the subject in April 1971. It was titled "And Now, the Biggest Shortchange of Them All":

> *Leroy (Satchel) Paige was named to the Baseball Hall of Fame in Cooperstown, N. Y. Well, he really wasn't named to the Hall of Fame, seems he just didn't qualify for that honor. He didn't play ten years in the majors. Instead of being named to the Hall of Fame, he was given a niche in the National Baseball [Hall of Fame and] Museum, a separate wing where they are inaugurating a special exhibit from the famed black baseball leagues. Each year a black player from the past will be voted into the museum and finally everyone who visits the museum will get to see and read about Paige, Gibson, Foster and the others—in the separate exhibit, of course. The Baseball Writers' Association won this hollow victory from The National Baseball Museum and Hall of Fame, Inc., the private trust endowed by a scion of the Singer Sewing Machine fortune and operated by his estate.*
>
> *When it comes to baseball, the so-called all-American game, Satchel Paige and other black stars who were kept out of organized ball for so many years do not belong in any anteroom. They belong in the Hall of Fame proper and the Baseball Writers' Association should have continued its fight a little longer. If state and national constitutions can be rewritten and amended to correct injustices, surely something can be done to the rules governing something so mundane as a sports Hall of Fame.*
>
> *The Hall of Fame needs to take another look at how it has shortchanged Satchel Paige. Black people will not in this day and age settle for just half a loaf.*

It took Cooperstown only a few months to understand the stupidity of its decision. On June 10, the Hall announced that a ten-member committee would pick worthy Negro leaguers, starting with Paige, for full membership. Before the committee was disbanded in 1977, it chose Josh Gibson, Buck Leonard, Monte Irvin, Cool Papa Bell, Judy Johnson, Oscar Charleston, Martin Dihigo, and Pop Lloyd.

Robert W. Peterson, whose 1970 book *Only the Ball Was White* had a powerful influence on the baseball establishment, argued that the number of Negro-leagues inductees should be proportional to the number of Negroes in the country.

"There are now in the Hall of Fame sixty-eight players whose careers in the major leagues covered the period from 1900 to 1947," he wrote. "During the 1900–47 era, the Negro percentage of America's population remained fairly consistent at ten percent. Arbitrarily, then, it could be assumed that ten percent of the Hall of Fame members for that era should be Negroes."

The idea of establishing a quota wasn't seriously studied, but it did serve as a rough guideline when the Hall, in 1977, turned the job of choosing Negro leaguers over to the Veterans Committee, which chose nine more players: Leon Day, Willie Foster, Willie Wells, Bullet Joe Rogan, Smokin' Joe Williams, Turkey Stearnes, Rube Foster, Ray Dandridge, and Hilton Smith.*

Ted Spencer came to the Hall of Fame as curator in 1982, just as the museum was making a leap from the glass-case era to a more modern sensibility. "We don't elect the members, we tell the story of baseball." A big part of that job has been to find ways of making black baseball fit into the story of America without alienating fans who didn't think the game's history needed tweaking.

"Race has always been the hottest potato," he says. "After 1990, we decided we needed to apply a cultural approach to the black

* This form of reparation infuriated Bill James and other purists. "The simultaneous election of a large number of Negro League players and executives—many of whom had frankly no credentials whatsoever worthy of inclusion—was one of the sorriest episodes in the Hall of Fame's history," James wrote of the 2006 mass induction of pre-integration players.

history exhibit we wanted to create. We didn't want it to be just a bunch of small-town white people telling a black story. We brought together a group of experts from around the country for advice. This was a breakthrough for us. We weren't talking about hits, runs, and errors: we were providing an American narrative that showed the evolution of black baseball along the timeline of the general black experience."

The decision to put up this exhibit was made by the board of directors, and it was regarded, Spencer recalls, as highly controversial. There were compromises. Focusing on the integration of baseball, for example, was relatively easy; but discussing the way individual franchises dealt with the issue was more complicated, especially since most of those franchises didn't have much to brag about.

Spencer is from Boston; his home team, the Red Sox, was the last franchise in baseball to integrate. The Sox got their first black player, Pumpsie Green, in 1959. The Sox hadn't won a World Series for forty-one years before Green arrived, and it took them another forty-five. Many people called it the Curse of the Bambino; Boston's punishment for letting Babe Ruth go. But the post–World War II part of the long dry spell is more correctly called the Curse of Isadore Muchnick.

In 1945, Muchnick, a Boston city councilman, began raising hell over the failure of the big leagues to integrate. He threatened to challenge the permit of the Red Sox and Boston Braves to play baseball in Boston on Sundays (there were still Sabbath blue laws making Sunday games illegal, a legacy of Puritan New England). Under political pressure, the Sox and the Braves offered tryouts to three Negro leaguers: outfielder Sam Jethroe, second baseman Marvin Williams, and Robinson. The players were brought to Boston by journalist Wendell Smith, who had been championing the case of baseball integration for many years.

Dave Egan of the *Boston Daily Record*, a talented columnist (and, incidentally, Ted Williams's most biting local media critic), wrote in favor of giving the tryouts a fair chance. General manager Eddie Collins, himself a Hall of Famer, proclaimed that that was his intention: "It is beyond my understanding how anyone can insinuate or believe that all ballplayers, regardless of race, color, or creed, have not been treated in the American way as far as having an equal opportunity to play for the Red Sox."

But in 1945, racial exclusion *was* the American way, especially the American League way. Larry MacPhail, the Yankees GM, publicly supported integration and privately worked to prevent it. "We can't afford to ignore the problem," he wrote to commissioner Happy Chandler shortly after Chandler replaced Judge Landis. "If we do, we will have colored players in the minor leagues in 1945 and in the major leagues shortly thereafter." MacPhail, like Eddie Collins, is a Hall of Famer. Supporting segregation wasn't a disqualifier in 1939 when Collins got in, and it still wasn't a problem in 1978, when MacPhail was selected by the Veterans Committee.

As for Robinson's tryout in Boston, it was a failure. The Red Sox brought Robinson, Jethroe, and Williams to the park and had them shag flies and hit some batting-practice pitching. Manager Joe Cronin wasn't there. Neither were any of the Red Sox players. When the session was over, one of the coaches who had been in charge told Jethroe, "You boys look like pretty good players. I hope you enjoyed the workout." That was the last word that was heard from the Red Sox. The team finished seventh in the American League that year with infielders like Catfish Metkovich, Ben Steiner, and Ty LaForest. Who needed Jackie Robinson?

I asked Spencer if he had considered detailing the way the Red Sox and other teams, like the Tigers and Yankees, dragged their feet on integration. "I just never went there," Spencer told me. "To be honest, I don't know why not."

The museum's exhibit on integration also skips over the resistance of many white players to their new black teammates, as well as the conspicuous absence of black managers. "We recognized that issue was out there, but we didn't get into it. Those are judgment calls."

Eventually, Major League Baseball gave the Hall $250,000 to find even more Negro leaguers suitable for enshrining. A screening committee of five members was established and produced a list of thirty-nine candidates. The Hall appointed a team of twelve baseball historians ("academic cranks," in Bill James's phrase) to make the final picks. Nine votes were needed for selection. Seventeen players and executives from the Negro-leagues and pre-Negro-leagues period were selected and, in 2006, inducted.

Major League Baseball meant well. The Hall meant well, too. But the gesture went largely unappreciated. These new guys were all dead and long forgotten. Their inclusion at Cooperstown had about as much impact on the black community—especially alienated young black sports fans—as inducting the 1935 Tuskegee marching band.

Even worse, some of the choices actually engendered fresh bitterness. Somehow, the committee managed to ignore the one candidate who was still alive and kicking. Buck O'Neil was a former teammate of Satchel Paige, Josh Gibson, and other legends; a gifted storyteller who described the Negro-leagues experience with humor, affection, and a minimum of rancor, he had been featured in Ken Burns's PBS documentary *Baseball.* America knew and loved him.

The committee rejected O'Neil on the grounds that he wasn't a good enough player. This seemed arbitrary—after all, some of the other choices had no statistics all; some had even played on pre-Negro-leagues teams. O'Neil had a fifteen-year career as a slick-fielding, good-hitting first baseman. He had gone on to become the first black major-league coach (with the Chicago Cubs). As a scout, he helped sign Ernie Banks, Lou Brock, Billy Williams, and Elston Howard. He might not have been a Hall of Fame–caliber player, but he was certainly as good as many of the white mediocrities stuffed into Cooperstown by Frankie Frisch.

In any case, the 2006 Negro-leagues selections were not intended as a scientific assessment of talent: they were supposed to be a public relations gesture. Major League Baseball put out a press release slamming the Hall of Fame for its "glaring omission" and noting that "even democratic elections do not always produce perfection." Of course, there had been no democratic election, just a dozen guys with paper ballots and tin ears.

Jane Forbes Clark blithely hailed this public relations disaster as a triumph for the Hall. "The Board of Directors is extremely pleased with how this project has evolved over the last five years—culminating in today's vote," she said. "This committee has held discussions in great detail, utilizing the research and statistics now available to determine who deserves baseball's highest honor—a plaque in the Hall of Fame Gallery in Cooperstown."* In 2007, the Hall of Fame announced that it was erecting a statue of Buck O'Neil and naming an award in his honor. O'Neil said nothing, since he had died in the interim.

Joe Morgan is one of two blacks on the Hall of Fame's board of directors (the other is Frank Robinson), and he is often Cooperstown's designated spokesman on matters of race. At a press conference announcing the O'Neil statue and award, he said, "I don't think this is necessarily trying to right a wrong. I think we're just trying to honor a person—there are a lot of people who are not elected to the Hall of Fame that the public, myself included, think should be in the Hall of Fame." The statement was a perfect example of Cooperstown's racial bumbling.

But the Hall is still trying. In June 2008, the board of directors declared a special day to honor Jackie Robinson. A new plaque was mounted, lauding Robinson as a civil rights pioneer as well as a

* This quote appears in the "Baseball Hall of Fame Balloting, 2006" entry in Wikipedia. The reference is to a press release on the Hall of Fame's Web site, baseball.org. That Web site now has a notice that reads: "The page you requested no longer exists." If only public relations were that easy.

.311 hitter. Robinson's widow, Rachel, came to Cooperstown to say thank-you with her customary grace. But nothing she said could change the fact that her husband had died angry, frustrated, and alienated from baseball—and that millions of black baseball fans feel the same way.

EIGHT . . . *The Marvin Miller Affair*

The first time I met Marvin Miller, I was half an hour late. I actually arrived at his apartment house on the Upper East Side of Manhattan almost an hour early, just to make sure I could find it, and then went around the corner to a coffee shop to read the paper. I was back at exactly 10:30 A.M., right on the dot. Miller was past ninety, and you don't waste the time of a man that age.

I rang, and Miller opened the door. "You're late," he said. "You said you'd be here at ten."

"Ten-thirty," I said. "I'm positive."

"It was ten," Miller said, "but come in and sit down anyway." His voice startled me. It was the voice of a much younger man, relaxed and utterly charming. Miller would hate the comparison, but it reminded me of Ronald Reagan on the radio.

I sat down on the couch, Miller facing me. He had a keen look in his brown eyes, but he *had* mixed up the hour of our appointment and I wondered—as you always wonder about very old people—if he was completely focused.

Miller was wearing a sweater and a pair of khakis. As the executive director of the baseball players' union, he generated vast fortunes for the men he organized and led. A few years ago, Alex Rodriguez introduced Miller to his wife at a party and told her, "Say thank you to this man. He's the one who bought us our big, fine house."

There was no hint of big money here. The living room was comfortable and unassuming, books stacked neatly on the glass coffee table, some interesting pieces of artwork on the walls, a few family photos. It was the sort of living room a retired college professor would have, or an honest judge. Later I learned that Miller's wife, Terry, whom he met in Brooklyn in 1936, *had* been a professor of psychology. She walked through the living room, nodded hello, and then sat a table in the kitchenette, absorbed in the *New York Times*. They had been married almost seventy years, and she probably wasn't expecting to hear her husband tell an inquisitive stranger anything she didn't already know.

Miller wasn't exactly surprised by my questions, either. A lot of reporters had been calling lately, wondering if he thought he was going to make it into the Hall of Fame, after losing out in 2007 when the Veterans Committee, including many players who had become multimillionaires due to his efforts, turned him down. For 2007 the Hall had once again changed its rules, appointing a twelve-member body to consider the candidacies of former executives like Miller. A lot of people, including me, thought that Miller was a lock. He had never worked for a major-league team, but he was nonetheless, in the words of the venerated broadcaster Red Barber, "along with Babe Ruth and Jackie Robinson, one of the two or three most influential men in baseball history."

Marvin Miller walked his first picket line at the age of ten, side by side with his father, in front of the clothing store where Alexander Miller worked as a salesman, on the Lower East Side of New York. This was a rare moment of father-son solidarity. Alexander Miller was an Orthodox Jew who insisted his son study Hebrew four days a week and prepare to become a bar mitzvah boy. He did, under protest, but the rift this argument caused never healed completely.

Miller grew up during the Depression, rooting for the labor unions and the Brooklyn Dodgers. His favorite player was an already-over-the-hill Dazzy Vance. Miller went to college at Miami of Ohio for a while, graduated from NYU, and during World War II worked as a staff economist on the War Production Board. In 1950, he was hired as a research economist by the United Steel Workers, where he collaborated with future Supreme Court justice Arthur Goldberg developing negotiating strategies. When Goldberg left for Washington to work as secretary of labor under JFK, Miller took over as chief economist and assistant to Steel Workers' president David McDonald. That turned out to be a bad career move. McDonald lost his post to I. W. Abel in a contentious 1965 election; Miller was McDonald's man. He briefly considered running for a union office himself, but his wife vetoed it. Labor politics were rough in those days; candidates had a habit of getting shot. So Miller decided to look elsewhere for a job.

In December 1965, Miller ran into Dr. George W. Taylor, the dean of the Wharton School of Business at the University of Pennsylvania. He and Miller were old friends and fellow baseball fans. Robin Roberts, the Phillies ace pitcher, had recently asked Taylor to suggest a good candidate to run the players' association. Taylor asked Miller if he wanted the job.

Miller met with Robin Roberts and his fellow search committee members, Jim Bunning and Harvey Kuenn. Bunning and Roberts are now in the Hall of Fame, and Kuenn ought to be; he was the best-hitting shortstop in the American League in the fifties, and a Detroit Tiger at that. The players were looking for someone who could help them set up an association that would bargain with the owners over pension rights. They wondered if Miller would be interested in the job of executive director.

It sounded great—Miller had never lost his boyhood love of the game—until Roberts told him that his general counsel would be Richard Nixon. There was a logic to the suggestion. There had never before been an effective independent players' association, and a lot of the guys, especially from small towns and rural areas, were dubious about joining a union. Baseball players weren't very political, but if they thought about it, they were mostly conservatives (even Jackie Robinson was a Republican). Miller was a Democrat, a labor leader, and a New York Jew with slicked-back hair and a moustache. Roberts thought that hiring Nixon, who was between presidential runs, would balance out the ticket and make the association seem somehow more *American.*

Miller said no. He liked the idea, but he didn't need a job bad enough to work in tandem with Tricky Dick. Roberts and the others thought it over and decided to go with Miller. A meeting of team player representatives ratified the choice. Not everyone was happy with the decision. Lew Burdette of the Braves, Dodgers first baseman Ron Fairly, Ron Santo of the Cubs, future Hall of Famer Eddie Mathews, and others publicly attacked the very idea of organizing. Braves first baseman Joe Adcock spoke for many: "Pro sports," he said, "has no place for unions."

Miller very quickly came to a few basic conclusions about baseball. First, it was a business—an *American* business—that ought to be subject to the same rules of labor relations as any other. Players were employees. Team owners were not their friends or patrons: they were their bosses. The owners were also the boss of the commissioner of baseball, who served at their pleasure.

Miller also realized that his new members were very young, mostly unsophisticated men with little experience in the real world. This made them easy prey for owners who wrapped baseball in mythology and appealed to the players' sense of responsibility to team.

The players had organized because they wanted a decent pension, but Miller decided that what they really needed was a crash course in economics. The game was awash in television and radio money. Meanwhile, the average player salary was $19,000 and the minimum was $6,000—up a thousand bucks from 1947. A lot of players thought they had a sweet deal. Hell, they were making more than their buddies back home—the average annual salary for American men was about $5,000—and they got to play baseball instead of doing real work. Miller went from training camp to training camp and patiently disabused them of this idea. In his reasonable, mellifluous way, he explained that they were getting screwed. Not just anyone could play major-league ball; it was a rare and specialized skill. Baseball might be fun, but careers were short and hard and often ended suddenly. The players, not the owners, were the show, and they had a right—and a responsibility to their families—to negotiate and demand a free market price for their services.

This ran counter not only to the interests of the owners but, weirdly, to American jurisprudence. Baseball contracts came with a "reserve clause" that essentially bound players to their teams for life. In 1922, the Supreme Court of the United States ruled that baseball is exempt from antitrust rules because baseball games, even played by traveling teams, did not represent interstate commerce. A game, the court held, took place in only one state, and "personal effort, not related to production, is not a subject of commerce." Justice Oliver Wendell Holmes Jr. himself wrote that "exhibitions of baseball are purely state affairs." The Supreme Court reaffirmed baseball's special status and exemptions in rulings in 1953 and 1972. It was the law of the land.

Miller's first few years at the Players' Association were filled with consciousness-raising and salary-boosting; but he knew that to effect real change, sooner or later he would have to challenge baseball's cartel. When Curt Flood decided to take the Cardinals to court over the reserve clause, Miller backed his play.

By the standards of 1969 baseball, Curt Flood was cerebral, artistic—and rebellious. When the Cards traded him to Philadelphia at the end of the 1969 season, Flood was thirty-one, at the height of a very good career. He was a sensational center fielder and lifetime .293 hitter.

Flood didn't especially love St. Louis, but than again he didn't want to be traded without any say in the matter. He decided to sue Major League Baseball. Flood went to the players' union for support.

Tom Haller, one of the members of the union board, asked him if he was making his protest as a black man.

"I'd be lying if I told you that as a black man in baseball I hadn't gone through worse times than my white teammates," he said. "I'd also say that, yes, the change in black consciousness in recent years has made me more sensitive to injustice in every area of my life. But I want you to know that what I'm doing, here I'm doing as a ballplayer, a major league baseball player . . . [the reserve clause is] improper, it shouldn't be allowed to go any further, and the circumstances are such that, well, I guess this is the time to do something about it."

With the help of Marvin Miller and the players' union, Flood took his case to the Supreme Court. And lost.

"I wasn't optimistic that we'd win the case, and of course we didn't," says Miller. "In 1972, the reserve clause was upheld by a 5–3 vote. Justice Harry Blackmun wrote for the majority. He admitted that baseball was, in fact, interstate commerce. He conceded that the game's legal status was an "anomaly" and an "aberration." But he didn't care.

Harry Blackmun was the Supreme Court justice who wrote *Roe v. Wade* and other landmark Constitutional opinions. But when it came to baseball, he was a nine-year-old boy. Here is how he prefaced his legal argument:

> *It is a century and a quarter since the New York Nine defeated the Knickerbockers 23 to 1 on Hoboken's Elysian Fields June 19, 1846, with Alexander Jay Cartwright as the instigator and the umpire. The teams were amateur, but the contest marked a significant date in baseball's beginnings. That early game led ultimately to the development of professional baseball and its tightly organized structure.*
>
> *The Cincinnati Red Stockings came into existence in 1869 upon an outpouring of local pride. With only one Cincinnatian on the payroll, this professional team traveled over 11,000 miles that summer, winning*

56 games and tying one. Shortly thereafter, on St. Patrick's Day in 1871, the National Association of Professional Baseball Players was founded and the professional league was born.

The ensuing colorful days are well known. The ardent follower and the student of baseball know of General Abner Doubleday; the formation of the National League in 1876; Chicago's supremacy in the first year's competition under the leadership of Al Spalding and with Cap Anson at third base; the formation of the American Association and then of the Union Association in the 1880's; the introduction of Sunday baseball; interleague warfare with cut-rate admission prices and player raiding; the development of the reserve "clause"; the emergence in 1885 of the Brotherhood of Professional Ball Players, and in 1890 of the Players League; the appearance of the American League, or "junior circuit," in 1901, rising from the minor Western Association; the first World Series in 1903, disruption in 1904, and the Series' resumption in 1905; the short-lived Federal League on the majors' scene during World War I years; the troublesome and discouraging episode of the 1919 Series; the home run ball; the shifting of franchises; the expansion of the leagues; the installation in 1965 of the major league draft of potential new players; and the formation of the Major League Baseball Players Association in 1966.

Then there are the many names, celebrated for one reason or another, that have sparked the diamond and its environs and that have provided tinder for recaptured thrills, for reminiscence and comparisons, and for conversation and anticipation in-season and off-season: Ty Cobb, Babe Ruth, Tris Speaker, Walter Johnson, Henry Chadwick, Eddie Collins, Lou Gehrig, Grover Cleveland Alexander, Rogers Hornsby, Harry Hooper, Goose Goslin, Jackie Robinson, Honus Wagner, Joe McCarthy, John McGraw, Deacon Phillippe, Rube Marquard, Christy Mathewson, Tommy Leach, Big Ed Delahanty, Davy Jones, Germany Schaefer, King Kelly, Big Dan Brouthers, Wahoo Sam Crawford, Wee Willie Keeler, Big Ed Walsh, Jimmy Austin, Fred Snodgrass, Satchel Paige, Hugh Jennings, Fred Merkle, Iron Man McGinnity, Three-Finger Brown, Harry and Stan Coveleski, Connie Mack, Al Bridwell, Red Ruffing, Amos Rusie, Cy

> *Young, Smokey Joe Wood, Chief Meyers, Chief Bender, Bill Klem, Hans Lobert, Johnny Evers, Joe Tinker, Roy Campanela, Miller Huggins, Rube Bressler, Dazzy Vance, Edd Roush, Bill Wambsganess, Clark Griffith, Branch Rickey, Frank Chance, Cap Anson, Nap Lajoie, Sad Sam Jones, Bob O'Farrell, Lefty O'Doul, Bobby Veach, Willie Kamm, Heinie Groh, Lloyd and Paul Waner, Stuffy McInnis, Charles Comiske, Roger Bresnahan, Bill Dickey, Zack Wheat, George Sisler, Charlie Gehringer, Eppa Rixey, Harry Heilmann, Fred Clarke, Dizzy Dean, Hank Greenberg, Pie Traynor, Rube Waddell, Bill Terry, Carl Hubbell, Old Hoss Radbourne, Moe Berg, Rabbit Maranville, Jimmie Foxx, Lefty Grove. The list seems endless.*
>
> *And one recalls the appropriate reference to the "World Serious," attributed to Ring Lardner, Sr.; Ernest L. Thayer's "Casey at the Bat"; the ring of "Tinker to Evers to Chance"; and all the other happenings, habits, and superstitions about and around baseball that made it the "national pastime" or, depending upon the point of view, "the great American tragedy."*

Even leaving aside the misspellings ("Comiske") and Blackmun's omission of the racial integration of baseball in his chronicle of the game's notable "happenings," this was a bizarre note to strike in the most powerful courtroom in the world. Some of the concurring justices dissociated themselves from Blackmun's preface. Thurgood Marshall, the Court's only African-American, reportedly demanded a new, more diverse preface. As for the decision itself, it was clear: the reserve clause would stand. Once more, the U.S. Supreme Court had proven unwilling to subject Major League Baseball to the rule of law.

The court of public opinion, though, ruled in favor of Flood. Major League Baseball couldn't continue to argue that its players had no rights and were merely chattel property. In 1975, it dropped the reserve clause and promptly turned its players into millionaires.

Flood himself didn't gain much. He was branded a traitor and a radical by the owners, and ostracized from the game.

The Veterans Committee was invented for a man like Curt Flood, whose contribution can best be appreciated in the fullness of time. In 2007, the committee had eighty-four members, a majority of whom were Hall of Fame players. Some of them were multimillionaires because of Flood's courage. They gave him exactly fourteen votes.

In 1972, Marvin Miller led the players out on strike over pension benefits, and the baseball establishment was scandalized. Cards owner Gussie Busch told the press that the owners were unanimous. "We're not going to give them a goddamn cent. If they want to strike, let them strike." "Walter O'Malley, the owner of the Dodgers, called me a 'little Jewboy from Brooklyn,'" Miller recalled with a smile.

A few baseball journalists like Red Smith and Leonard Koppett supported the strike, but most took the side of management. The *Sporting News,* which represented the BBWAA consensus, had opposed the integration of the game in 1947. Now its editor, C. C. Johnson Spink, called the players' labor action "the darkest day in sports history." Spink added that "the whole idea of pensions for major league players may have been a mistake growing out of a misconception over what constitutes a career."

In the cities where major-league baseball was played, journalists, including the baseball journalists, were themselves members of the guild, and sometimes went out on strike. But the idea that baseball players had the same rights struck the traditionalists (which included nearly all of the writers) as subversive, even sacrilegious.

The players went out for thirteen days. Eighty-six games were cancelled. The owners lost about $5 million, the players around

$600,000. The strike was settled more or less on the union's terms, but its significance was greater than money: it marked the first time the players had taken on the owners and won.

The balance of power was permanently tipped. Miller established the principle of arbitration, which undermined the reserve clause and brought about free agency. Players were now able to negotiate and sign with the highest bidder. The average baseball salary had, by 1979, reached $113,558—more than five times what it had been when Miller started.

In 1981, the owners demanded that a team which lost a free agent be compensated by the signing team. This was an obvious effort to undermine free agency and the players struck again, this time for more than six weeks. A third of the season was lost. A compromise was finally reached, and Miller called it the players' finest hour. "Unlike in 1972, almost all the players had nothing to gain," he told an interviewer. "They were striking for free agency rights for players to come."

Miller had taken a collection of unsophisticated, often suspicious jocks and molded them into a real union.

Miller retired in 1983, but he remained a powerful figure in the union. When the owners attempted to roll back salaries through collusion, Miller was the lead witness for the players. Three lawsuits in the eighties cost the owners upward of $280 million. Some of the teams were barely able to make their payments. It was a terrible financial blow, and it left the baseball establishment furious at Marvin Miller.*

A Hall of Fame vote was coming up at the end of 2007, and there had been a lot of speculation that Miller would be selected by the

* And for good reason. The spirit of those judgments hovers over Barry Bonds's collusion case.

Veterans Committee. "People call up and tell me I'm a sure thing, and it makes me laugh," he said. "I'm not going to be chosen. The people who run Cooperstown still haven't forgiven me."

I found this hard to believe, and politely said so. Miller had been retired for twenty-five years. Sure, he had cost baseball teams a lot of money, but the game was now more profitable than ever. Yes, owners and traditionalists had hated Miller's guts in the old days, but he was a living legend now. How long could they hold a grudge?

"I'll tell you a story," Miller said. "The year before Roberto Clemente died, he contacted me. He was negotiating with Joe Brown, the Pirates general manager, and Roberto was asking for a very large percentage of the money in deferred payments. He had a premonition that he would die young, and he wanted to make sure his family would be taken care of.

"I asked Roberto how much interest the Pirates were offering on the deferred money. He said that Joe Brown hadn't mentioned any interest on the deferred payments. In other words, the team would hold and use Clemente's money for free.

"The next time I saw Roberto he told me, 'Boy, was Joe Brown mad when I asked him for interest on my money. He wanted to know where I had heard about interest. I told him I talked to you.' "

"What does that have to do with the Hall of Fame?" I asked.

Miller gave me an indulgent smile. "For twenty years, Joe Brown was chairman of the committee that picked Hall of Fame executives. His deputy was Bob Broeg, a St. Louis baseball writer who was viciously antiunion and wrote that the only way I'd get into the Hall of Fame was through the janitors' entrance. They didn't even allow my name on the ballot. I was told by a member of the committee that Brown and Broeg had refused to even put me on the ballot. They said I didn't qualify as a baseball executive."

"Well," I said, "that might explain why you didn't get in before, but Brown and Broeg aren't there any more. Right?"

"There are twelve members of the committee, and to get elected you need nine votes," Miller said. "Seven of the twelve are former management people. Don't worry, I'm not going to be elected. I'm retired, but I haven't forgotten how to count votes."*

I left Miller's apartment that day feeling happy to have met him, but a little sad, too. The man had been a great visionary in his time, but now he was living in the past, imaging that he was haunted by the ghosts of long-dead enemies. I decided I'd call him after the election to congratulate him. When I got to the car, I opened my date book, to write myself a reminder, and saw the note I had written for that morning's interview: "Marvin Miller. 10:00."

On December 3, 2007, the Hall of Fame announced the members of the class of 2008. Three executives were selected: Barney Dreyfuss, who owned the Pirates between 1901 and 1932; Walter O'Malley; and former commissioner Bowie Kuhn. Ewing Kauffman came in fourth. John Fetzer came in fifth. Miller finished in a tie for sixth with Bob Howsam. He got three votes.

Fay Vincent, a former commissioner of baseball who had his own battles with Miller, wrote, "The members of the committee that elected Bowie Kuhn and passed on Marvin Miller should be ashamed . . . they almost surely believe that Miller and the union won the war, but they refuse him the honor of victory. This is a set of actions by little men making small minded decisions. Electing Kuhn and Miller together might have been a tolerable result. But

* The committee, appointed by the Hall, included two former players: Harmon Killebrew, who works for the Twins as a broadcaster, and Monte Irvin, a long-time associate of Bowie Kuhn. Executives were Bobby Brown, former president of the American League; John Harrington of the Red Sox, with whom Miller tangled over the free agency of Carlton Fisk; Bill Giles and Andy MacPhail, Miller's adversaries in the collusion cases of the 1980s; David Glass of the Kansas City Royals (a senior executive of Wal-Mart); Jerry Bell of the Twins and Bill DeWitt of the Cards; and baseball writers Paul Hagen, Rick Hummel, and Hal McCoy.

electing Kuhn alone is intolerable . . . These are old men trying to turn back time, to reverse what has happened. Theirs is an act of ignorance and bias. I am ashamed for them. I am ashamed that they represent our game."

Vincent spoke for most of the serious baseball thinkers in the country; choosing Kuhn and not Miller was like putting Custer in the Little Bighorn Hall of Fame instead of Sitting Bull. Miller dismissed it as "degrading," and baseball experts agreed.

Jane Forbes Clark, however, begged to differ. "There was no concerted effort other than to have very qualified committee members evaluate very qualified candidates," she said in a press statement. "There was a very open and frank discussion about each of the candidates. Everyone on that committee knows Marvin and respects what he did for the game. And that showed in the discussions." And in their vote.

When I next saw Miller, shortly after the result was announced, he didn't remind me that he had forecast the outcome. He would have preferred to be wrong. It would have been a thrill for him to belong to the same club as Dazzy Vance. But Marvin is a realist. A few people had tried to console him with the thought that he would get in next time, but he wasn't having any of that. In May, he wrote a letter to Jack O'Connell, the secretary of the BBWAA and one of the chief coat-holders of the Hall of Fame establishment:

Dear Mr. O'Connell,

Paradoxically, I'm writing to thank you and your associates for your part in nominating me for Hall of Fame consideration, and, at the same time, to ask that you not do this again. The anti-union bias of the powers who control the Hall has consistently prevented recognition of the historic significance of the changes to baseball brought about by collective bargaining.

As former Executive Director (retired since 1983) of the Players' Union that negotiated these changes, I find myself unwilling to contemplate one more rigged Veterans Committee whose members are hand picked to reach a particular outcome while offering the pretense of a democratic vote. It is an insult to baseball fans, historians, sports writers and especially to those baseball players who sacrificed and brought the game into the 21st century. At the age of 91 I can do without farce.

Sincerely,
Marvin J. Miller

In his introduction to Marvin Miller's book *A Whole Different Ballgame,* Bill James wrote, "If baseball ever buys itself a mountain and starts carving faces on it, one of the first men to go up is sure to be Marvin Miller." But, as usual, who gets remembered depends on who owns the mountain.

NINE . . . *Lost in Translation*

In 2002, the Hall of Fame museum launched its first traveling exhibit, "Baseball as America." More than five hundred baseball relics, many of which had never left Cooperstown, were dispatched on a four-year run to fifteen museums around the United States. They included an 1860 lithograph of Abraham Lincoln playing baseball; a picture of A. G. Spalding's world-touring all-star team arrayed on the face of the Sphinx; and the first known photograph of a women's team, the Vassar College Resolutes, circa 1876. There was also a recording of Roy Campanella, Phil Rizzuto, and other stars of the fifties singing "Take Me Out to the Ball Game," a copy of Ted Williams's 1966 Induction Speech on the need to put Negro leaguers into Cooperstown, Andy Warhol's painting of Tom Seaver, and a host of other treasures.

The mission statement of the exhibit was clear. "Baseball as America," as ambassador for the museum in Cooperstown, was mounted to celebrate "enduring American values of freedom, patriotism, opportunity and ingenuity."

These are great values, but they don't always go together. When the Hall took up the issue of Hispanic baseball, "freedom and patriotism" crashed rudely into "opportunity and initiative," and it cost Dale Petrosky his job.

Petrosky was the president of the Hall of Fame, but he wasn't one of the monks. He came to Cooperstown in July 1999 from an executive job with the National Geographic Society. His background was political: he had served as a deputy spokesman in the second Reagan administration.

Petrosky, in his early fifties, looks like a local TV anchorman and carries himself with the wholesome self-assurance of the suburban high-school quarterback he once was. He didn't have any particular background in baseball (although, on the plus side, he is a Tigers fan); presumably Jane Forbes Clark hired him for his administrative and fund-raising abilities. It didn't hurt that Petrosky, like Clark, was a Republican. America was changing, and the Hall had to change with it—the decision to induct seventeen Negro-leagues players was an example of that change—but there was no point in getting carried away. Petrosky was the sort of man who could be counted on to protect Clark family values. Or so she thought.

In 2003, Petrosky caused a stir when he disinvited actor Tim Robbins from a Cooperstown event honoring the fifteenth anniversary of the baseball film *Bull Durham*. Robbins had been an outspoken critic of the war in Iraq; Petrosky's letter to him, which soon became public, noted, "Public figures, such as you, have platforms much larger than the average American's, which provides you an extraordinary opportunity to have your views heard—and an equally large obligation to act and speak responsibly. We believe your very public criticism of President Bush at this important—and sensitive—time in our nation's history helps undermine the U.S. position, which ultimately could put our troops in even more danger. As an institution, we stand behind our President and our troops in this conflict."

Robbins responded with a letter of his own: "I'm sorry that you have chosen to use baseball and your position at the Hall of Fame to make a political statement. I know there are many baseball fans that disagree with you, and even more that will react with disgust to realize baseball is being politicized."

It turned out to be a public relations disaster. Petrosky wrote an apology to Robbins. "I wish I had a do-over on that one," he told me ruefully. It was a manful performance, but nobody who knows the Hall of Fame believed that Petrosky had stiffed Tim Robbins on his own. Insiders conjecture that such a letter could not have been sent without the approval of June Forbes Clark.*

Just about the time Dale Petrosky arrived in Cooperstown, the Hispanic Heritage Baseball Museum was founded in San Francisco. The Hall did not want a repeat of its racial fiascos. Hispanics were rapidly becoming the largest ethnic group in America, and many were huge baseball fans. It seemed essential to connect to them—without, of course, losing the traditional American values and ideals of the Hall of Fame.

Baseball first came to Latin America in 1866, when a Cuban named Nemesio Guilló returned from his studies in the U.S. with a bat and ball and founded the first team in Havana. Within a decade, skilled Cuban players were looking for work on American diamonds. Among the Hall of Fame's most treasured possessions is a baseball used in an 1871 contest between the New York Mutuals and the Troy Haymakers of the National Association of Professional Base Ball Players. Esteban Bellán, the first Hispanic in professional baseball, played third base in that game. There have been Latino players ever since. The first such major-league star was pitcher Adolfo Luque, who broke in with the Miracle Braves in 1914 and compiled a 194–179 record in twenty National League seasons. Luque was light-skinned enough to be given the benefit of the doubt in the Jim Crow era. So were forty or so other Cubans who played in the majors before integration. They got called "Cuban Niggers" by fans and bench jockeys, but they benefited from the Desi Arnaz Exception: straight

* In September 2008, the Hall celebrated the twentieth anniversary of *Bull Durham*. Tim Robbins was there, along with the other stars of the film and its director, Ron Shelton. Petrosky was long gone. The Hall of Fame press release on the event made no mention of the disinvitation five years earlier.

hair and pale skin could make a Cuban racially acceptable, even as the husband of the red-headed Lucille Ball.

The racial integration of baseball opened the door for darker-skinned Cubans. In 1949, the definitely black Orestes "Minnie" Minoso signed with the Cleveland Indians. He was already in his mid-twenties, a star for the New York Cubans in the Negro leagues.* Goose Tatum, the great Harlem Globetrotters star, played baseball with Minoso and brought him to the attention of Globetrotters owner Abe Saperstein. Saperstein, in turn, brought Minoso to his fellow super-promoter Bill Veeck of the Cleveland Indians, who signed him shortly thereafter, and then hired him again when he moved to the Chicago White Sox in 1951.

Minoso has a special place in the hearts of Hispanic players. "Minnie Minoso is to Latin players what Jackie Robinson is to black ballplayers," writes Orlando Cepeda in his autobiography, *Baby Bull*. "As much as I love Roberto Clemente and cherish his memory, Minnie is the one who made it possible for all of us Latins. Before Roberto Clemente, before Vic Power, before Orlando Cepeda, there was Minnie Minoso . . . He was the first Latin player to become a superstar."

Minoso was, unlike most American Leaguers of the stolid fifties, an exciting player. Three times he led the league in steals and in triples. Perhaps as a result, he was the perennial leader in getting hit by pitches. He was also a good outfielder who won three Gold Gloves. And he was a lifetime .298 hitter.

Minoso cut a flamboyant figure in Chicago and around the American League. He drove a green Cadillac, sported diamond rings and wide-brimmed hats (his nickname was "El Charro Negro," the black cowboy), and was known as a soft touch. Minoso was married, but he wasn't a fanatic about it. On the other hand, he was cautious.

* The Cubans were owned by Alex Pompez, who was a well-known numbers king in Harlem, a former associate of Dutch Schultz and Lucky Luciano, who was in exile in Havana. Pompez lived to a ripe old age and eventually became a member of the Hall of Fame's special committee on Negro-leagues ballplayers.

Unlike his fellow Latino All-Star Vic Power, he didn't flaunt relationships with white women. The writers approved of that, and when he got hit with a paternity suit by an African American waitress in Chicago, they kept it out of the papers.

Minoso led the way for an influx of Spanish-speaking players. Like Minoso, many were furnished by their teams with American names. Roberto "Beto" Avila, a Mexican who led the American League in batting average in 1954, was christened Bobby. Antonio Oliva Lopez Hernandes Javique became Tony Oliva. Vic Power started out as Victor Pellot. And Roberto Clemente's early baseball cards identified him as Bob Clemente. Ted Williams didn't need renaming, because nobody had the slightest idea that he had a Mexican-American mother and a whole family of Spanish-speaking relatives back on the West Coast.*

After Fidel Castro came to power in 1959, Cuba became inaccessible as a source of major-league talent. It was replaced by Puerto Rico, Mexico, Panama, Venezuela, the Dominican Republic, and other countries that produced stars like Cincinnati Reds shortstop Davey Concepcion, Pirates catcher Manny Sanguillen, and Dodgers pitcher Fernando Valenzuela. Then, in the mid-eighties, baseball experienced a great wave of Latino excellence that continues to roll in today. First came Rafael Palmeiro and Jose Canseco, followed by Roberto Alomar, Omar Vizquel, Juan Gonzalez, and Sammy Sosa. Within a decade, they were followed by Vinny Castilla, Bernie Williams, Ivan Rodriguez, Pedro Martinez, Manny Ramirez, Carlos Delgado, Alex Rodriguez, Mariano Rivera, Edgar Renteria, Nomar Garciaparra, Vladimir Guerrero, Magglio Ordonez, Miguel Tejada, Carlos Guillen, Carlos Beltran, Alfonso Soriano, and Albert Pujols. This was an explosion of ethnic talent unequaled since the arrival of

* In 1973, Clemente became the first Hispanic (not counting Williams) inducted into the Hall of Fame. His Cooperstown plaque read "Roberto Walker Clemente." His actual name was Roberto Clemente Walker. In 2000, the Hall rectified this with what it called a "culturally correct plaque," explaining that in Latin America the mother's maiden name traditionally follows a surname. A special ceremony was held in Puerto Rico, and the family pronounced itself satisfied.

Mays, Aaron, Robinson, and the other black superstars of the post-integration years.

For more than a hundred years, baseball was the American Game. Teachers from the U.S. brought it to their students in Tokyo in the 1870s. After a stay in the U.S., Cuban Nemesio Guilló founded the first team in Havana in 1866. In 1887–88, A. G. Spalding took a professional squad around the world. Babe Ruth barnstormed Japan with a team of major-leaguers in 1934. (The trip, billed as a goodwill tour, was a short-term success, but it was also a lesson in the limitations of international public relations; seven years later, the Japanese attacked Pearl Harbor.) The United States was an exporter of baseball and baseball players to the Cuban and Caribbean winter leagues, Mexico, and Japan.

But by the start of the twenty-first century, America had become an importer of talent. In 2006, the first World Baseball Classic was held, pitting national teams against one another. The U.S. sent its best players, and lost to Mexico in the second round. Japan beat Cuba for the gold. The spin was that the Americans weren't really in game shape, but the results demonstrated what many in the U.S. had feared for years: American-born baseball players were no longer necessarily the best in the world.

Some Americans have found this disconcerting. It seemed like a reversal of the natural order, an echo of what happened back when Honda and Toyota started beating Ford and General Motors. In the summer of 2007, CBS commentator and syndicated columnist Andy Rooney put it into words: "I know all about Babe Ruth and Lou Gehrig, but today's baseball stars are all guys named Rodriguez to me. They're apparently very good, but they haven't caught my interest."*

The BBWAA doesn't publish demographic information on its

* In the middle of the 2008 season, the New York Yankees further confused Rooney by acquiring catcher Ivan "Pudge" Rodriguez from the Detroit Tigers. Now, with A-Rod, they had two guys named Rodriguez.

members (actually, it doesn't publish a list of members, period), but the best estimate is that no more than 3 percent are Hispanic. Most writers no longer quote Latinos in pidgin English, as was customary a generation ago, or make mocking remarks about the imagined characteristics of Hispanics. But the same demographic and cultural gap that frustrated Roberto Clemente and other Latinos forty years ago still exists, and it very much affects the reputations of foreign players.

There were baseball writers who believed Latino players were bringing more than foreign-sounding names to the game. In 2006, *Newsweek* reported that eight of the twelve major-league players who tested positive for steroids in the previous season were Hispanic, and that half the positives in the minors were Latinos (the magazine didn't mention that about half the *players* in the minors were Latinos, too). "The data raise a troubling possibility that few in baseball would like to address head on: are players from Latin America simply too driven to succeed?"

The *New York Times* sent a reporter to the Dominican Republic and found that anabolic steroids were readily available there without a prescription. "Strength coaches in the major leagues say players often obtain steroids while playing winter ball in Latin America.

"Young ballplayers at San Pedro de Macorís, a town that has produced many major league players, said it was common to find aspiring baseball players shooting up steroids. Some Dominican players said their colleagues who used steroids have often resorted to veterinary drugs, which are even easier to obtain."

The self-proclaimed "godfather of steroids," Jose Canseco, is a Cuban-~~American~~ whose best-selling book *Juiced* made his name virtually synonymous with performance-enhancing drugs. Canseco has admitted to introducing steroids to at least two all-American heroes—Mark McGwire and Roger Clemens—and has, in his opinion, been demonized for it. "I remember one time Harmon Killebrew was doing commentary for a game between the A's and the Twins," he writes.

"When I came to bat he said: 'I saw Canseco in the minor leagues and I've never seen a player change so much so drastically.' What a joke. How about Mark McGwire? He went through an even more dramatic change than I did . . . But nobody ever cared what McGwire was doing." Canseco's conclusion is that McGwire got a pass because he was an Anglo.

Canseco isn't the only Hispanic ballplayer who suspects that there is a certain amount of nativist sentiment behind reports of the Latino Connection. In the summer of 2007, Chicago White Sox manager Ozzie Guillen complained about it to the Associated Press. "I meet with, like, five people [investigating steroids in baseball]. The only thing that made me upset was they tried to mention too many Latino players. I think they try to put Latinos to be the bad cloud in this thing . . . everything they asked [was] 'Do you ever see this in Venezuela?'

"They were like, 'You never see any of the players bring this thing to the States?'" Guillen said. "I said, 'Wait a second, BALCO is not [in] Venezuela, is not [in] Puerto Rico, is not Dominican, is not [in] Mexico. BALCO is in California. Then why do you keep blaming players from Latin America for the problem that we have in the States?'"

It wasn't just old grouches like Andy Rooney and suspicious reporters who had a problem with the Latino invasion: a lot of African-Americans nodded in agreement with Gary Sheffield's observation that baseball was using Hispanics as cheap replacement players. *New York Times* columnist William C. Rhoden wrote, "At a time when immigration is a searing topic, Sheffield raised a crucial issue about a delicate subject: the competition for jobs between African-American and Latino players in Major League Baseball."

Surprisingly, a lot of Latinos in baseball seconded Sheffield's analysis. "We know if we don't agree [with managers] or do what they say, it's 'Bye-bye, you are going back to the Dominican,'" Sheffield's Tigers teammate Neifi Perez said. "That's what Sheffield is talking about. It's true. It's easier to control a Latino than an American. We come here, we play baseball and do our job. If you do anything against baseball, you get labeled a bad person and every organization believes it. There is nothing new about that." (Perez may not be the most neutral observer. In 2007, he was suspended for a third time for testing positive for a banned stimulant.)

"Maybe when we come to this country, we're hungry," added Guillen. "We're trying to survive. Those [American players] sign for $500,000 or $1 million, and they're made. We have a couple of dollars . . . Look at how many Latin players have won Cy Youngs or MVP awards the last couple of years, how many Latin players have been in the All-Star Game; it's quantity and quality. You go to the minor-league camps, and there are 100 kids from Latin America—maybe because it's easier to sign them and cheaper and better talent right now."

By the time the Hall of Fame came to grips with the issue of how to present Latino baseball, there were already seven Latino players in Cooperstown (not counting Williams): Martin Dihigo, Roberto Clemente, Orlando Cepeda, Rod Carew, Luis Aparicio, Juan Marichal, and Tony Perez. And more are on the way. Catcher Ivan Rodriguez, pitchers Pedro Martinez and Mariano Rivera, and sluggers Manny Ramirez, Alex Rodriguez, and David Ortiz are sure bets; Vladimir Guerrero, Roberto Alomar, and—if the voters get past their steroid use—Sammy Sosa, Rafael Palmeiro, and Miguel Tejada have a shot. And there are lots more where they came from.

Telling the story of Latino baseball was never going to be as easy as tossing a little pepper into the great American melting pot. But Dale Petrosky and his boss, Jane Forbes Clark, complicated matters by going into it with a partner, the CITGO Petroleum Corporation. The Hall announced that CITGO would be the sponsor of a permanent Cooperstown exhibit on Hispanic baseball.

The Hall had not previously taken on partners in its museum, but

Ernst & Young had sponsored the traveling "Baseball as America" show, and Jane Forbes Clark had pronounced it an example of "a great American tradition—that of patronage—providing support for the artistic and intellectual endeavors that better our society." But CITGO wasn't Ernst & Young: it is the national energy company of Venezuela, which means that it is controlled by Hugo Chavez, an outspoken socialist and sworn enemy of the United States.

How this happened is a mystery, even to Jeff Idelson, the current president of the Hall. "Chavez and his political views didn't come into play when we were considering the sponsorship with CITGO," he told me. Idelson is an experienced public relations expert, and I'm sure he wouldn't lie. Evidently, the two Republicans running the Hall of Fame simply joined forces with the biggest America-hater in the Western Hemisphere without giving it a thought.

In April 2006, the "¡Béisbol Baseball!" project was launched with great fanfare. "We want to explore the growing Latino influence in the game, the way the game is played and loved throughout Latin America," Dale Petrosky announced. "Over the next five years, we want to bring the rich history of Latin American baseball to the largest American audience ever."

Frank Gygax, CITGO chief operating officer, confirmed that his company had given a five-year commitment to the Hall of Fame, and he contemplated a long and happy partnership. "We hope this display will find a permanent home in Cooperstown," he said.

For the next few months, a temporary "panel" exhibit was displayed in major-league parks, under the Hall of Fame/CITGO banner. Arranged by countries, it featured pictures and artifacts from the Caribbean and Winter leagues, including a photograph of the 1955 Santurce Crabs, a Puerto Rican team whose outfielders included Willie Mays and Roberto Clemente. The exhibit was seen by fans in Atlanta, Boston, Baltimore, Detroit, Houston, Milwaukee, San Diego, Tampa Bay, and Cincinnati, and it was still circulating when Hugo Chavez appeared before the United Nations General

Assembly in September. There, in an unforgettable televised speech, he denounced George W. Bush, president of the United States (and former owner of the Texas Rangers), as the incarnation of Satan.

"The devil came here yesterday," Chavez said from the podium of the UN General Assembly, "and it smells of sulfur still today . . . As the spokesman of imperialism, he came to share his nostrums to try to preserve the current pattern of domination, exploitation, and pillage of the peoples of the world . . . The American empire is doing all it can to consolidate its hegemonistic system of domination, and we cannot allow him to do that. We cannot allow world dictatorship to be consolidated."

Chavez's feelings about the U.S. were not exactly a secret. In May 2006, as "¡Béisbol Baseball!" toured the country, Chavez accused America of committing genocide. Somehow this had escaped the attention of the Hall's board of directors, but the televised diatribe at the UN was hard to miss. Not all of them loved George W. Bush; but if he was an imperialist, what did that make them? They suddenly noticed that Chavez was accusing Major League Baseball of "exploiting" Latino raw material, in the form of talent, for decades. He was even talking about taxing the majors for the privilege of mining ballplayers. Who had decided to go into partnership with this guy?

Of course, nobody asked this question out loud; Cooperstown is a shrine, and shrines keep their secrets. Besides, the answer was clear. President Petrosky had proposed the deal, and the directors themselves, led by Jane Forbes Clark, had approved it. The agreement with CITGO was suspended in the spring of 2007 and then very quietly cancelled. There was virtually no press coverage.

In March 2008, the Hall of Fame announced that Petrosky was out as president. "The resignation is the result of our finding that Dale Petrosky failed to exercise proper fiduciary responsibility, and it follows other business judgments that were not in the best interest of the National Baseball Hall of Fame and Museum." ("Fiduciary" is the English word for Chavez.)

Once again, there was barely a ripple in the media. One of America's most iconic national institutions had made, and cancelled, an alliance with Hugo Chavez, and nobody noticed.

Jeff Idelson, who was one of the few people who had counseled against the deal, was appointed president. When I asked him what had happened, he answered that "it is our policy not to reveal financial considerations." According to him, the project fell apart because the Hall of Fame couldn't find suitable locations—an odd answer considering that the permanent exhibition was intended for Cooperstown.

Petrosky went quietly. "After almost nine productive years at the Hall of Fame, I have offered my resignation to the Hall's Executive Committee, and it has been accepted," he said. "The Hall of Fame is a world-class institution, and I am proud of all we have accomplished through vision, hard work, and teamwork. I serve at the pleasure of the Board, and accept the judgment of the Executive Committee."

Petrosky moved to Texas, where he was hired by George Bush's old team, the Rangers, as director of marketing. CITGO swore on a stack of bibles that the cancellation had nothing to do with Hugo Chavez. Jane Forbes Clark said absolutely nothing. It is good to be the Queen.

In the spring of 2009, the Hall is planning to mount a permanent exhibit, "Viva Béisbol!" It will, in Jeff Idelson's words, "explore the exciting story of Latin American baseball, viewing the game through both its cultural history in the Caribbean Basin and the impact of Latino players on Major League Baseball." Meanwhile, the Hall is looking for a new sponsor. Latin American dictators need not apply.

TEN . . . *Mitchell and Clemens*

I was in Cooperstown during the great snowfall of December 2007, marooned at the Hall with the monks, when Senator George Mitchell delivered his report on the use of steroids in Major League Baseball. The steroids issue had been hovering over the Hall for several years. More than 70 percent of the BBWAA voters had kept Mark McGwire off their Hall of Fame ballots because he was known to have used performance-enhancing drugs (PEDs) during his epic home run spree of the nineties. The *Freeman's Journal* editorial of the previous summer had made it clear that the Hall's establishment considered Barry Bonds persona non grata. But these had been treated as isolated cases, to be dealt with at some future time. "Nothing has been proven yet, one way or the other," Ted Spencer told me earlier that day over lunch. "There are allegations. There are stories. But there is nothing to say that there is such a thing as the steroid era like there was a dead-ball era. There is no consensus on that. Two years from now, five, twenty, who's to say? But right now, it's just an elephant in the room."

Now, according to leaks in the media, Mitchell was going to let the elephant out. A televised press conference was scheduled for 2:00 P.M., and a few minutes before two the monks filed in to the Grandstand Theater to watch on the Hall's big screen.

Even the most pessimistic monks were dismayed by what Mitchell delivered—dozens of names, from Manny Alexander to Gregg Zaun. He named some of baseball's greatest players. McGwire and Bonds,

Mo Vaughn and Miguel Tejada, Gary Sheffield, Kevin Brown, Lenny Dykstra, Jason Giambi, Juan Gonzalez, David Justice, Rafael Palmeiro, Andy Pettitte, and dozens more. And, worst of all, Roger Clemens.

"For more than a decade there has been widespread illegal use of anabolic steroids and other performance enhancing substances by players in Major League Baseball, in violation of federal law and baseball policy," Mitchell reported. "Club officials routinely have discussed the possibility of such substance use when evaluating players. Those who have illegally used these substances range from players whose major league careers were brief to potential members of the Baseball Hall of Fame. They include both pitchers and position players, and their backgrounds are as diverse as those of all major league players."

Mitchell made it clear that he hadn't caught everyone. "Other investigations will no doubt turn up more names and fill in more details, but that is unlikely to significantly alter the description of baseball's 'steroids era,' as set forth in this report . . . the evidence we uncovered indicates that this has not been an isolated problem involving just a few players or a few clubs. It has involved many players on many clubs. In fact, each of the thirty clubs has had players who have been involved with performance enhancing substances at some time in their careers."

Mitchell couldn't say exactly how many current players had been using PEDs. "There have been many estimates of use," he noted. "In 2002, former National League Most Valuable Player Ken Caminiti estimated that 'at least half' of all major league players were using anabolic steroids. Dave McKay, a longtime coach for the St. Louis Cardinals and the Oakland Athletics, estimated that at one time thirty percent of players were using them. Within the past week, the former Cincinnati Reds pitcher Jack Armstrong estimated that between twenty percent and thirty percent of players in his era, 1988 to 1994, were using large doses of steroids while an even higher percentage of players were using lower, maintenance doses of steroids. There have been other estimates, a few higher, many lower, all impossible to verify."

In 2004, MLB had instituted anonymous testing, but the program was widely recognized as a joke. Five to seven percent of the players tested were shown to be using—a ridiculously low figure. Human growth hormone wasn't screened for, and the players had known in advance they were going to be examined. Worse, as Mitchell said, "A negative test does not necessarily mean that a player has not been using performance enhancing substances."

At the outset of his investigation, Mitchell had promised to conduct a "deliberate and unbiased examination of the facts that will comport with basic American values of fairness." His demeanor at the press conference made it clear that he was very satisfied that he had delivered. Mitchell seemed untroubled by the fact that most of his "cases" relied on nothing more than newspaper reports or hearsay. He also wasn't troubled by allegations that his relations with the Boston Red Sox, on whose board of directors he sat, compromised his objectivity. "Judge me by my work," he said. "You will not find any evidence of bias, special treatment for the Red Sox or anyone else. That had no effect on this investigation, none whatsoever."

George Mitchell, a former federal judge and Democratic Senate majority leader, has been, since he left the Senate in 1996, America's Most Available Man. Bill Clinton reportedly offered him a place on the Supreme Court. Al Gore considered him for the number two spot on the ticket in 2000, and after Gore picked Joe Lieberman instead, Mitchell was said to be his choice for secretary of state. In 2004, there was speculation that John Kerry might appoint Mitchell to a senior cabinet position. Mitchell served briefly as chairman of the board of directors of the Disney Corporation. Under Bill Clinton, he was made U.S. envoy to Northern Ireland, where he helped broker a peace agreement; and later to the Middle

East, where he didn't.* More than once, he was mentioned as a future commissioner of baseball. Instead, Bud Selig made him the game's High Inquisitor.

At the start of the press conference, when Mitchell named Roger Clemens, there had been an audible gasp in the Grandstand Theater. One of the monks sitting nearby said, "This is as bad as the Black Sox." Actually, it was potentially worse. After the 1919 scandal, baseball brought in an honest-looking federal judge, picked out a handful of scapegoats to point to as the only gamblers in the game, and waited for the sporting public's attention to turn from the age-old sin of gambling to the newfangled thrill of the home run. That wasn't going to happen this time: things were different. For starters, Mitchell lacked Judge Landis's dramatic flair. And Commissioner Selig, as owner of the Milwaukee Brewers, was one of the owners who had ignored steroids for years. The players had a union now, and nobody was going to get railroaded out of the game by an arbitrary decision. There were far too many names in the Mitchell Report to pick out individual scapegoats. If you believed that PEDs were rotten, then the entire game of baseball was rotten.

Mitchell advised amnesty. An exhaustive investigation into the pharmacological practices of every player would be counterproductive. He had learned from his experience in Northern Ireland that sometimes progress is served by leaving certain stones unturned. The use of performance-enhancing drugs, he said, was wrong "legally and ethically," but the time had come to institute real testing procedures and put it all in the past.

This approach was not quite as magnanimous as it seemed. Mitchell (and Selig) knew full well that a full-scale legal investigation, with players put under oath, would result in disaster. The union might shut the game down. Players (and trainers, managers, and owners) could go to jail for perjury.

* In 2009, President Obama sent Mitchell back to the Middle East for a second try as U.S. special envoy.

And all for what? Mitchell had no actual proof of anything. In fact, during much of the two decades he labeled the Era of Steroids, most of the substances weren't illegal or even banned. There would be no criminal charges. Nobody was going to jail for using performance enhancers (perjury, in the Bonds case, could be a different matter). They could put asterisks on the baseballs, but the records would stand—nobody could expunge twenty years of statistics. And no one would wind up on skid row, either. The players, especially the stars, were rich men.

No, the ultimate penalty—the only penalty, really—would be administered in Cooperstown. After the press conference, Dennis Eckersley, who had been Clemens's teammate, summed it up in an interview. "It all comes down to the Hall of Fame, really," he said. "That's what we're talking about. Should a guy be in there?"

For the monks assembled in the Grandstand Theater, there was a more immediate question: what to say when the media came calling. Jeff Idelson was the senior Hall of Fame staffer that day, and he gave the monks their marching orders. "No actual Hall of Famers were named by Mitchell," he noted. "That's good news. We will be getting a permanent copy of the report, which we will put in our archives. Tonight, we'll be issuing a statement. It will include talking points. Until then, please don't give anyone your personal opinion."* I was the only journalist present, and a few heads turned in my direction.

Everyone went back to work and I found myself in the deserted

* The statement, issued December 13, 2007, read as follows: "The National Baseball Hall of Fame and Museum preserves and exhibits baseball history through the collection of artifacts and documents, and, it also honors the game's greatest players, managers, umpires and executives, through election.

"The Mitchell Report is an important historical document that researchers and historians will study for generations. Our role as a history museum and educational research center is to make this document available to researchers and fans, and, over time, exhibit the impact of the findings in a manner appropriate to its place in the game's history."

plaque room. All alone, I passed by the bronzed likenesses. Here was White Sox owner Charles Comiskey, whose penurious treatment of his players was said to have helped inspire the 1919 fix. And Grover Cleveland Alexander, the great pitcher whose performance-enhancing substance came in a bottle. I stopped in front of John J. McGraw, probably the fiercest competitor in the history of the game. "There has only been one manager, and his name is John McGraw," Connie Mack once said. McGraw's team captured ten pennants, and he was famous for his willingness to do almost anything to win. What, I wondered, would John McGraw have done about players who used drugs to improve their performance? Would he have demanded that they stay clean, even if the other side was using? Would he have insisted his men put their concern about health risks ahead of winning baseball games? Would he have refused to help his team duck urine tests on the grounds that it would have been unethical to do so?

I may be mistaken but standing there in the silence, I thought I heard McGraw laughing at me.

A few weeks later, I met Jane Forbes Clark in New York City and asked her how the Hall of Fame was going to deal with the aftermath of the Mitchell Report. She seemed surprised by the question. "I like to think of us as neutral," she said. "Like Switzerland."

If she truly believes that will be possible, Ms. Clark belongs with Gary Sheffield in the Optimists' Hall of Fame.

Assuming he doesn't un-retire again, Roger Clemens will become eligible for the Hall of Fame in 2012. If the voters snub him, as they have Mark McGwire, Cooperstown will be without the greatest pitcher of the last forty years. Not only that: if you leave out Clemens on the grounds that he cheated by taking steroids, how do you elect Barry Bonds? Both Clemens and Bonds have denied for the record taking steroids. And who knows what other superstars on performance enhancers will be discovered? In February 2009, *Sports Illustrated* reported that Alex Rodriguez was one of 104 players who tested positive in the 2003 season. In retrospect, maybe this should have been evident. Over his career, Rodriguez had bulked up his body in a manner highly reminiscent of Barry Bonds. But sportswriters had credulously attributed this to his superhuman work ethic.

Other superstars have had unusual longevity or physical stamina, and in the age of steroids any example of excellence could be grounds for suspicion. How did Cal Ripken amass that iron-man streak? What has enabled Greg Maddux and Tom Glavine to pitch so effectively at an age when most ballplayers are hobbling out of the game? Why did Mike Mussina win 20 games for the first time at what should be the end of his career? While none of these players have been accused of anything, start asking questions like this and the list is endless.

In 2001, Tom Verducci wrote an article in *Sports Illustrated* about Clemens and his amazing longevity:

> *Throughout almost 18 major league seasons (the first 13 with the Red Sox and the next two with the Toronto Blue Jays), Clemens has been a fitness fanatic. He so refined his training sessions with Blue Jays strength coach Brian McNamee that Toronto catcher Darrin Fletcher nicknamed them "Navy SEAL workouts"* . . .
>
> *Between outings Clemens religiously adheres to McNamee's tightly choreographed program of distance running, agility drills, weight training, 600 daily abdominal crunches and assorted other tortures.*

McNamee, as we now know, is the guy who allegedly supplied Clemens with performance-enhancing drugs, and then told the Mitchell Committee.

> *Clemens takes great pride in having stopped his baseball biological clock. He will tell you that he still runs three miles in 19 to 20 1/2 minutes, that he still weighs 232 pounds, that he still wears slacks with a 36-inch waist (though they must be tailored to allow for his massive thighs) and that he can still reach for a mid-90s fastball at will—the same specs he had at least 10 years ago. "He's a freak of nature, the kind of pitcher who comes along once in a generation, maybe every 25 to 30 years," says Devil Rays pitching coach Bill Fischer . . . "He's like Tom Seaver or Nolan Ryan . . . He can pitch as long as he wants."*

Tom Seaver? Nolan Ryan? Hmmm.

By 2001, when this article appeared in *SI*, steroid use in baseball was not a secret. Ten years earlier, Commissioner Fay Vincent had sent out a memo banning "all illegal drugs and substances, including steroids." In 1995, San Diego general manager Randy Smith publicly estimated that between 10 and 20 percent of the players in the majors were using. "It's like the big secret we're not supposed to talk about," Tony Gwynn told a reporter for the *Los Angeles Times*. "I think we all have our suspicions who's on the stuff, but unless someone comes out and admits to it, who'll ever know for sure?" During the 1998 home run duel between Mark McGwire and Sammy Sosa, an enterprising reporter noticed (and, more remarkably, actually reported noticing) a bottle of androstenedione in McGwire's locker. The substance was legal and available in health-food stores, and it wasn't banned by baseball. McGwire freely admitted using it to make himself bigger and stronger.* It evidently didn't occur to Tom

*In 2002, Ken Caminiti revealed to *Sports Illustrated* that he used performance enhancers and estimated that half the players in the majors did likewise. The following year, federal agents raided BALCO, a Burlingame, California, drug lab whose clients included Barry Bonds. Suddenly sportswriters began noticing—in print—that Bonds was a lot bigger than he used to be. It took another four years for them to make the same observation about Clemens, a difference that was not lost on Bonds himself or other black and Latino players.

Verducci that Clemens might be bigger and stronger for the same reason as McGwire.

This isn't too hard to understand. Reporters often miss the most obvious stories. Twenty years ago, the entire American press corps in Moscow was shocked to discover that the Soviet Union—which they had been covering for years on a daily basis—was going out of business. They weren't bad reporters, necessarily; they simply worked with a narrative that didn't allow for the collapse of an empire.

Steroids in baseball had a narrative, too. They were a slugger's brew. Guys who used them went from line-drive hitters to long-ball monsters. These guys paid a price, of course—everyone knew steroids were poison in the long run—but they were willing to pollute their bodies, sacrifice their souls, and sell out the game of baseball for glory and profit.

But Roger Clemens? He was a *pitcher*—and a good ole boy to boot. He achieved greatness by working like a Navy SEAL to develop the special body God had given him. *SI* is a sophisticated and influential publication. Regular baseball writers, BBWAA types, had no reason to question the magazine's take on the Rocket's longevity. On the contrary, they burnished the legend with their own stories about his maniacal fitness regimen.

And then along came the Mitchell Report, and suddenly everyone could see what had been right in front of their eyes the whole time. And the same writers who had not raised the possibility before suddenly were certain of guilt and became outraged. Of *course* Clemens had been using steroids—just look at him! He was bigger than Bonds. Nastier, too—that time he threw a bat at Mike Piazza? 'Roid rage. He was a cheater. He lied to the children of America. Hell, forget the children, he lied to *us*!

A few days after the Mitchell Report, the *Rocky Mountain News* asked nineteen BBWAA members how they would vote on Clemens when the time came. Barely half said they would cast a ballot for the Rocket—far fewer than the 75 percent he'd need to get into Cooperstown. Dan Graziano of the Newark *Star-Ledger* said, "My personal feeling on this is that the Hall of Fame is a reward, and I don't intend to reward people who cheated in an effort to get there. I did not vote for Mark McGwire last year and have no plans to vote for him in the future. Similarly, I have no plans to vote for Barry Bonds." Mark Gonzales of the *Chicago Tribune* said, "I'm leaning strongly on Rule 5 of the Hall of Fame ballot that states a player's candidacy shall be based upon a list that includes 'integrity, sportsmanship and character' as well as contributions." Pat Reusse of the *Minneapolis Star Tribune* made the Cooperstown point in reverse. "I've been voting for McGwire, so I suppose I'll vote for Clemens," he said. "Baseball wouldn't let us vote for Rose. If they don't want the steroid boys in the Hall, do the same."

"Baseball" meant the Commissioner's Office. The Hall of Fame is theoretically independent, but it has usually bowed to the decisions of MLB. It honored Judge Landis's ban on Joe Jackson with a gentleman's handshake. But it's very doubtful that MLB is going to ban the "steroid boys." The owners can collude to keep certain players off the field or deny them post-baseball jobs, but banning players for life is not so simple. Great stars have great personal fortunes, good lawyers, and a solid union. They won't be easily deprived of their rights—including their right be enshrined in Cooperstown and participate in the haul of fame.

That means that it will be up to the Hall itself to decide how to handle the performance-enhancers. There are three basic choices. Option 1: keep Rule 5 and seriously enforce it. This means excluding the players who juiced, or deciding that juicing, even with banned or illegal substances, is not a form of cheating that violates Cooperstown's standard of good sportsmanship. The upside of this decision is that it is unambiguous. The downside is that it would exclude the modern Walter Johnson (Clemens), the modern Babe Ruth (Bonds), and potentially most of the great players of the current era.

Option 2: keep Rule 5 but enforce it selectively (which will look like bias) or not at all. The upside is that this is what Cooperstown has always done. The downside is that—in the era of YouTube, citizen bloggers, and ESPN—you can't count on hiding the truth from the public.

Then there is Option 3: drop Rule 5 and the pretense that baseball greatness is inextricably linked with good character. Make the price of admission to the Hall of Fame simple professional excellence, judged by the standards of the day.

Number 3 is the right choice. For one thing, honesty is always the best policy, especially when dishonesty is impossible to pull off. If the Hall of Fame wants to be regarded reverentially, it will first have to be taken seriously. That will require facing some uncomfortable truths about the nature of baseball, the nature of human beings, and the nature of nature.

There are baseball purists who believe that the use of steroids has altered the very essence of the game. One of the most eloquent is George F. Will, whose baseball book, *Men at Work,* is a great favorite in Cooperstown. In an influential column written in 2004, Will argued the case against PEDs on moral and historical grounds:

> *In recent decades, athletes have learned that, using nutrition, strength training and other means, it is possible to enhance performance. But not all that is possible should be permissible. Some enhancements devalue performance while improving it, because they unfairly alter the conditions of competition. Lifting weights and eating your spinach enhance the body's normal functioning. But radical and impermissible chemical intrusions into the body can jeopardize the health of the body and mind, while causing both to behave abnormally.*
>
> *. . . Professional athletes stand at an apex of achievement because they have paid a price in disciplined exertion—a manifestation of good character. They should try to perform unusually well. But not unnaturally well. Drugs that make sport exotic drain it of its exemplary power by making it a display of chemistry rather than character—actually, a display of chemistry and bad character.*

If a baseball fan from the last decade of the 19th century were placed in a ballpark in the first decade of the 21st, that fan would feel in a familiar setting. One reason baseball has such a durable hold on the country is that, as historian Bruce Catton said, it is the greatest topic of conversation America has produced. And one reason is the absence of abrupt discontinuities in the evolution of this game with its ever-richer statistical sediment. This makes possible intergenerational comparisons of players' achievements.

Until now, only one radical demarcation has disrupted the game's continuity—the divide, around 1920, between the dead ball and lively ball eras. (A short-lived tampering with the ball produced the lurid offensive numbers of 1930—nine teams batted over .300; the eight-team National League batted .304.) Now baseball's third era is ending—the era of disgracefully lively players.

I have great respect for George Will, but I think he's wrong on just about every count of his indictment of steroids in baseball, starting with the notion that current medical performance enhancement pollutes the "continuity" of the game that makes it possible to use statistics to compare players separated by generations.

Baseball stats go back to the middle of the nineteenth century. Stats can tell us, for example, that in 1877, Lipman Pike hit .298. In 2008, Derek Jeter hit .300. Does that mean that Pike and Jeter were similar hitters? In 1877, Pike led the National League in home runs—with 4. In 2008, Ryan Howard led the NL with 48. There are sports, like track or swimming, where we can objectively measure the abilities of athletes over time. But batting averages or ERAs are only comparative figures; they tell you how players did against one another at a certain time, under similar rules and conditions.

The plaques on the walls at Cooperstown put players from the Pike era on the walls next to Goose Gossage and Cal Ripken. These old-timers were great at what they did, but it wasn't much like modern baseball. Until 1883, pitchers threw underhand.

Catchers had no mitts. There was only one umpire. Sometimes a walk consisted of six balls. "You reach a point at which the players of different eras can no longer interact," says Bill James. "A team from the 1920s still has some chance to win playing 2007 baseball; a team from 2007 still would have some chance to win if they went to 1926 and had to play under the conditions of the game in 1926 . . . A team from 1897, in my view, might *never* win a game under modern rules and modern conditions, whereas a team from 2008 might hardly ever win if forced to play under the conditions of 1897."

An 1890s fan, plopped down at, say, Yankee Stadium, would feel like a Victorian ballroom dancer at a Brooklyn hip-hop club. What are the stadium lights for? How did the field get so smooth? Why are they playing the "Star Spangled Banner" (which didn't even become the national anthem until 1931)? What are the players doing with huge gloves on their hands, helmets on their heads, and body armor? How did the outfield fences get so distant? Why are there four umpires on the field? What is a "designated hitter"? And why on earth are there women in the stands, blacks on the diamond, and cars in the parking lot?*

Since the 1890s, science and technology have changed the game, too. There was no cortisone to prolong Smoky Joe Wood's career, but John Smoltz wrung another fifty wins out of his arm after undergoing Tommy John surgery. Players these days have videotapes to study, and managers use computers instead of (or along with) gut feelings. Stadium lights improve twilight visibility. Game balls are much cleaner and less scuffed than they once were. Players of the dead-ball era

* I am sympathetic to Will's longing for historical continuity. When I first started learning Hebrew, I was motivated by the conceit that, theoretically, I could carry on a conversation with King David. Once I actually *learned* modern Hebrew, though, I realized that the king and I might know the same words but we wouldn't have spoken the same language (and, anyway, I doubt we would have had much to say to one another).

didn't wear glasses, because they thought it made them look like nerds; nowadays they get LASIK surgery.*

Some experts attribute the home run explosion of the mid-nineties not to steroids but to the new "impact bats" major-leaguers are using.† Strike zones shrink and grow over time, as MLB tinkers with the balance between offense and defense. Even the field itself is a historic variable. "Jim Bunning keeps saying that he's opposed to steroids because he wants a 'level playing field,'" says Marvin Miller. "When Bunning was playing, they raised the height of the mound."

Pitchers are no longer allowed to hit batters with impunity—players are too valuable to be used for target practice. Today's American players are about an inch and a half taller than in Ruth's day. They also have a completely different attitude toward conditioning. "When I was playing [back in the 1960s], you came to spring training with a ten-pound winter beer belly on," said Jim Leyland when he was managing the Pirates. "Now players do Nautilus all winter, they play racquetball, they swim, they exercise, and they come to spring training looking like Tarzan." (One of the players he managed in Pittsburgh was an outfielder named Barry Bonds.)

One thing an 1890s fan *would* have recognized about today's game is the willingness of players to do whatever they can get away with. All those umpires are on the field now because John J. McGraw, in his playing days, tripped and pushed so many baserunners around third base that additional authority was needed to keep the peace. Decades later, Gaylord Perry threw his way into the Hall of Fame

* In 1921, George "Specs" Toporcer, a Cardinals infielder, became the Jackie Robinson of eyeglasses. The first Hall of Famers to wear them were Mel Ott, Chick Hafey, and Paul Waner. In 1971, the Braves Darrell Evans became the first major-leaguer to use contact lenses. By the end of the seventies, 20 percent of major-leaguers were artificially enhancing their vision. In 1974, even umpires won the contractual right to wear glasses to work.

† Bats are now given multiple coats of shellac. This is legal and, some experts believe, it makes today's bats more potent than the corked bats of yesteryear.

using illegal spitters. As Buck O'Neil once said, "The only reason we didn't use steroids when I was playing is because we didn't have them."

Anabolic steroids were invented in the 1930s. By the fifties, athletes used them openly to train for strength sports like weight-lifting and wrestling. Most baseball trainers believed that big muscles hurt performance, so it is possible that steroids weren't widely used in the fifties (although it would have been interesting to ask Ted Kluszewski how he got those biceps).

Gary Wadler, a professor at New York University's School of Medicine, is one of America's leading crusaders against PEDs in sports. He is also a realist. He knows chemical enhancement didn't start with Barry Bonds and Roger Clemens. "I don't know how long steroids have been in baseball," he told me, "but clearly they have been around at least since the seventies."

In 1959, pitcher Jim Brosnan kept a diary of his year with the St. Louis Cardinals and the Cincinnati Reds. *The Long Season* was the first prolonged, honest account of life inside major-league clubhouses. Jimmy Cannon, a pioneer of realistic sports writing, called it "the greatest baseball book ever written."

The Long Season is filled with drugs. "Your pills are in that little plastic bottle on the shelf," Doc Bauman, the Cards trainer, tells Brosnan in spring training. Brosnan recalls how Bauman "uncapped a bottle of Decadron and counted out a three-days' supply to Alex Grammas."*

Brosnan also mentions a friendly rival who pitched on Equanil, a tranquilizer, to keep his throwing under control. Given a rare start, he asks the trainer for some "nine-inning pills."

In August, on the way to a West Coast road trip, Brosnan sug-

* Decadron is an anti-inflammatory so strong that it is sometimes used in cancer treatment. It is commonly given to treat arthritis, and is classified as a "glucocorticosteroid." It enables players to perform better than their "natural" physical state—i.e., injuries or infirmities—would otherwise permit.

gested to a teammate, Ellis "Cot" Deal, that he ask the trainer for some Dexamyl, "to get you through the week." Dexamyl is an upper that came into commercial use in the mid-1930s and was given to American troops during World War II to increase stamina and enhance battlefield performance. Baseball players who returned from the service knew all about it. Brosnan's account of major-league drug use is completely casual (though he does make a big deal out of drinking martinis); for players, it was simply a fact of the game.

The world outside baseball learned more about the use of amphetamines (affectionately known as "greenies") in Jim Bouton's classic first-person diary *Ball Four.* Bouton was an All-Star pitcher for the New York Yankees. In 1964, aided by uppers, he led the American league in starts.

Bouton's book, set in the 1969 season, was filled with stories about girl-chasing, pill-popping ballplayers. In one scene, he describes a conversation with teammate Don Mincher about another player who had just received a supply of five hundred amphetamine pills.

"That ought to last about a month," Bouton says. He asks Mincher, who had played on several teams, how many players he thought used uppers. "Half? More?"

"Hell, a lot more than half," Mincher says. "Just about the whole Baltimore team takes them. Most of the Tigers. Most of the guys on this club. And that's just what I know for sure."

Greenies weren't banned from baseball. They weren't even classified as a Schedule Two drug until 1971. And nobody in the baseball establishment cared what players in far-off outposts like Detroit and Baltimore were doing. What rattled baseball was the stories Bouton told about his days with the New York Yankees.

Bouton revealed, among other things, that Mickey Mantle was a boozer and womanizer. This wasn't exactly a secret—Mantle later died of alcoholism—but baseball writers had covered up for him for years, attributing his frequent absences to "injuries" and dismissing his nocturnal antics as good-old-fashioned high spirits. Mantle was so offended by Bouton's breach of *omerta* that he refused to speak to him again. The Yankees declared the pitcher persona non grata and banned him from old-timer games until 1998.

In truth, Bouton went easy on the Mick. "Once," Bouton wrote, "Mantle got a vitamin shot from a quack who used an unsterile needle and almost missed a World Series with a bleeding abscess on his hip." The real story was more interesting. The quack Mantle went to was Max Jacobson, known to his celebrity clientele as "Doctor Feelgood." Jacobson, an immigrant from Germany, specialized in dispensing "vitamin injections," a home-brewed serum of thirty to fifty milligrams of amphetamine mixed with multivitamins, steroids, enzymes, and solubilized placenta, bone marrow, and animal organ cells.

Jacobson's practice was located on New York's Upper East Side, but he also did more than thirty White House calls for President Kennedy. Dr. Feelgood even went on a road trip with JFK, to the Vienna summit with Soviet Premier Nikita Khrushchev in 1961. Bobby Kennedy warned his brother that Jacobson's medicine could be dangerous; nobody knew exactly what was in it. "I don't care if it's horse piss, it works," the president told his younger brother.*

After Dr. Feelgood returned from the summit, Mickey Mantle came to see him, based on a referral by the Yankees Hall of Fame broadcaster Mel Allen. We don't know how often Jacobson shot Mantle up with his concoction, but on the one occasion Mantle got infected, it caused him to miss several games in September, putting him out of the home run record race with Roger Maris. If Jacobson's

* Kennedy blew the summit anyway, as he later ruefully admitted. PEDs are usually about as good as the guy who is using them.

needle had been clean, Mantle might have been the first to break Babe Ruth's 60 in a season—with chemical assistance.

Did other Yankees (and their out-of-town friends) visit Dr. Feelgood? It's impossible to say; nobody wrote about such things at the time. There is a hint in *Ball Four*, though: Bouton mentions that Mantle's close friend and teammate, Hall of Fame pitcher Whitey Ford, also bypassed the Yankees team physician and used outside doctors.

In 1985, a Pittsburgh grand jury uncovered widespread use of cocaine and other stimulants in Major League Baseball. The players who testified got immunity. All-Star outfielder Tim Raines of the Expos admitted that he snorted cocaine during games, kept a vial of it in his uniform pocket, and avoided sliding into bases feet-first to protect his dope. Keith Hernandez of the Mets estimated that 40 percent of major-league players were using, although he later said it was just a guess. Mets first baseman/outfielder John Milner testified under oath that Willie Mays kept a bottle of red liquid amphetamine in his locker, and said that Pirates Hall of Famer Willie Stargell was also using, accusations that both men denied.

Even Hank Aaron, the anti-Bonds, confessed in his autobiography that he scored a greenie to counter a slump. Aaron implied—but didn't actually say—that he only used once. And Bill Clinton never inhaled.

Baseball players are young men in a stressful, sometimes dangerous profession. They perform in front of millions of critics. They have short careers that can be ended by a single injury. If there are drugs that make them better (or make them *believe* they are better), heal them quicker, or allow them to work out more effectively, why shouldn't they use them?

A study conducted in 1987 found that 25 percent of the members of America's fifty-one largest classical orchestras use Inderal to fight stage fright. Trial lawyers use beta blockers for similar reasons. Millions of ordinary people take Prozac or other antidepressants to function better at work and at home. Former presidential candidate Bob Dole did commercials for Viagra, a performance enhancer if ever there was one.

Pilots and surgeons stay sharp with "cognition enhancers" like Provigil. Even scientists do: *Nature* magazine recently reported that 20 percent of its readers used Ritalin, Provigil, or some other "smart pill." "These are individuals that are actively participating in science or have a very active interest in science," said Dr. Nora Volkow, director of the U.S. National Institute on Drug Abuse. "[They] are more educated about the potential negative consequences of taking a stimulant medication. That's why it's so strikingly surprising. This highlights how prevalent the use of these medications is as potential cognitive enhancers."

Does anyone really think that baseball players are going to just say no when biochemists, trial lawyers, Broadway actors, fighter pilots, symphony conductors, and Bob Dole are using new drugs to solve old problems?

Yes, but what about testing? Why can't baseball players be *forced* to eschew PEDs by a rigid, aggressive, intrusive regime imposed by MLB? I can think of at least two reasons why this isn't going to happen. First, many baseball players are citizens. They have rights, including the right to protection against arbitrary searches. True, the Supreme Court ruled, de facto, in the Flood case in 1972 that Major League Baseball stands above the Constitution. But a lot has changed in America since then. Does baseball really want to go to court to find out how much? Baseball would lose—if it was lucky. But if it "won" and the courts agreed that a ballplayer, to earn a living, must turn in samples of his urine (and saliva and blood) on demand, what would happen then? There would be strikes, busts, suspensions, and convictions that would cast a shadow over everything else in baseball. The game would find itself drowning in its own bodily fluids. Does anyone believe that MLB—or the Hall of Fame—would be self-destructive enough to bring this on themselves?

Even more important: testing doesn't actually work. "Because advances in biotechnology have outpaced advances in laboratory science, the detection of certain drugs or biologicals is today either impractical or impossible," says Gary Wadler. "To wit, human growth hormone, erythropoietin and, most recently, IGF-1 . . . Those are some of the drugs we know. But what about those we don't know . . ."

Hein Verbruggen, head of the International Cycling Federation, has suggested that "undetectable drugs are 90 percent of estimated doping cases." In other words, most current performance-enhancing drugs cannot easily be detected. Some, like HGH, require a blood test to be found. This country doesn't permit mandatory drug testing for lethally contagious blood diseases—and it's going to impose them on baseball players?

The march of biochemical progress will continue. In testimony before Congress in the aftermath of the Mitchell Report, Don Fehr, head of the players' union, talked about what progress might well look like. "Gene doping will make what we see now look quaint. And the reason that it will make it look quaint is that if it is done right—my understanding is that people are trying to develop it so it will be done in utero and you would be penalizing someone for something—something his parents did at the time he was still being carried by his mother. That is a very serious issue. And I don't pretend to have a handle on the ethical or scientific or policy questions that relate to that. It is a very difficult issue."

"Recombinant DNA technology (genetic engineering) faces our society with problems unprecedented not only in the history of science but life on earth," said the late Nobel Prize–winning biologist George Wald. What is "natural" when a baby is born with engineered athleticism? When do we go from A-Rod to Superman?

Here's the great irony of the Hall of Fame steroids debate: *There is no proof at all that steroids, or other PEDs, improve baseball performance in a way that changes the competitive balance of the game or alters the measure of "greatness."*

I didn't say there are no anecdotes, urban legends, theories, suppositions, or accusations. I'm talking about actual empirical data. There is no evidence that anabolic steroids or other chemicals help a hitter hit or a pitcher pitch. None.

What there is is a conviction in the court of public opinion. Exhibit A—the fact that Mark McGwire and Barry Bonds hit more home runs while taking substances than they had hit previously, and more than any other players had hit in the past—is interesting but not dispositive. McGwire's 70 home runs in the 1998 season was a leap of about 9 percent over Roger Maris's total. In 1920, Babe Ruth hit 29; the previous record was 24, held by Gavvy Cravath of the Phillies—roughly twice that differential. The next year, Ruth hit 54—more than double Cravath's record. Is that proof that he was taking a chemical substance? Spitballs were outlawed in 1920 (although current spitballers were grandfathered in); and corked bats were being used. But still, that year Babe Ruth hit more homers than any other *team* except the Phillies. Sometimes transcendent performances are simply transcendent.

The argument that steroids helped Bonds and McGwire also completely misses the nature of baseball competition. In track, the contest is between the runner and other runners. In baseball, it is between a hitter and a pitcher. In other words, there are two sides to every statistic. If only one side has access to a (supposedly) magical potion, it would obviously change the balance. But what if both sides are using the same thing? Doesn't that even things out? In fact, the Mitchell Report found a higher percentage of pitchers than position players using PEDs.

Jonathan R. Cole, a professor of sociology at Columbia, and Stephen M. Stigler, a professor of statistics at the University of Chicago, analyzed the performance of the players named by the Mitchell Report. Of the twenty-three pitchers, sixteen had *higher* ERAs in the year they are suspected of first using drugs than they did the previous season. Among forty-eight hitters, home runs and batting average were actually lower in the "after" season than in the "before." Maybe this means steroid use actually hurts performance on average. But that's just speculation of course; it all is.

The authors concluded that there is "no example of a mediocre player breaking away from the middle of the pack and achieving stardom with the aid of drugs."

Some see the fact that Bonds and Clemens improved with age as proof they were getting pharmaceutical help. Asked about Bonds by the *Cincinnati Enquirer*, Frank Robinson said, "You don't get better as you get older." What person out of his teenage years can argue with that? Still, Warren Spahn pitched almost 260 innings and went 23–7 at the age of forty-two. Ted Williams hit .388 when he was thirty-eight, led the American League again the following year, and finished his career at forty-one hitting .316—with a higher on-base percentage than he had as a twenty-year-old rookie phenom. Pitcher Early Wynn went 22–10 at the age of thirty-nine. Stan Musial had a better statistical year in 1962 than he did in 1942. Nolan Ryan struck out 203 batters at forty-four. If great geriatric performance is a proof of chemical dependency, what were these guys on?

Cole and Stigler pointed out that Babe Ruth hit 198 homers in the last six years of his twenty-two-year career, 28 percent of his career total of dingers. In the last six years of *his* career, Barry Bonds hit 195, or 26 percent. "There is no convincing way," the study said, "to demonstrate that Bonds' performance owed to drugs more than Ruth's did to his prodigious use of alcohol and tobacco." Which, of course, was nothing.

It seems perverse and counterintuitive to say that steroids add *nothing* to baseball ability. If they didn't make a difference, why would players use them? Can't we see that guys like Bonds and Clemens get big and strong on steroids? "Bonds's hat size went up two and a half inches," Steve Garvey told me at Cooperstown. "That's supposed to be natural growth?"

And yet, even antisteroid experts like Gary Wadler concede that it is impossible to quantify the possible advantages provided by anabolic steroids to baseball players. He believes that these drugs increase acceleration—runners get off their mark a little faster and bat swings might be quicker. And he is pretty sure that steroids can help players, especially pitchers, come back from injuries more quickly. (Baseball has a long tradition to this kind of thing. In Tom Verducci's 1999 *Sports Illustrated* profile of Sandy Koufax, he describes the great left-hander's struggle with arthritis. Only drugs kept him going. "His elbow was shot full of cortisone several times a season," Verducci reported. "His stomach was always queasy from the cocktail of (legal) anti-inflammatories he swallowed before and after games, which he once said made him 'half-high' on the mound.") What Wadler is saying, essentially, is that anabolic steroids appear to be a therapeutic aid and they may help a player who trains with them to increase the speed of his first step or the velocity of his swing. They will not help a batter connect with a baseball, or a pitcher throw one with control and movement. Steroids *might* make a great player greater, but they will not send a mediocrity to Cooperstown. They are a factor—among many, many factors—in the changes since the 1890s. Steroids (in their present form, at least) are no more a historical "discontinuity" than the abolition of the spitball, night baseball, greenies, sabermetrics, or racial integration.

• • •

On January 20, 2004, President George W. Bush delivered his first State of the Union Address since the Iraq invasion. It was a busy time. Bush reported on the battlefronts in Iraq and Afghanistan, warned North Korea against developing nuclear weapons, and once again declared his intention to fight "the manmade evil of terrorism." But he also found room in the speech to address the scourge of steroids in baseball.

"To help children make right choices, they need good examples," the president said. "Athletics play such an important role in our society, but, unfortunately, some in professional sports are not setting much of an example. The use of performance-enhancing drugs like steroids in baseball, football, and other sports is dangerous, and it sends the wrong message—that there are shortcuts to accomplishment, and that performance is more important than character. So tonight I call on team owners, union representatives, coaches, and players to take the lead, to send the right signal, to get tough, and to get rid of steroids now."

The president's challenge was met with loud bipartisan applause. Only a few snide political commentators mentioned that when Bush had been an owner (and the managing general partner) of the Texas Rangers, he brought Jose Canseco, already a famous steroid user, to the team. (The Bush-era Rangers had five players who were subsequently mentioned in the Mitchell Report: Canseco, Juan Gonzalez, Rafael Palmeiro, Kevin Brown, and Mike Stanton.

Did George W. Bush know what was going on in his clubhouse? Canseco is certain that he did. It is a matter of speculation; Bush is not known as an especially acute observer of things he would prefer to ignore. Besides, during the 2000 presidential campaign, he brushed off questions about drugs by saying "When I was young and foolish, I was young and foolish." Bush's players were pretty young themselves, and had a lot more on the line.

• • •

Steroids are baseball's gift to politicians. Representative Tom Davis, chairman of the House Government Reform Committee, denounced steroids as a "crisis in national health," convened a nationally televised hearing, and dragged players before the committee to build the audience. These hearings led to the Mitchell Report, and the Mitchell Report led to more hearings. The congressmen got the players' autographs in private meetings off-camera, and then savaged them on television as dangerously unhealthy role models.

Soon, health officials and concerned headline writers launched a campaign, full of horror stories about athletes gone mad with 'roid rage or brought low by terrible side effects.

Anecdotal reports hardened into conventional wisdom. But there was something slightly elusive about the problem steroids actually caused. In 2007, an ESPN reporter asked Gary Wadler about the specific health hazards of anabolic steroids.

"There can be a whole panoply of side effects, even with prescribed doses. Some are visible to the naked eye and some are internal. Some are physical, others are psychological," said Wadler. "With unsupervised steroid use, wanton 'megadosing' or stacking (using a combination of steroids), the effects can be irreversible or undetected until it's too late." The ESPN.com report continues, "Also, if anabolic steroids are injected, transmitting or contracting HIV or Hepatitis B through shared needle use is a very real concern."

Wadler added that, "unlike almost all other drugs, all steroid-based hormones have one unique characteristic—their dangers may not be manifest for months, years, even decades. Therefore, long after you gave them up you may develop side effects."

Well, yes. You get sick from shooting steroids with a dirty needle. You shouldn't take medication without supervision. Overdoses are a mistake. Medicine you take today could prove to be deleterious decades from now. (So might food. I belong to a generation raised on the belief that lots of eggs and butter are good for you.)

As for effects that can actually be observed, Wadler mentioned reduced sperm count, impotence, development of breasts, shrinking of the testicles, and difficulty or pain while urinating. These are undoubtedly unpleasant. Still, it is not hard to imagine a pro baseball player deciding that temporarily shrunken testes and low sperm counts are a price worth paying for a big-league life and big-league money. I personally wouldn't make that choice for a million dollars. But for ten?

In April 2008, the government escalated the war on steroids. In an interview in *US News and World Report*, Barry Hoffer, the director of the National Institute on Drug Abuse's Intramural Division, was asked if steroids are really bad physically.

"Yes, they are," he replied. "In fact, many professional athletes who have taken steroids to enhance their performance have died from heart failure, liver failure and cancers like lymphomas. Teenagers who abuse anabolic steroids might never grow as tall as they would have, and may experience emotional problems and suicidal thoughts."

I called the National Institute on Drug Abuse and asked for details. Spokeswoman Jan Lipkin responded by saying that the NIDA does not have a list of athletes killed by steroids and neither does Dr. Hoffer. She suggested contacting Professor Linn Goldberg at the University of Oregon—like Gary Wadler, an internationally famed expert on sports and steroids.

Goldberg sent me a list of deceased weightlifters and wrestlers who took anabolic steroids, but he cautioned that there were too many variables to determine the cause of death. No baseball players were on the list. "What scientific tests have been conducted that demonstrate that steroids, used in the way baseball players are alleged to use them, cause death or permanent injury?" I asked.

Dr. Goldberg's reply surprised me. "Who knows how baseball players use steroids? I don't. No one has done a study on the way baseball players use steroids. It is all by allegation, and there is really only one person"—Jose Canseco—"who described the way he took steroids. You can't do 'scientific tests' on a population one is not studying, and not subjecting themselves to tests. You have to have willing subjects to perform tests and subjects that describe use patterns (dose/duration/frequency); family history; medical and surgical history; drug and alcohol use history; medication history. Without that, you can't draw much of a conclusion."

Let's recap the conclusions you can draw.

We know that there is no scientific evidence that anabolic steroids, as they are currently used, are physically dangerous to adult male athletes, including baseball players.

We know that steroids can help a player get bigger and stronger and quicker by increasing his workout capacity, and they can probably help injured players heal faster. But we do not know if steroids have a quantifiable influence on baseball performance skills or, if they do, what the effect is. If Bonds faces Clemens, who has the advantage? If a steroid-using shortstop gets to a ball quicker on a grounder that's hit by a steroid-using batter, who is helped more by the drug? Where is the unfair advantage if everyone is using the same enhancements? How, for that matter, are comparative statistics affected?

We know that there have been so many changes in baseball since the days of Lipman Pike or even Ty Cobb that one-to-one statistical comparisons with today's players are sheer fantasy (although they gain some meaning when we know about, and can weigh, all the variables). We know that greatness is *measurable* (if at all) only by contrast to other players within a similar era.

We also know that baseball players have always used whatever they could find—cork, cocaine, saliva, emery boards, uppers, downers, booze, steroids—to gain a competitive advantage, real or imagined. We know that today's players are no different.

We know that biochemistry is a fact of life, and that there is no likely way that sophisticated drug use can be detected; we also know that today's fans live in the same culture as players. Do a blood test in the bleachers (or the press box) and you will find everything from Ritalin and Prozac to Vitamin B and Viagra.

And we know that modern media technology makes it impossible to keep secret the things we now know (and suspect) about performance-enhancing drugs and baseball.

Some people fear that baseball players who use steroids will become role models for kids, and this isn't easily dismissed. There is some evidence that anabolic steroids can be harmful to adolescent males (and to women of any age). And some kids do idolize baseball players. A few even hope to get to the majors themselves.

Kids aren't dumb. They know, for example, that ballplayers drink alcohol (and if they don't know it, they can read about major-league DUI's on the Internet). Does that inspire them to drink? Maybe it does. But the alternative is to reinstate Prohibition for adult baseball players.

Honesty, not fake purity, is what baseball players should be displaying to young fans. Right now, every player is a suspected cheater. Legalize the use of PEDs, and that cloud goes away. The players should be open about what they are doing to improve their performance—list the substances on baseball cards along with the training regime and diet. Fans will then know what they are watching. If MLB makes sure that steroids are prescribed and administered safely, by team doctors, the message will be: chemistry can be helpful, but only when it is used carefully, responsibly, and legally. There needs to be realistic steroid education in schools, especially for athletes. Telling a kid who dreams of getting rich playing baseball to "just say no" to anabolic steroids is about as productive and realistic as keeping birth control out of the hands of horny teenagers.

For many of the strongest opponents of steroids in baseball, practical issues are beside the point. "A society's recreation is charged with moral significance," George F. Will writes. "Sport—and a society that takes it seriously—would be debased if it did not strictly forbid things that blur the distinction between the triumph of character and the triumph of chemistry."

Will assumes that baseball players once existed in a pure state, and that chemicals disturb the game's natural order. This is a profoundly backward-looking view, akin to the critics of the Wright Brothers who said that if God had wanted man to fly, he would have given us wings.

I doubt very much that there was ever an ancient time when baseball players conformed to some Platonic ideal of virtue. Plato himself was not only a philosopher but a wrestler. The name "Plato" (which means "broad") was actually bestowed on him by his wrestling coach. Some historians say he competed at the Isthmian Games. If so, I bet he took the same potions the other guys were using.

George Will's belief in a baseball Atlantis, lost in the mists of time, is moralistic. He is a Luddite. (I say this with empathy; I myself believe that rock 'n' roll died the day the Beatles stepped off the plane in New York in 1963.) "It still is unclear if there will be judicially imposed punishment in [the case of Barry Bonds]," he wrote in 2006. "But condign punishment for a man as proud as Bonds would be administered by the court of public opinion and by exclusion from the Hall of Fame."

George Will is a great favorite at the Hall of Fame, and what he suggests—withholding immortality from steroid users—will tempt the Cooperstown establishment. From its first embrace of the

Abner Doubleday myth to the snubbing of Marvin Miller, the Hall's instinct has been reactionary. Cooperstown generally lags a generation or so behind the norms of American society. It experiences social changes as a series of rude shocks. It integrated fifteen years after the rest of baseball. (I know, Jackie Robinson didn't become eligible until 1962. But the Hall knows how to make exceptions when it wants to.) Almost a third of the players in the majors are Latinos, but at the end of 2008 there was still no Hispanic exhibit.

When the Hall *does* wake up, it tends to lurch wildly in the direction of what it sees as progress. The mass induction of Negro-leagues players, most of whom were unknown and unknowable (while leaving Buck O'Neil out), is an example. So was the bizarre partnership with Hugo Chavez on "¡Béisbol Baseball!" It's not that the Hall doesn't mean well; it simply works on a different calendar than the rest of the world. In the summer of 2008, as Barack Obama was on the verge of becoming America's first black president, Cooperstown was still fussing around trying to get the wording of Jackie Robinson's plaque right.

Barack Obama is America's first basketball president, a high-school hoopster who still plays recreation-league ball. On the day after the election, he relaxed on his home court in a Chicago gym. He replaces George W. Bush, retired Little League catcher and the only American chief executive whose signature—on the owner's line of Nolan Ryan's Texas Ranger contract—rests in the Hall of Fame.

On the eve of the presidential election, Obama and John McCain were interviewed on *Monday Night Football.* Host Chris Berman asked them what single thing they would change in sports. Obama talked about fixing the college bowl system. McCain gave a sermonette about steroids. "I'd take significant action to prevent the spread and use of performance-enhancing substances," he said. "I think it's a game we're going to be in for a long time. What I mean by that is there is somebody in a laboratory right now trying to develop some type of substance that can't be detected and we've got to stay ahead of it. It's not good for the athletes. It's not good for the sports. It's very bad for those who don't do it, and I think it can attack the very integrity of all sports."

The interview made McCain sound old (which he is), pompous (which he usually is not), and as out-of-touch as a candidate from the 1950s raving about reefer madness. The election of Obama demonstrated that a majority of Americans are now comfortable with a black man in the White House—and my guess is they will be equally okay with Barry Bonds and Roger Clemens in Cooperstown. Young people these days are used to sports realism and applied biochemistry and are unlikely to see steroids as a Satanic device. On the other hand, if the Hall of Fame decides to exclude the greatest players in baseball because a bunch of baseball writers—in conformity to Clark family values—think they lack character, Cooperstown will become about as relevant and as interesting as Colonial Williamsburg.

ELEVEN . . . *A Few Closing Thoughts*

The great sportswriter Red Smith once suggested blowing up the Hall of Fame and starting over. Smith didn't normally advocate the violent overthrow of sports museums, but the Hall is special. If the Pro Football Hall of Fame disappeared tomorrow, nobody except the Canton city council would notice. Sure, Cooperstown is a baseball museum. But it is also an ideal, the shrine of the American pastime and standard-bearer for a historical narrative and set of values that influence succeeding generations.

Guys like Red Smith and Bill James and other critics of Cooperstown usually focus on the baseball side of the Hall, especially the arbitrary nature of the selection process and the very uneven results. Many ask, how can Babe Ruth and Bill Mazeroski both be HoFers? This problem is inherent in institutionally conferred immortality. There were greater and lesser gods on Mount Olympus, too.

Some critics have suggested establishing an inner sanctum of the fifty greatest of the greats. I thought this would be a good corrective until I realized that it could very well exclude Hank Greenberg. If there is a heaven, I don't want to explain someday to Uncle Pinchus why I advocated giving Hammering Hank the heave-ho. I imagine other fans feel the same about their heroes. Better to let sleeping plaques hang. Let's concentrate on the future.

The Hall of Fame is theoretically independent of MLB, but it has surrendered a lot of autonomy over the years. The worst example is the Pete Rose Rule: "Any person designated by the Office of the Commissioner of Baseball as ineligible shall not be an eligible candidate." That's like saying that the Pope can confer sainthood subject to the approval of the directors of the Vatican Bank.

The Hall itself should get out of the moral-judgment game by repealing the Character Clause. Nothing drains an institution's integrity like fake claims of integrity. Honesty clears the way for judging players solely on their professional excellence, meaning that Bonds, Clemens, and the other "steroid boys"—and there will be more—go in. Keeping them out is the surest way to transform Cooperstown from a vital and relevant institution into a joke.

Most of the great scandals in Hall of Fame history have come about because of the Veterans Committee, which, in various permutations, has been either too generous or too stingy.

The stars of the pre-video age have all been discovered. Today's players are highly visible, and fifteen years of postretirement evaluation should be more than enough. I think they should convene the Veterans Committee one more time, induct the top ten veteran vote-getters (my ballot is marked for Rose, Dick Allen, Ron Santo, Curt Flood, Steve Garvey, Mickey Lolich, Harvey Kuenn, Minnie Minoso, Luis Tiant, and Joe Jackson), and then shut the committee down permanently.

The electoral college has to change, too. "Baseball writer for a daily newspaper" is an occupational category as antiquated as "telex operator" or Western Union delivery boy. And the membership of the BBWAA is about as diverse and culturally attuned as the Pontiac Elks Club bowling league, circa 1959. The writers should still have a vote, but not a monopoly. How about giving a vote to every living major- and minor-league player or manager, members of SABR, radio and TV sportscasters, proprietors of the most-visited baseball Web sites, and any regular fan who can pass a baseball SAT exam devised and administered by the monks of Cooperstown? (Test-takers would be encouraged to chemically enhance their performance).

The Hall of Fame was born looking backward into the mists of American history. Thomas Jefferson and John Adams were still alive when Abner Doubleday, whose supposed creation the Hall commemorated, was born. Judge Kenesaw Mountain Landis and Stephen Clark were creatures of the Victorian, Protestant, small-town America of the nineteenth century. All five of the first inductees were born before the year 1900; Ty Cobb, in Sam Crawford's recollection, reached Detroit still fighting the Civil War. When Cooperstown opened its doors, the country was less than two years from World War II.

Today's Hall of Fame is almost as distant in time from 1939 as 1939 was from the presidency of Abraham Lincoln. Lincoln couldn't have imagined what the country would become in seven decades after his death; or how baseball, a game he loved, would change. What would Honest Abe have made of Babe Ruth? Or fielders with mitts? Or night games broadcast on the radio?

America and baseball have changed at least that much since 1939. The men who gathered at Cooperstown would be astonished to see a black man in a major-league dugout, much less the White House. .235 hitters with million-dollar contracts? Games from Japan broadcast by satellite? Baseball players endorsing Viagra and posing for underwear ads?

Time moves on, even in Cooperstown. America is a better place than it was in 1839, or 1939. Baseball is a better game, too; fairer to its players, more accessible to its fans, and, nostalgia aside, played at a higher level of excellence. Does anyone really believe that the 1927 Yankees would win a World Series today? Sure, and the 1939 Chicago Bears would win the Super Bowl. And so what? The stars of the future will be even bigger, stronger, smarter, faster, and better coached. That is what's called progress, and nothing—certainly not a sport that wants to hold the imagination of fans—can flourish without it.

The one thing that is not likely to change much is human nature.

The guys on the plaques in Cooperstown are a mixed bag, heroes and scoundrels just like the rest of humanity. The players who arrive in the future won't be any different. The Hall of Fame doesn't enshrine saints, and it never has. It enshrines baseball greatness. And for millions of people who love the game, that's more than enough.

Acknowledgments

Many people helped me with this book. I am especially grateful to Bill James, who was inexplicably generous with his time; Marvin Miller, Robert Lipsyte, Daniel Okrent, George Cantor, Marty Appel, Tim Gay, Gene Orza, Joe Dimino, and Danny Sheridan.

Richard Lapchick, Richard Ben Cramer, John T. Bird, Leigh Montville, Dave Parker, Steve Garvey, Mickey Lolich, George Brett, Maury Brown, Gary Gillette, Goose Gossage, Andrew Levy, Dr. Linn Goldberg and Dr. Gary Wadler, and Dan Rosenheck.

Thanks to the Hall of Fame staff, led by the always helpful Jeff Idelson, curator Ted Spencer, Brad Horn, Jim Gates, Gabriel Schechter, Freddy Berowski, and Tim Wiles. Special thanks to Dale Petrosky.

I am indebted to Skip McAfee, a member of the SABR Bibliography Committee, for a fine-tooth-combing of the manuscript, and for preparing the index as part of the SABR Bibliography Committee's tasks to provide indexes for baseball books; and to Luca Marzorati, one of SABR's youngest members, for his sharp fact-checking and comments. Naturally I alone am responsible for any errors in fact or interpretation.

I am indebted to Steve Verkman, founder of Clean Sweep Auctions, for educating me about the memorabilia business, and for letting us photograph some of his treasures to illustrate this book.

Thanks, as always, to my agent, Flip Brophy. She's the best.

Finally, I want to thank my editor, Nick Trautwein. This book is a tribute to his enthusiasm, his energy, his unerring editorial judgment, his willingness to roll up his sleeves—and his friendship. My name is on the cover, but he has been my partner and collaborator all the way.

Appendix 1: Rules for Election

1. **Authorization:** By authorization of the Board of Directors of the National Baseball Hall of Fame and Museum, Inc., the Baseball Writers' Association of America (BBWAA) is authorized to hold an election every year for the purpose of electing members to the National Baseball Hall of Fame from the ranks of retired baseball players.

2. **Electors:** Only active and honorary members of the Baseball Writers' Association of America, who have been active baseball writers for at least ten (10) years, shall be eligible to vote. They must have been active as baseball writers and members of the Association for a period beginning at least ten (10) years prior to the date of election in which they are voting.

3. **Eligible Candidates—Candidates to be eligible must meet the following requirements:**

A. A baseball player must have been active as a player in the Major Leagues at some time during a period beginning twenty (20) years before and ending five (5) years prior to election.

B. Player must have played in each of ten (10) Major League championship seasons, some part of which must have been within the period described in 3 (A).

C. Player shall have ceased to be an active player in the Major Leagues at least five (5) calendar years preceding the election but may be otherwise connected with baseball.

D. In case of the death of an active player or a player who has been retired for less than five (5) full years, a candidate who is otherwise eligible shall be eligible in the next regular election held at least six (6) months after the date of death or after the end of the five (5) year period, whichever occurs first.

E. Any player on Baseball's ineligible list shall not be an eligible candidate.

4. **Method of Election:**

A. BBWAA Screening Committee—A Screening Committee consisting of baseball writers will be appointed by the BBWAA. This Screening Committee shall consist of six members, with two members to be elected at each Annual Meeting for a three-year term. The duty of the Screening Committee shall be to prepare a ballot listing in alphabetical order eligible candidates who (1) received a vote on a minimum of five percent (5%) of the ballots cast in the preceding election or (2) are eligible for the first time and are nominated by any two of the six members of the BBWAA Screening Committee.

B. Electors may vote for as few as zero (0) and as many as ten (10) eligible candidates deemed worthy of election. Write-in votes are not permitted.

C. Any candidate receiving votes on seventy-five percent (75%) of the ballots cast shall be elected to membership in the National Baseball Hall of Fame.

5. **Voting:** Voting shall be based upon the player's record, playing ability, integrity, sportsmanship, character, and contributions to the team(s) on which the player played.

6. **Automatic Elections:** No automatic elections based on performances such as a batting average of .400 or more for one (1) year, pitching a perfect game or similar outstanding achievement shall be permitted.

7. **Time of Election:** The duly authorized representatives of the BBWAA shall prepare, date and mail ballots to each elector no later

than the 15th day of January in each year in which an election is held. The elector shall sign and return the completed ballot within twenty (20) days. The vote shall then be tabulated by the duly authorized representatives of the BBWAA.

8. **Certification of Election Results:** The results of the election shall be certified by a representative of the Baseball Writers' Association of America and an officer of the National Baseball Hall of Fame and Museum, Inc. The results shall be transmitted to the Commissioner of Baseball. The BBWAA and National Baseball Hall of Fame and Museum, Inc. shall jointly release the results for publication.

9. **Amendments:** The Board of Directors of the National Baseball Hall of Fame and Museum, Inc. reserves the right to revoke, alter or amend these rules at any time.

Appendix 2: Hall of Fame Members

Year Inducted	Name	Position	Years Played	Percent of HoF Votes
1936	Ty Cobb	CF	1905–1928	98.23%
	Walter Johnson	P	1907–1927	83.63%
	Christy Mathewson	P	1900–1916	90.71%
	Babe Ruth	RF-P	1914–1935	95.13%
	Honus Wagner	SS	1897–1917	95.13%
1937	Morgan Bulkeley	Executive	1874–1876	†
	Ban Johnson	Executive	1900–1927	†
	Nap Lajoie	2B	1896–1916	83.58%
	Connie Mack	Mgr	1894–1950	†
	John McGraw	Mgr-3B	1899, 1901–1932	†
	Tris Speaker	CF	1907–1928	82.09%
	George Wright	Pioneer	1867–1882	†
	Cy Young	P	1890–1911	76.12%
1938	Grover Cleveland Alexander	P	1911–1929	80.92%
	Alexander Cartwright	Pioneer		†
	Henry Chadwick	Pioneer		†
1939	Cap Anson	1B	1871–1897	†
	Eddie Collins	2B	1906–1930	77.74%
	Charles Comiskey	Mgr-Executive	1900–1931	†
	Candy Cummings	Pioneer		†
	Buck Ewing	C	1880–1897	†
	Lou Gehrig	1B	1923–1939	
	Willie Keeler	RF	1892–1910	75.55%
	Charles Radbourn	P	1881–1891	†

† Percentage unavailable for players selected by the Veterans Committee prior to 2001.

Year Inducted	Name	Position	Years Played	Percent of HoF Votes
	George Sisler	1B	1915–1922, 1928–1930	85.77%
	Albert Spalding	P-Executive	1871–1878	†
1940–1941	No elections			
1942	Rogers Hornsby	2B	1915–1937	78.11%
1943	No election			
1944	Kenesaw Mountain Landis	Executive	1920–1944	†
1945	Roger Bresnahan	C	1897, 1900–1915	†
	Dan Brouthers	1B	1879–1896, 1904	†
	Fred Clarke	LF-Mgr	1894–1915	†
	Jimmy Collins	3B	1895–1908	†
	Ed Delahanty	LF	1888–1903	†
	Hugh Duffy	CF	1888–1906	†
	Hughie Jennings	SS-Mgr	1891–1918	†
	King Kelly	RF-C	1878–1893	†
	Jim O'Rourke	LF	1872–1904	†
	Wilbert Robinson	C-Mgr	1902, 1914–1931	†
1946	Jesse Burkett	LF	1890–1905	†
	Frank Chance	1B-Mgr	1898–1914	†
	Jack Chesbro	P	1899–1909	†
	Johnny Evers	2B	1902–1917, 1917, 1922	†
	Clark Griffith	P-Executive	1891–1914	†
	Tommy McCarthy	RF	1884–1896	†
	Joe McGinnity	P	1899–1908	†
	Eddie Plank	P	1901–1917	†
	Joe Tinker	SS	1902–1916	†
	Rube Waddell	P	1897, 1899–1910	†
	Ed Walsh	P	1904–1917	†
1947	Mickey Cochrane	C	1925–1937	79.5%
	Frankie Frisch	2B	1919–1937	84.47%
	Lefty Grove	P	1925–1941	76.4%
	Carl Hubbell	P	1928–1943	86.96%
1948	Herb Pennock	P	1912–1934	77.69%
	Pie Traynor	3B	1920–1935, 1937	76.86%
1949	Mordecai Brown	P	1903–1916	†
	Charlie Gehringer	2B	1924–1942	85.03%
	Kid Nichols	P	1890–1901, 1904–1906	†

Year Inducted	Name	Position	Years Played	Percent of HoF Votes
1950	None elected			
1951	Jimmie Foxx	1B	1925–1942, 1944–1945	79.2%
	Mel Ott	RF	1926–1947	87.17%
1952	Harry Heilmann	RF	1914, 1916–1931	86.75%
	Paul Waner	RF	1926–1940	83.33%
1953	Ed Barrow	Executive	1921–1945	†
	Chief Bender	P	1903–1917, 1925	†
	Tommy Connolly	Umpire	1898–1931	†
	Dizzy Dean	P	1930, 1932–1941, 1947	79.17%
	Bill Klem	Umpire	1905–1941	†
	Al Simmons	LF	1924–1941, 1943–1944	75.38%
	Bobby Wallace	SS	1894–1918	†
	Harry Wright	Mgr-Pioneer	1871–1893	†
1954	Bill Dickey	C	1928–1943, 1946	80.16%
	Rabbit Maranville	SS	1912–1933, 1935	82.94%
	Bill Terry	1B	1923–1936	77.38%
1955	Home Run Baker	3B	1908–1914, 1916–1919, 1921–1922	†
	Joe DiMaggio	CF	1936–1942, 1946–1951	88.84%
	Gabby Hartnett	C	1922–1941	77.69%
	Ted Lyons	P	1923–1942, 1946	86.45%
	Ray Schalk	C	1912–1929	†
	Dazzy Vance	P	1915, 1918, 1922–1935	81.67%
1956	Joe Cronin	SS	1926–1945	78.76%
	Hank Greenberg	1B	1930, 1933–1941, 1945–1947	84.97%
1957	Sam Crawford	RF	1899–1917	†
	Joe McCarthy	Mgr	1926–1946, 1948–1950	†
1958	None elected			
1959	Zack Wheat	LF	1909–1927	†
1960	None elected			
1961	Max Carey	CF	1910–1929	†

Year Inducted	Name	Position	Years Played	Percent of HoF Votes
	Billy Hamilton	CF	1888–1901	†
1962	Bob Feller	P	1936–1941, 1945–1956	93.75%
	Bill McKechnie	Mgr	1915, 1922–1926, 1928–1946	†
	Jackie Robinson	2B	1945, 1947–1956	77.5%
	Edd Roush	CF	1913–1929, 1931	†
1963	John Clarkson	P	1882, 1884–1894	†
	Elmer Flick	RF	1898–1910	†
	Sam Rice	RF	1915–1934	†
	Eppa Rixey	P	1912–1917, 1919–1933	†
1964	Luke Appling	SS	1930–1943, 1945–1950	84%
	Red Faber	P	1914–1933	†
	Burleigh Grimes	P	1916–1934	†
	Miller Huggins	2B-Mgr	1913–1929	†
	Tim Keefe	P	1880–1893	†
	Heinie Manush	LF	1923–1939	†
	John Montgomery Ward	P-SS	1878–1894	†
1965	Pud Galvin	P	1875, 1879–1892	†
1966	Casey Stengel	Mgr	1934–1936, 1938–1943, 1946–1960, 1962–1965	†
	Ted Williams	LF	1939–1942, 1946–1960	93.38%
1967	Branch Rickey	Executive	1925–1955	†
	Red Ruffing	P	1924–1942, 1945–1947	86.93%
	Lloyd Waner	CF	1927–1942, 1944–1945	†
1968	Kiki Cuyler	RF	1921–1938	†
	Goose Goslin	LF	1921–1938	†
	Joe Medwick	LF	1932–1948	84.81%
1969	Roy Campanella	C	1948–1957	79.41%
	Stan Coveleski	P	1912, 1916–1928	†
	Waite Hoyt	P	1918–1938	†
	Stan Musial	LF-1B	1941–1944, 1946–1963	93.24%

Year Inducted	Name	Position	Years Played	Percent of HoF Votes
1970	Lou Boudreau	SS	1938–1952	77.33%
	Earle Combs	CF	1924–1935	†
	Ford Frick	Executive	1934–1951, 1951–1965	†
	Jesse Haines	P	1918, 1920–1937	†
1971	Dave Bancroft	SS	1915–1930	†
	Jake Beckley	1B	1888–1907	†
	Chick Hafey	LF	1924–1935, 1937	†
	Harry Hooper	RF	1909–1925	†
	Joe Kelley	LF	1891–1906, 1908	†
	Rube Marquard	P	1908–1925	†
	Satchel Paige	P	1927–1953, 1955, 1965	‡
	George Weiss	Executive	1947–1966	†
1972	Yogi Berra	C	1946–1963, 1965	85.61%
	Josh Gibson	C	1930–1946	‡
	Lefty Gomez	P	1930–1943	†
	Will Harridge	Executive	1909–1925	†
	Sandy Koufax	P	1955–1966	86.87%
	Buck Leonard	1B	1933–1950	‡
	Early Wynn	P	1939–1945, 1946–1962	76.01%
	Ross Youngs	RF	1917–1926	†
1973	Roberto Clemente	RF	1955–1972	92.69%
	Billy Evans	Umpire	1906–1927	†
	Monte Irvin	LF	1937–1942, 1945–1956	‡
	George Kelly	1B	1915–1917, 1919–1930, 1932	†
	Warren Spahn	P	1942, 1946–1965	82.89%
	Mickey Welch	P	1880–1892	†
1974	Cool Papa Bell	CF	1922–1938, 1942, 1947–1950	‡
	Jim Bottomley	1B	1922–1937	†
	Jocko Conlan	Umpire	1941–1965	82.89%
	Whitey Ford	P	1950, 1953–1967	77.81%
	Mickey Mantle	CF	1951–1968	88.22%
	Sam Thompson	RF	1885–1898, 1908	†

‡ Percentage unavailable for players selected by the Negro Leagues Committee or committee on African-American Baseball.

Year Inducted	Name	Position	Years Played	Percent of HoF Votes
1975	Earl Averill	CF	1930–1941	†
	Bucky Harris	Mgr	1924–1943, 1947–1948, 1950–1956	†
	Billy Herman	2B	1931–1943, 1946–1947	†
	Judy Johnson	3B	1918–1937	‡
	Ralph Kiner	LF	1946–1955	75.41%
1976	Oscar Charleston	CF	1915–1950, 1954	‡
	Roger Connor	1B	1880–1897	†
	Cal Hubbard	Umpire	1936–1951	†
	Bob Lemon	P	1946–1958	78.61%
	Freddie Lindstrom	3B	1924–1935	75.41%
	Robin Roberts	P	1948–1966	86.86%
1977	Ernie Banks	SS-1B	1953–1971	83.81%
	Martín Dihigo	P-2B	1923–1931, 1935–1936, 1945	‡
	John Henry "Pop" Lloyd	SS	1906–1932	‡
	Al Lopez	C-Mgr	1951–1965, 1968–1969	†
	Amos Rusie	P	1889–1895, 1897–1898, 1901	†
	Joe Sewell	SS	1920–1933	†
1978	Addie Joss	P	1902–1910	†
	Larry MacPhail	Executive	1933–1942, 1945–1947	†
	Eddie Mathews	3B	1952–1968	79.42%
1979	Warren Giles	Executive	1937–1951, 1951–1969	†
	Willie Mays	CF	1948–1973	94.68%
	Hack Wilson	CF	1923–1934	†
1980	Al Kaline	RF	1953–1974	88.31%
	Chuck Klein	CF	1928–1944	†
	Duke Snider	CF	1947–1964	86.49%
	Tom Yawkey	Executive	1933–1976	†
1981	Rube Foster	P-Mgr	1902–1926	†
	Bob Gibson	P	1959–1975	84.04%
	Johnny Mize	1B	1936–1942, 1946–1953	†

Year Inducted	Name	Position	Years Played	Percent of HoF Votes
1982	Hank Aaron	RF	1952, 1954–1976	97.83%
	Albert "Happy" Chandler	Executive	1945–1951	†
	Travis Jackson	SS	1922–1936	†
	Frank Robinson	RF	1956–1976	89.16%
1983	Walter Alston	Mgr	1954–1976	†
	George Kell	3B	1943–1957	†
	Juan Marichal	P	1960–1975	83.69%
	Brooks Robinson	3B	1955–1977	91.98%
1984	Luis Aparicio	SS	1956–1973	84.62%
	Don Drysdale	P	1956–1969	78.41%
	Rick Ferrell	C	1929–1945, 1947	†
	Harmon Killebrew	1B-3B	1954–1975	83.13%
	Pee Wee Reese	SS	1940–1942, 1946–1958	†
1985	Lou Brock	LF	1961–1979	79.75%
	Enos Slaughter	RF	1938–1959	†
	Arky Vaughan	SS	1932–1943, 1947–1948	†
	Hoyt Wilhelm	P	1952–1972	83.8%
1986	Bobby Doerr	2B	1937–1944, 1946–1951	†
	Ernie Lombardi	C	1931–1947	†
	Willie McCovey	1B	1959–1980	81.41%
1987	Ray Dandridge	3B	1933–1939, 1942, 1944, 1949	†
	Catfish Hunter	P	1965–1979	76.27%
	Billy Williams	LF	1959–1976	85.71%
1988	Willie Stargell	LF	1962–1982	82.44%
1989	Al Barlick	Umpire	1940–1943, 1946–1955, 1958–1971	†
	Johnny Bench	C	1967–1983	96.42%
	Red Schoendienst	2B	1945–1963	†
	Carl Yastrzemski	LF-1B	1961–1983	94.63%
1990	Joe Morgan	2B	1963–1984	81.76%
	Jim Palmer	P	1965–1984	92.57%
1991	Rod Carew	2B-1B	1967–1985	90.52%
	Ferguson Jenkins	P	1965–1983	75.4%
	Tony Lazzeri	2B	1926–1939	†

Year Inducted	Name	Position	Years Played	Percent of HoF Votes
1991	Gaylord Perry	P	1962–1983	77.2%
	Bill Veeck	Executive	1946–1949, 1951–1953, 1959–1961, 1975–1980	†
1992	Rollie Fingers	P	1968–1982, 1984–1985	81.16%
	Bill McGowan	Umpire	1925–1954	†
	Hal Newhouser	P	1939–1955	†
	Tom Seaver	P	1967–1986	98.84%
1993	Reggie Jackson	RF	1967–1987	93.62%
1994	Steve Carlton	P	1965–1988	95.82%
	Leo Durocher	Mgr	1939–1946, 1948–1955, 1966–1973	†
	Phil Rizzuto	SS	1941–1942, 1946–1956	†
1995	Richie Ashburn	CF	1948–1962	†
	Leon Day	P	1934–1939, 1941–1943, 1946, 1949–1950	†
	William Hulbert	Executive	1876–1882	†
	Mike Schmidt	3B	1972–1989	96.52%
	Vic Willis	P	1898–1910	†
1996	Jim Bunning	P	1955–1971	†
	Bill Foster	P	1923–1938	†
	Ned Hanlon	Mgr	1889–1890, 1892–1907	†
	Earl Weaver	Mgr	1968–1982, 1985–1986	†
1997	Nellie Fox	2B	1947–1965	†
	Tommy Lasorda	Mgr	1976–1996	†
	Phil Niekro	P	1964–1987	80.34%
	Willie Wells	SS	1923, 1924–1936, 1942, 1944–1948	†
1998	George Davis	SS	1890–1909	†
	Larry Doby	CF	1942–1943, 1946–1959	†
	Lee MacPhail	Executive	1958–1984	†

Year Inducted	Name	Position	Years Played	Percent of HoF Votes
1998	Bullet Rogan	P	1917, 1920–1938	†
	Don Sutton	P	1966–1988	81.6%
1999	George Brett	3B	1973–1993	98.19%
	Orlando Cepeda	1B	1958–1974	†
	Nestor Chylak	Umpire	1954–1978	†
	Nolan Ryan	P	1966, 1968–1993	98.79%
	Frank Selee	Mgr	1890, 1892–1905	†
	Smokey Joe Williams	P	1910–1932	†
	Robin Yount	SS-CF	1974–1993	77.46%
2000	Sparky Anderson	Mgr	1970–1995	†
	Carlton Fisk	C	1969, 1971–1993	79.56%
	Bid McPhee	2B	1882–1899	†
	Tony Pérez	1B	1964–1986	77.15%
	Turkey Stearnes	CF	1920–1942, 1945	†
2001	Bill Mazeroski	2B	1956–1972	†
	Kirby Puckett	CF	1984–1995	82.14%
	Hilton Smith	P	1932–1948	†
	Dave Winfield	RF	1973–1988, 1990–1995	84.47%
2002	Ozzie Smith	SS	1978–1996	91.74%
2003	Gary Carter	C	1974–1992	78.02%
	Eddie Murray	1B	1977–1997	85.28%
2004	Dennis Eckersley	P	1975–1998	83.2%
	Paul Molitor	DH-3B	1978–1998	85.2%
2005	Wade Boggs	3B	1982–1999	91.86%
	Ryne Sandberg	2B	1981–1994, 1996–1997	76.16%
2006	Ray Brown	P	1931–1945	‡
	Willard Brown	RF	1935–1950	‡
	Andy Cooper	P	1920–1941	‡
	Frank Grant	2B	1886–1903	‡
	Pete Hill	LF	1899–1926	‡
	Biz Mackey	C	1920–1947	‡
	Effa Manley	Executive	1935–1948	‡
	José Méndez	P	1908–1926	‡
	Alex Pompez	Executive	1916–1950	‡
	Cumberland Posey	Executive	1920–1946	‡
	Louis Santop	C	1909–1926	‡
	Bruce Sutter	P	1976–1988	76.9%

Year Inducted	Name	Position	Years Played	Percent of HoF Votes
2006	Mule Suttles	1B - LF	1921, 1923–1944	‡
	Ben Taylor	1B	1908–1929	‡
	Cristóbal Torriente	CF	1913–1928	‡
	Sol White	Pioneer		‡
	J.L. Wilkinson	Executive	1912–1948	‡
	Jud Wilson	3B - 1B	1922–1945	‡
2007	Tony Gwynn	RF	1982–2001	97.61%
	Cal Ripken, Jr.	SS	1981–2001	98.53%
2008	Barney Dreyfuss	Executive	1899–1932	83.33%
	Rich "Goose" Gossage	P	1972–1989, 1991–1994	85.82%
	Bowie Kuhn	Executive	1969–1984	83.33%
	Walter O'Malley	Executive	1950–1979	75.00%
	Billy Southworth	Mgr	1929, 1940–1951	81.25%
	Dick Williams	Mgr	1967–1969, 1971–1988	81.25%
2009	Joe Gordon	2B	1938–1950	83.33%
	Rickey Henderson	LF	1979–2003	94.81%
	Jim Rice	LF	1974–1989	76.44%

Appendix 3: The Honor Rolls of Baseball

Writers:

Walter Barnes (Boston)
Tim Murnane (Boston)
Harry Cross (New York)
William Hanna (New York)
Sid Mercer (New York)
Bill Slocum (New York)
George Tidden (New York)
Joe Vila (New York)
Frank Hough (Philadelphia)
Frank Richter (Philadelphia)
Irving Sanborn (Chicago)
John B. Sheridan (St. Louis)

Umpires:

Bill Klem*
Tommy Connolly*
Bill Dinneen
Billy Evans*
John Gaffney
Thomas Lynch
Tim Hurst
John Kelly
Silk O'Loughlin
Jack Sheridan
Bob Emslie

Managers:

Ned Hanlon*
Bill Carrigan
John M. Ward*
Miller Huggins*
Frank Selee*

Executives:

Ed Barrow*
Bob Quinn
Ernest S. Barnard
John Bruce
John T. Brush
Barney Dreyfuss
Charles H. Ebbets
August Herrmann
John A. Heydler
Arthur Soden
Nicholas Young

*Now in Hall of Fame

Notes

22 *The village itself had been founded about 1800:* Louis C. Jones, *Cooperstown.*

23 *"that swine and treacherous sneak":* The material on the Clark family is based largely on Nicholas Fox Weber's *The Clarks of Cooperstown.* Jane Forbes Clark made it clear that she does not hold the book in high regard. As an antidote, she sent me *Cooperstown* by Louis C. Jones, originally published by the Otsego County Historical Society. Unsurprisingly, the book contains a highly sanitized view of the Clarks and their beneficence.

23 *Sterling despised Franklin Roosevelt:* Weber, *Clarks of Cooperstown*, p 183.

24 *"a threat to our very way of government":* Ibid., p. 205, quoting Jules Archer's book, *The Plot to Seize the White House* (Hawthorne Books, 1973), pp. 213–16.

26 *Despite its official-sounding name, the commission:* The material on this dispute and the Mills Commission is based on: James A. Vlasich, *A Legend for the Legendary: The Origin of the Baseball Hall of Fame*; Jim Reisler, *A Great Day in Cooperstown*; Ken Smith, *Baseball Hall of Fame*; and James Mallinson, *A.G. Mills* (SABR, The Biography Project, undated).

30 *It was inspired by a recent visit to the Hall of Fame for Great Americans:* Bill James, *Whatever Happened to the Hall of Fame?* p. 5.

34 *"Cooperstown . . . now a bustling little village and a shrine":* Smith, *Baseball's Hall of Fame.*

35 *"most fitting that the history":* Quoted in Vlasich, *Legend for the Legendary*, p. 175.

35 *"They started something here":* Smith, *Baseball's Hall of Fame*, p. 19.

36 *"Each of the major league teams had sent two representatives":* Smith, *Baseball's Hall of Fame*, pp. 21–22.

40 *Irish players dominated the nineteenth-century game:* John Mooney, "Honoring the Irish," *Irish Examiner*, March 7, 2007.

43 *"George Kelly was a good ballplayer":* Bill James, *The New Bill James Historical Baseball Abstract* (Free Press, 2001), p. 458.

51 *"[I] lashed away until the man was faceless":* Al Stump, *Cobb: The Life and Times of the Meanest Man Who Ever Played Baseball* (Algonquin, 1994) p. 212.

51 *Baseball historian Doug Roberts combed through:* Doug Roberts, *The National Pastime, Ty Cobb Did Not Commit Murder* (SABR, 1996), pp. 25–28.

52 *Ban Johnson, the president of the American League, suspended Cobb:* Charles Alexander, *Ty Cobb*, pp. 105–7.

52 *"When a spectator calls me a half nigger": Detroit Free Press*, May 16, 1912, p. 10.

53 *"These players have not been, nor are they now, found guilty":* Quoted in Alexander, *Ty Cobb*, p. 194.

54 *"Babe Ruth is not only a great athlete":* Quoted in Montville, *The Big Bam*, pp. 157–58.

56 *Four years later, Anson threatened to cancel a White Stockings exhibition game:* Brian Wilson, "Unfortunate Situation: Color Line Takes Stove Out of Big Leagues," MLB.com, http://mlb.mlb.com/mlb/history/mlb_negro_leagues_profile.jsp?player=stovey_george.

58 *"When I broke in . . . the only advice [the sports editor] gave me":* Quoted in Jerome Holtzman, *No Cheering in the Press Box*, p. 166.

58–59 *"When athletes are no longer heroes to you anymore":* Quoted in Jerome Holtzman, *No Cheering in the Press Box*, p. 109.

59 *He actually brokered at least one of Ruth's salary negotiations:* Jerome Holtzman, *No Cheering in the Press Box.*

59 *"It's one of the great boasts of all journalists":* Jerome Holtzman, *No Cheering in the Press Box*, p. 276.

62 *"I won't say I haven't done some foolish things in my life":* "Another Shadow," *Time*, March 9, 1970.

63 *In 1946, the new commissioner of baseball, Happy Chandler, confronted Durocher:* Daniel E. Ginsburg, *The Fix Is In*, pp. 213–27.

63 *"a powerful force for undermining the moral and spiritual training":* Ginsburg, *The Fix Is In*, p. 225.

64 *"I got a special request, an unusual request":* Hank Greenberg with Ira Berkow, *The Story of My Life*, pp. 140–41.

65 *"Joe let those thousands and tens of thousands pile up":* Richard Ben Cramer, *Joe DiMaggio: The Hero's Life* (Simon and Schuster Paperback, 2001), pp. 246–47.

88 *"Gentlemen," he told them, "we have the only legal monopoly":* Heylar, *Lords of the Realm*, p. 268.

96 *"Just about every Hall of Famer in baseball is hanging on these walls":* Quoted in Pete Rose, *My Prison Without Bars*, p. 2.

97 *"Regardless of the verdict of juries":* Jonathan Fraser Light, *The Cultural Encyclopedia of Baseball*, p. 98.

110 *"thrilled that we now have the opportunity":* Quoted in Ken Daley, "Bonds Baseball to Be Branded with Asterisk," *New York Times*, September 26, 2007.

110 *"I will never be in the Hall of Fame. Never.":* Mike Fitzpatrick, "Bonds: Asterisk Would Force Boycott of Hall of Fame," Associated Press, November 2, 2007.

112 *they were both referred to "publicly and frequently as 'nigger'":* Hank Aaron, *I Had a Hammer*, pp. 310–13.

112 *As a boy at St. Mary's Orphanage in Baltimore:* Robert W. Creamer, *Babe*, p. 38.

112 *"I never have slept under the same roof":* Quoted in Fred Leib, *Baseball as I Have Known It*, p. 186.

112 *"Even players in the Negro Leagues":* Robert W. Creamer, *Babe,* p. 185.

113 *"When I see the footage of Aaron's 715th home run":* Stephen Cannella, "My Sportsman: Hank Aaron," SI.com, November 21, 2007, http://sportsillustrated.cnn.com/2007/magazine/specials/sportsman/2007/11/20/cannella.aaron/.

114 *Chandler: (Claps hands and calls) Robbie-eee! Robbiee!:* As reported in Jules Tygiel, *Baseball's Great Experiment*, p. 92.

115 *"The baseball writers at that time were very conservative":* Quoted in Jerome Holtzman, *No Cheering in the Press Box*, p. 316.

115 *"I'm telling you as a friend":* Quoted in Jackie Robinson and Alfred Duckett, *I Never Had it Made* (HarperPerennial, 2003), p. 96.

116 *The* Sporting News *denounced him for this:* Tygiel, *Baseball's Great Experiment*, p. 323.

119 *"Don't come back again, nigger.":* Quoted in Craig R. Wright, "Another View of Dick Allen," *Baseball Research Journal* 24 (1995): 2–14.

123 *"First ballot, second ballot, whatever":* "Talkin' Beisbol: Sheffield Speaks Out," MLB.com, June 8, 2007, http://mlb.mlb.com/news/article.jsp?ymd=20070607&content_id=2011367&vkey=perspectives&fext=.jsp&c_id=mlb.

127 *Twenty-five years ago, almost a third of major-league players:* Richard Lapchick, *The 2008 Racial and Gender Report Card: Major League Baseball* (Institute for Diversity and Ethics in Sports, 2008).

127 *"[but] I'm going to be tremendously more pleased and more proud":* John Helyar, "Robinson Would Have Mixed View of Today's Game," ESPN.com, April 9, 2007, http://sports.espn.go.com/mlb/jackie/news/story?id=2828584.

129 *"Until now, there has been one failing":* Bill Francis/National Baseball Hall of Fame Library, "Decades Later, Negro Leaguers Got Their Due," March 28, 2008, http://web.baseballhalloffame.org/news/article.jsp?content_id=6649&vkey=hof_news&ymd=20080325.

130 *"I was just as good as the white boys":* Quoted in James, *Whatever Happened to the Hall of Fame?*, p. 187.

131 *"There are now in the Hall of Fame sixty-eight players":* Robert Peterson, *Only the Ball Was White*, p. 254.

131 *"The simultaneous election of a large number of Negro League players":* Bill James, e-mail message to author, January 19, 2008.

133 *"It is beyond my understanding how anyone can insinuate":* Dave Egan, *Boston Daily Record*, April 16, 1945 (cited in Tygiel, *Baseball's Great Experiment*, p. 43).

135 *Major League Baseball put out a press release: "O'Neil Must Wait Longer for Hall Call"* MLB.com, February 27, 2006, http://mlb.mlb.com/news/article.jsp?ymd=20060227&content_id=1324873&vkey=perspectives&fext=.jsp&c_id=mlb.

135 *"I don't think this is necessarily trying to right a wrong":* Interview with *Jane Forbes Clark, Joe Morgan, Dale Petroskey*, and *Bud Selig*, ASAP Sports, October 24, 2007, http://www.asapsports.com/show_interview.php?id=46375.

142 *"I'd be lying if I told you that as a black man in baseball":* Quoted in Marvin Miller, *A Whole Different Ballgame*, p. 186.

153 *Baseball first came to Latin America in 1866:* Michael M. Oleksak and Mary Adams Oleksak, *Beisbol: Latin Americans and the Grand Old Game* (Masters Press, 1996).

154 *"Minnie Minoso is to Latin players":* Quoted in Tim Wendel, *The New Face of Baseball*, p. 11.

157 *the best estimate is that no more than 3 percent are Hispanic:* Based on a survey by SABR member Luca Marzorati, July 2008.

158 *"What a joke. How about Mark McGwire?"* Jose Canseco, *Juiced*, pp. 88–90.

158 *"They were like, 'You never see any of the players bring this thing to the States?' ":* Associated Press, "Guillen Says MLB Drug Probe Targeting Latinos," June 7, 2007, http://nbcsports.msnbc.com/id/19080493/.

158 *"We know if we don't agree [with managers]":* MLB.com, "Talkin' Beisbol."

160 *"We want to explore the growing Latino influence in the game":* Jim Molony, "Baseball! Beisbol! Debuts in Houston," MLB.com, April 21, 2006, http://mlb.mlb.com/news/article.jsp?ymd=20060421&content_id=1411344&vkey=news_mlb&fext=.jsp&c_id=mlb.

164 *"For more than a decade, there has been widespread illegal use of anabolic steroids":* George L. Mitchell, *Mitchell Report.*

165 *"Judge me by my work":* Joe Mathews, "Mitchell Drawn to Thorny Issues," *Los Angeles Times,* December 15, 2007.

167 *"It all comes down to the Hall of Fame, really":* Ben Walker, "Clemens for the Hall? Mitchell Report Throws That in Doubt," Associated Press, December 15, 2007, http://www.boston.com/sports/baseball/articles/2007/12/15/clemens_in_the_hall_it_may_be_in_doubt/.

176 *Today's American players are about an inch and a half taller:* Jonah Keri, ed., *Baseball Between the Numbers*, p. xxiii.

Bibliography

Aaron, Hank. *I Had a Hammer*. HarperCollins, 1991.

Alexander, Charles E. *Ty Cobb*. Oxford University Press, 1984.

Angell, Roger. *The Summer Game*. Viking, 1972.

Bird, John T. *Twin Killing: The Bill Mazeroski Story*. Esmerelda Press, 1995.

Boswell, Thomas. *Why Time Begins on Opening Day*. Penguin Sports Library, 1985.

Bouton, Jim. *Ball Four*. Midpoint Trade Books, 2008.

________. *Glad You Didn't Take it Personally*. William Morrow, 1971.

Bradbury, J. C. *The Baseball Economist*. Dutton, 2007.

Brosnan, Jim. *The Long Season*. Ivan R. Dee, 2002.

Bryant, Howard. *Juicing the Game*. Viking, 2005.

Canseco, Jose. *Juiced*. HarperEntertainment, 2006.

________. *Vindicated*. Simon Spotlight Entertainment, 2008.

Connor, Anthony J. *Voices of Cooperstown*. Collier Books, 1984.

Creamer, Robert W. *Babe*. Simon & Schuster, 1974.

________. *Stengel*. Simon & Schuster, 1984.

Dawidoff, Nicholas. *The Catcher Was a Spy*. Pantheon, 1994.

Dreifort, John E., ed. *Baseball from Outside the Lines*. University of Nebraska Press, 2001.

Entine, Jon. *Taboo*. Public Affairs, 2001.

Evans, Christopher H., and William Herzog, eds. *The Faith of 50 Million*. Westminster John Knox, 2002.

Fainaru-Wada, Mark, and Lance Williams. *Game of Shadows*. Gotham, 2006.

Fleder, Rob, ed. *Sports Illustrated: Great Baseball Writing*. Time, 2005.

Ginsburg, Daniel E. *The Fix Is In*. McFarland & Company, 2004.

Gmelch, George, ed. *Baseball without Borders*. Bison Books, 2006.

Greenberg, Hank, with Ira Berkow. *The Story of My Life*. Benchmark Press, 2001.

Heylar, John. *Lords of the Realm*. Ballantine Books, 1995.

Holtzman, Jerome. *No Cheering in the Press Box*. Holt, Rinehart & Winston, 1974.

James, Bill. *Whatever Happened to the Hall of Fame?* Free Press, 1995.

Jones, Louis C., ed. *Cooperstown*. The Farmers' Museum, 2006.

Kahn, Roger. *The Boys of Summer*. Harper Perennial Modern Classics, 2006.

Keri, Jonah, ed. *Baseball Between the Numbers*. Perseus, 2006.

Klein, Allen M. *Growing the Game*. Yale University Press, 2006.

Lacey, Robert. *Little Man*. Little, Brown, 1991.

Leib, Fred. *Baseball as I Have Known It*. Coward, McCann & Geoghegan, 1977.

Light, Jonathan Fraser. *The Cultural Encyclopedia of Baseball*. McFarland & Company, 2005.

Maranis, David. *Clemente*. Simon & Schuster, 2006.

Miller, Marvin. *A Whole Different Ball Game*. Ivan R. Dee, 2004.

Mitchell, George L. *Report to the Commissioner of Baseball of an Independent Investigation into the Illegal Use of Steroids and Other Performance Enhancing Substances by Players in Major League Baseball* ("*The Mitchell Report*"). United States Government Printing Office, 2008.

Montville, Leigh. *The Big Bam*. Doubleday, 2006.

________. *Ted Williams*. Anchor, 2005.

National Baseball Hall of Fame. *Baseball as America*. National Geographic, 2002.

National Baseball Hall of Fame and Museum. *2007 Annual*.

Okrent, Daniel. *Nine Innings*. McGraw-Hill, 1985.

Peterson, Robert. *Only the Ball Was White*. Gramercy, 1999.

Pierce, G. F. A., ed. *How Bill James Changed Our View of Baseball.* ACTA Sports, 2007.

Reisler, Jim, ed. *Guys, Dolls, and Curveballs.* Da Capo Press, 2005.

________. *A Great Day in Cooperstown.* Da Capo Press, 2006.

Rhoden, William C. *Forty Million Dollar Slaves.* Crown, 2006.

Rose, Pete. *My Prison Without Bars.* Rodale Books, 2004.

Russo, Frank, and Gene Racz. *Bury My Heart at Cooperstown.* Triumph, 2006.

Schweizer, Peter and Rochelle Schweizer. *The Bushes.* Doubleday, 2004.

Smith, Ken. *Baseball's Hall of Fame.* New York, Grosset & Dunlap, 1970.

Stanton, Tom. *The Road to Cooperstown.* Thomas Dunne Books, 2003.

Thorn, John, ed. *The Complete Armchair Book of Baseball.* Galahad, 1997.

________. *Total Baseball.* Warner Books, 2004.

Tygiel, Jules. *Baseball's Great Experiment.* Oxford University Press, 1983.

Vlasich, James A. *A Legend for the Legendary.* Popular Press, 1990.

Weber, Nicholas Fox. *The Clarks of Cooperstown.* Knopf, 2007.

Wendel, Tim. *The New Face of Baseball.* Rayo, 2003.

Williams, Ted, and John Underwood. *My Turn at Bat.* Simon & Schuster, 1969.

Zimbalist, Andrew. *In the Best Interests of Baseball?* Wiley, 2006.

Zoss, Joel, and John Bowman. *Diamonds in the Rough.* Bison Books, 2004.

Film

Baseball, 10-disc DVD set. Directed by Ken Burns. PBS, 1994.

Web Sites

National Baseball Hall of Fame & Museum, http://web.baseball halloffame.org/index.jsp

Society for American Baseball Research, http://www.sabr.org/

Statistics.com

The Business of Baseball, http://bob.sabrwebs.com

The Biz of Baseball, http://www.bizofbaseball.com

Index

Aaron, Hank, 17, 90, 93, 105, 108, 110–13, 126, 129, 180
Abbott, Sam, 17
Adams, Margo, 70–71
Adcock, Joe, 140
Adonis, Joe, 63, 65
African-American players, 14, 19–20, 101, 111–36
alcoholism, 61–62
Alexander, Grover Cleveland, 33, 55–56, 58, 90, 168
All-American Girls Professional Baseball League (AAGPBL), 80–83
Allen, Dick, 48, 118–20, 195
Allen, Mel, 179
Alomar, Roberto, 101, 159
Alvarez, Jose, 74
amphetamines, 178–80
Anson, Cap, 39, 56
antitrust exemption, 141–44
Aparicio, Luis, 159
Armstrong, Jack, 164–65
Arnovich, Morris, 36
autographs, 95–96, 99–108, 187
Avila, Bobby, 155
Bancroft, Dave, 42
Banks, Ernie, 129, 134
Barber, Red, 138
barnstorming, 54–55
baseball, changes in, 174–76
baseball, economics of, 87–88
baseball, origin of, 24–28, 34
Baseball Annies, 61
Baseball Writers' Association of America, 7–8, 38–39, 44, 58, 61, 93, 129–30, 145, 156–57, 171–72, 195
Bauman, Doc, 177
Bell, Cool Papa, 131
Bell, Jerry, 148
Bellán, Esteban, 153
Belle, Albert, 120–21
Bench, Johnny, 79, 94, 106
Bender, Chief, 79, 103
Berg, Moe, 36
Bernstein, Abe, 64–65
Berowski, Freddy, 74–75
Berra, Yogi, 17, 90, 105–6
Biggio, Craig, 101
bigotry, 52
Bird, John T., 91–93

Blackmun, Herry, 142–43
Black Sox Scandal, 53, 97–98, 166–67, 172
Blyleven, Bert, 89, 93
Boggs, Wade, 70–71, 118
Bonds, Barry, 16–17, 19, 97, 101, 110–11, 113–14, 123–25, 146, 163, 167–72, 176, 183–85, 191, 193, 195
Bonds, Bobby, 17
Boone, Ray, 12
Boston Braves, 132
Boston Red Sox, 45, 132–33, 165
Bottomley, Jim, 42
Boudreau, Lou, 104, 116
Bouton, Jim, 178–79
Boyer, Clete, 76
Bracigliano, Molly, 104–8
Bresnahan, Roger, 40
Brett, George, 7, 86–87, 108
Brock, Lou, 134
Broeg, Bob, 147
Brosius, Scott, 107
Brosnan, Jim, 177–78
Brouthers, Dan, 40
Brown, Bobby, 148
Brown, Joe, 93, 147
Brown, Kevin, 164, 186
Bulkeley, Morgan G., 26, 39
Bull Durham, 152–53
Bunning, Jim, 11, 19, 91, 105, 139, 176
Burdette, Lew, 140
Bush, George W., 152, 161, 186, 192
Caminiti, Ken, 164, 170
Campanella, Roy, 115–17, 129, 151
Cannella, Stephen, 113
Cannon, Jimmy, 59–60, 177
Canseco, Jose, 157–58, 169, 186, 189
Carew, Rod, 104–5, 159
Carpenter, Bob, 119
Carter, Gary, 86, 106, 117–18
Cartwright, Alexander, 33–34, 39
Cartwright, Bruce, 33–34
Cash, Norm, 124
centennial celebration, 31–35
Cepeda, Orlando, 154, 159
Chadwick, Henry, 24–27, 33, 39, 57
Chafets, Coby, 3–4
Chandler, Happy, 63, 133
Charleston, Oscar, 131
Chavez, Hugo, 160–62, 192
Cincinnati Reds, 94
Clark, Alfred, 28
Clark, Edward, 21–23
Clark, Jane Forbes, 8, 16, 18, 47, 85, 135, 148, 152–53, 159–62, 168
Clark, Stephen C., 18, 23–24, 29–32, 35–36, 38, 49, 196
Clark, Sterling, 23–24, 29
Clark, Will, 101
Clark Foundation, 23
Clarke, Fred, 40

Cleland, Alexander, 29, 36–37
Cleveland Indians, 52
Clemens, Roger, 101, 107–8, 157, 164, 166, 168–72, 184–85, 193, 195
Clemente, Roberto, 117, 147, 154–55, 157, 159–60
Cobb, Ty, 1, 11, 32–33, 50–53, 56, 70, 99, 102, 112–13, 196
cocaine, 180
Cochrane, Mickey, 1, 13, 39
Cody, Buffalo Bill, 78
Cole, Jonathan R., 184
Collins, Dottie, 82–83
Collins, Eddie, 33, 36, 133
Collins, Jimmy, 40
collusion, 124–26, 146
color line, 114–15
Comiskey, Charles, 39, 168
Concepcion, Dave, 94–95
Cooper, James Fenimore, 22, 29–30, 34–35
Cooper, William, 22
Cooperstown, NY, 8–9, 16–17, 22–23, 27–29, 34, 72
corked bats, 54, 183
Costas, Bob, 113
Costello, Frank, 65
Coveleski, Stan, 41–42, 129
Cramer, Richard Ben, 65–66
Cravath, Gavvy, 183
Crawford, Sam, 1, 41, 51, 196
Creamer, Robert, 112
Cronin, Joe, 133
Cummings, Candy, 39

Daley, Arthur, 114
Dandridge, Ray, 131
Davis, Chili, 107–8
Davis, George, 102
Davis, Tom, 187
Dawson, Andre, 118
Day, Laraine, 63
Day, Leon, 131
Deal, Ellis "Cot," 178
Dean, Dizzy, 36, 62, 129
Delahanty, Ed, 40
DeMint, Jim, 99
Deschaine, Alice Pollitt, 81–82
Detroit Tigers, 1, 11–14, 52
DeWitt, Bill, 148
Di Franza, Lenny, 77
Dihigo, Martin, 131, 159
DiMaggio, Joe, 59–60, 65–66, 70, 96, 139
Doby, Larry, 129
domestic abuse, 67
Donovan, John, 118
Doubleday, Abner, 27–28, 34–35, 192, 196
Doubleday Baseball, 31–32
Doubleday Field, 28, 30–31, 36, 77
Doyle, Charles J., 33
Drebinger, John, 59
Dreyfuss, Barney, 148
Duffy, Hugh, 40
Durbin, Dick, 47

Durocher, Leo, 63–64
Dykstra, Lenny, 164

Ebony magazine, 130
Eckersley, Dennis, 167
Ecko, Marc, 110
Egan, Dave, 132–33
Evers, Johnny, 100, 103
Ewing, Buck, 39

Fairly, Ron, 140
Farley, James, 33
Fehr, Don, 182
Feller, Bob, 48, 128–29
Fetzer, John, 148
Fischer, Bill, 170
Fisk, Carlton, 105, 125, 148
fixing games, 52–53, 97
Flood, Curt, 64, 141–42, 144–45, 195
Ford, Whitey, 180
Ford C. Frick Award, 47, 115
Foster, Rube, 130–31
Foster, Willie, 131
Fox, Nellie, 92
Foxx, Jimmie, 61
Freeman's Journal, 16–17
Frick, Ford C., 29–32, 37, 53, 59, 128
Frisch, Frankie, 39, 42, 134

gambling, 52, 57–58, 62–63, 95–96
Garvey, Steve, 68–70, 185, 195
Gates, Jim, 76
Gay, Tim, 94–95
Gehrig, Lou, 39, 104
Gehringer, Charlie, 1, 36, 39
ghostwriters, 59
Giambi, Jason, 164
Gibson, Bob, 116
Gibson, Josh, 19, 129, 131
Gibson, Kirk, 125
Giles, Bill, 148
Glass, David, 148
Glavine, Tom, 101, 169
Goings, William, 78
Goldberg, Linn, 188–89
Gomez, Lefty, 36, 39
Gonzales, Mark, 172
Gonzalez, Juan, 101, 164, 186
Gordon, Joe, 101–2
Gorman, Arthur Pue, 26
Goslin, Goose, 41–42
Gossage, Goose, 85–87, 89-91, 104, 107–9, 122
Grammas, Alex, 177
Grant, Eddie, 50
Grant, Jim "Mudcat," 9
Graves, Abner, 27–28, 31
Graziano, Dan, 172
Green, Pumpsie, 132
Greenberg, Hank, 1, 12–13, 36, 64–65, 103, 194
Griffey, Ken, Jr., 101

Grove, Lefty, 39, 61
Guerrero, Vladimir, 159
Guest, Edgar, 13
Guillen, Ozzie, 158–59
Guilló, Nemesio, 153, 156
Gwynn, Tony, 7, 16–19, 68, 90, 105, 117, 170
Gygax, Frank, 160

Hafey, Chick, 42–43, 176
Hagen, Paul, 148
Haines, Jess, 42–43
Haller, Tom, 142
Hall of Fame. *See* National Baseball Hall of Fame
Hall of Fame for Great Americans, 30, 38
Hanlon, Ned, 41
Harrington, John, 148
Hartnett, Gabby, 116
Harwell, Ernie, 76
Heilmann, Harry, 1, 62, 118
Henderson, Rickey, 89
Herman, Bill, 36
Hernandez, Keith, 180
Heydler, John, 28, 62
Hillsman, Bill, 93
Hodges, Gil, 48
Hodges, Russ, 76
Hoffer, Barry, 188
Hoffman, Trevor, 101
homosexuality, 83–84
Hooper, Harry, 41–42
Horn, Brad, 83
Hornsby, Rogers, 39, 56–57
Howard, Elston, 134
Howsam, Bob, 148
Hoyt, Waite, 129
Hubbell, Carl, 36, 39
Hummel, Rick, 148
Hunt, Marshall, 53–55, 59

Idelson, Jeff, 4, 46–47, 86–87, 89, 110, 160, 162, 167
Irvin, Monte, 131, 148
Israel, baseball in, 1–3

Jackson, Bo, 101
Jackson, Reggie, 17, 106
Jackson, Shoeless Joe, 53, 95, 97–99, 172, 195
Jackson, Travis, 42
Jacobson, Max, 179–80
James, Bill, 40, 42–47, 57, 97, 118–19, 131, 134, 150, 175, 194
Jenkins, Fergie, 93
Jennings, Hughie, 40
Jeter, Derek, 100
Jethroe, Sam, 132–33
J. G. Taylor Spink Award, 47, 115
Johnson, Ban, 39, 52–53
Johnson, Judy, 131
Johnson, Randy, 101
Johnson, Walter, 18, 33, 57, 100
Jordan, Ambrose, 21
Jorgens, Arndt, 36
Joss, Addie, 102
Justice, David, 164

Kaat, Jim, 48
Kahn, Roger, 77
Kaline, Al, 11–12, 14–16, 120
Kauffman, Ewing, 148
Keeler, Wee Willie, 33
Kelly, George, 42–43
Kelly, Mike "King," 40, 61
Kemp, Abe, 58
Kerr, Paul, 128
Killebrew, Harmon, 148, 157–58
Kling, Johnny, 103
Koufax, Sandy, 17, 90, 103, 105, 185
Kuenn, Harvey, 139, 195
Kuhn, Bowie, 111, 129, 148–49
Ku Klux Klan, 52, 57

Lajoie, Napoleon, 33, 100
Landis, Kenesaw Mountain, 31–34, 36, 38–40, 49–50, 53–54, 57, 76, 97–98, 166, 172, 196
Larkin, Barry, 101
Larsen, Don, 91
Lary, Frank, 11
Latin-American players, 153–62
Lawton, Matt, 113–14
League of Their Own, A, 81
Lemon, Bob, 93
Leonard, Buck, 131
Leonard, Hubert "Dutch," 52–53
Levy, Andrew, 89, 107
Leyland, Jim, 176
Lieb, Fred, 112
Limmer, Lou, 76
Lincoln, Abraham, 28, 151, 196
Lindstrom, Fred, 42–43
Lipkin, Jan, 188
Lipsyte, Bob, 1, 121
Littell, Walter, 31
Lloyd, Pop, 131
Lolich, Mickey, 91, 195
Lombardi, Ernie, 36
Lueker, Claude, 51–52
Luque, Adolfo, 153

Mack, Connie, 33, 39–41, 57, 62, 168
MacPhail, Andy, 148
MacPhail, Larry, 133
Madden, Bill, 121
Maddux, Greg, 101, 169
Major League Baseball Players Association, 60, 139–46
Mantle, Mickey, 9, 11, 62, 96, 100, 124, 178–80
Maranville, Rabbit, 61–62, 116
Marichal, Juan, 93, 159
Marquard, Rube, 41–42
Marshall, Thurgood, 144
Martin, Pepper, 36
Martinez, Pedro, 101, 159
Mathews, Eddie, 140
Mathewson, Christy, 32–33, 57
Mattingly, Don, 101
Maxwell, Charlie, 11
Mays, Willie, 17, 90, 100, 105, 108, 126, 129, 160, 180

Mazeroski, Bill, 48, 91–94, 194
McCain, John, 192–93
McCarthy, Joe, 40, 62
McCovey, Willie, 105
McCoy, Hal, 148
McGinnity, Joe, 40
McGraw, John, 39, 59, 62, 168, 176
McGwire, Mark, 97, 157–58, 163, 168, 170–72, 183
McKay, David, 164
McNamee, Brian, 169
McPhee, Bid, 48
memorabilia auctions, 99–100
Messersmith, Andy, 88
Miller, Alexander, 138
Miller, Marvin, 48, 60–61, 97, 125, 137–51, 176, 192
Miller, Terry, 138
Mills, Abraham G., 26–27
Mills Commission, 26, 35, 76
Milner, John, 180
Mincher, Don, 178
Minoso, Orestes "Minnie," 154, 195
Mitchell, George, 163–67
Mitchell Report, 72, 163–69, 171, 184, 186–87
MLB.com, 87–89
Molitor, Paul, 87
Montefusco, John, 10–11
Morgan, Joe, 94, 135
Muchnick, Isadore, 132
Murray, Eddie, 17
Musial, Stan, 90, 105, 184
Mussina, Mike, 169

National Baseball Day (June 12, 1939), 35
National Baseball Hall of Fame
  all-star game, 36
  business opportunities for HoFers, 48, 87, 89–91, 93, 98, 100–109
  Character Clause, 49–50, 58, 61–71, 172–73, 195
  CITGO Petroleum Corp., 159–62
  dedication of, 32–36
  election to, 9, 38–43, 47, 85, 116, 120, 131, 195, 201–3
  exclusivity, 40–43, 47–48, 117–23, 147–50, 163, 168–69, 191
  founding of, 29–32
  Honor Rolls of Baseball, 41, 215
  induction ceremonies, 7–8, 10, 17–20, 33, 35
  ineligibility list, 95
  Latin-American players, 153–55, 159–60
  lobbying for candidates, 91–96, 98–99
  museum staff, 72–81
  museum traveling exhibit, 151
  Negro leagues players, 101, 112, 128–31, 134–35, 192

National Baseball Hall of Fame (*con't*)
performance-enhancing drugs, policy on, 172–73
"pioneers," 39
sacred nature of, 4–6, 18
team logos on plaques, 106–7
Veterans Committee, 38–43, 47–48, 75, 91, 95, 102, 131, 133, 138, 145, 148–50, 195
voting procedures, 75
National Baseball Hall of Fame and Museum, 29–32, 36, 72–81, 151
Native Americans, 78–79
Newcombe, Don, 129
New York Yankees, 3–4, 116
Niekro, Phil, 125
Nixon, Richard, 139–40

O'Connell, Jack, 149–50
O'Connor, Jack, 85
Okrent, Daniel, 44
Oliva, Tony, 48, 155
Oliver, Al, 48
O'Malley, Walter, 148
O'Neil, Buck, 134–35, 177, 192
organized crime, 63–65
O'Rourke, Jim, 40
Ortiz, David, 159
Ott, Mel, 36, 176

Paige, Satchel, 19, 96, 126, 128–31
palimony, 70–71
Palmeiro, Rafael, 159, 164, 186
Palmer, Jim, 17
Parker, Dave, 117–18, 126
paternity suits, 70, 155
Pennock, Herb, 39
Perez, Neifi, 158–59
Perez, Tony, 94, 159
Perry, Gaylord, 93, 176–77
Peterson, Robert W., 131
Petrosky, Dale, 46, 110–11, 151–53, 159–62
Pettitte, Andy, 164
Philadelphia Phillies, 119
Piazza, Mike, 101, 171
Pike, Lipman, 74–75
Piniella, Lou, 108
Pinson, Vada, 48
Plank, Eddie, 102
Pollitt, Alice. *See* Deschaine, Alice Pollitt
Pompez, Alex, 154
Power, Vic, 126, 154–55
Puckett, Kirby, 66–68, 103, 117
Pujols, Albert, 101

Radbourn, Hoss, 39
Raines, Tim, 125, 180
Ramirez, Manny, 100, 159
Rawlings, Johnny, 112
Reese, Jimmie, 103
reserve clause, 141–44
Reulbach, Ed, 102–3
Reusse, Pat, 172
Reynolds, Harold, 89
Rice, Grantland, 58–59

Rice, Jim, 9–10, 89, 121–22
Richard, Ruth, 81–82
Richmond, J. Lee, 70
Rickey, Branch, 114–15
Ripken, Cal, Jr., 7–8, 14, 16–20, 90, 106, 169
Ritter, Lawrence, 41, 77, 117
Rivera, Mariano, 100, 159
Rizzuto, Phil, 151
Robbins, Tim, 152–53
Roberts, Doug, 51
Roberts, Robin, 90, 139–40
Robinson, Brooks, 17
Robinson, Frank, 8, 17, 116, 127, 135, 184
Robinson, Jackie, 64, 96, 114–16, 126–29, 132–33, 135–36, 138–39, 192
Robinson, Rachel, 136
Robinson, Wilbert, 40
Rock, Chris, 113
Rodriguez, Alex, 100, 137, 156, 159, 169
Rodriguez, Ivan "Pudge," 101, 156, 159
Rogan, Bullet Joe, 101, 131
Roosevelt, Franklin Delano, 35
Roosevelt, Theodore, 25
Rose, Pete, 19, 86, 95–97, 108, 195
Royko, Mike, 62
Russert, Tim, 83
Ruth, Babe, 8, 32–33, 35, 53–56, 58–59, 70, 76, 96, 100, 102, 111–13, 138, 156, 183–85, 194
Ryan, Nolan, 7, 106, 170, 184, 192

sabermetrics, 43–45, 92
salaries, 140, 146
Sample, Billy, 89
Sanchez, Jesse, 123
Santo, Ron, 47–48, 140, 195
Schechter, Gabriel, 73, 77
Schmidt, Mike, 19, 96, 119
Schoendienst, Red, 48
Seaver, Tom, 105–6, 151, 170
segregation, 56
Selig, Bud, 19, 96–98, 111, 128, 166
Selkirk, George, 36
Seymour, Harold, 77
Shandler, Ron, 45
Shaughnessy, Dan, 121
Sheffield, Gary, 101, 122–23, 158–59, 164, 168
Shelton, Ron, 153
Shipp, E. R., 113
Sierra, Ruben, 101
Simmons, Al, 61
Singer, Isaac Merritt, 21–22
Sisler, George, 33
Slater, Robert, 75
Smith, Hilton, 131
Smith, Ken, 34–36
Smith, Lee, 118
Smith, Randy, 170
Smith, Red, 194
Smith, Wendell, 114–15, 132
Smoltz, John, 101, 175

Society for American Baseball Research (SABR), 43
Sockalexis, Louis, 79
Sosa, Sammy, 159, 170
Southworth, Billy, 102
Spahn, Warren, 184
Spalding, Albert Goodwill "A. G.," 25–27, 33, 37, 39, 57, 151, 156
Speaker, Tris, 33, 52–53, 56, 58
Spencer, Ted, 72, 76–82, 84, 131–33, 163
Spink, C. C. Johnson, 145
Spink, J. G. Taylor, 115
spitballs, 183
Sports Illustrated, 44
sportswriters protecting players, 58–60, 70
stamp (postage), 33
Stansfield, George, 51
Stanton, Mike, 186
Stargell, Willie, 79, 116, 180
Stearnes, Turkey, 131
Steinbrenner, George, 88
Stengel, Casey, 61
steroids, 16–17, 46, 72, 85–86, 107, 110, 123, 125, 157–58, 163–74, 176–77, 179, 183–93, 195
Stigler, Stephen M., 184
Stump, Al, 51
suspensions, 53–54, 63
Sutter, Bruce, 100, 105
Sutton, Don, 6, 93, 105–6
Suzuki, Ichiro, 101
Swearingen, Randall, 9
Swope, Tom, 38

Taylor, George W., 139
Tejada, Miguel, 101, 159, 164
Terry, Bill, 42
testing (for drugs), 181–82
Texas Rangers, 186
Thomas, Frank Edward "Big Hurt," 101
Thomas, Frank Joseph, 118
Thome, Jim, 101
Thomson, Bobby, 76, 91
Thorpe, Jim, 79
Tiant, Luis, 48, 195
Toporcer, George "Specs," 176
Torgeson, Earl, 11
Torre, Joe, 48, 86, 100, 123
Traynor, Pie, 39
Turner, Ted, 88
Tuttle, Bill, 12

Ueberroth, Peter, 117, 125

Vance, Dazzy, 138, 148
Vander Meer, Johnny, 36
Vaughn, Mo, 164
Veeck, Bill, 55, 154
Verducci, Tom, 169–71
Verkman, Steve, 99–104
Veterans Committee. *See* National Baseball Hall of Fame, Veterans Committee

Vincent, Fay, 148–49, 170
Virgil, Ozzie [b. 1933], 14

Waddell, Rube, 39, 62
Wadler, Gary, 177, 182, 185, 187–88
Wagner, Billy, 101
Wagner, Honus, 33, 36, 57, 100
Walker, James J., 54–55
Walker, Moses Fleetwood, 56
Walla Tonka, 78–79
Waner, Lloyd, 36
Waner, Paul, 61, 176
Weaver, Earl, 17
Weber, Nicholas Fox, 32
Weiss, George, 87
Wells, Willie, 131
Wexler, Jonathan, 90, 93
Wheat, Zack, 79
Wheeler, Lonnie, 111–12
White, Sol, 76
Wiles, Tim, 75–77
Will, George F., 173–75, 191
Williams, Bernie, 107
Williams, Billy, 134
Williams, Joe, 131
Williams, Marvin, 132–33
Williams, Ted, 11, 19, 61, 70, 96, 124, 128–29, 132, 151, 184
Wills, Maury, 48
Wilson, Hack, 62
Winfield, Dave, 106, 116–17
Wood, Joe, 52, 175
World Baseball Classic, 156
World War II, 64–65, 79–80
Wright, George, 39, 100
Wright, Harry, 39, 100
Wrigley, Phil, 80
Wynn, Early, 79, 93, 184

Yastrzemski, Carl, 105–6
Young, Cy, 32–33, 103
Young, Dick, 61, 115–16, 129
Youngs, Ross, 42–43, 102
Yount, Robin, 7

A NOTE ON THE AUTHOR

Zev Chafets is the author of eleven books, including *A Match Made in Heaven*, *Members of the Tribe*, and *The Devil's Night*. He is a frequent contributor to the *New York Times Magazine* and other periodicals, a former columnist for the *New York Daily News*, and the founding managing editor of *Jerusalem Report*.